"This is a thoughtful and compelling book about power. Thinking of power as a gift which is meant for flourishing gives the reader much to consider. Institutions are meant for flourishing. Therefore, leaders of institutions must ask the question about how they are using the power gifted to them. Are they image bearers of that power or god players? The author's biblical and personal stories help the reader work through these and many other great questions."

**Mary Andringa,** president/CEO, Vermeer Corporation

"What do poverty, the cello, human trafficking, iPods, loan sharks, wine, the tower of Babel and the Olympics have in common? Crouch shows that all of these are expressions of power, God's unique gift to humanity. With unceasing eloquence, Crouch delivers a unique perspective on everyday life that opens readers' eyes to a whole new world of conflict, meaning and possibility. A truly transformative experience."

**Brian Fikkert,** coauthor of *When Helping Hurts*

"Once again, Andy Crouch cuts to the heart of the matter by challenging us to take seriously the One whose image we bear. *Playing God* is a clear and compelling call for Christians to steward the kind of power that enables flourishing."

**Gabe Lyons,** coauthor of *unChristian*

"In deft moves of integrating sound biblical theology with astute observations about culture, Andy Crouch wades into the immense topic of power—the powers, institutional power, cultural power, racial power—to offer the alternative Christian perception of power, a power that can be reshaped by the gospel about Jesus Christ, refashioned by love and reoriented by a new community called the church. In this book worldly power is deconstructed and replaced with a new kind of gospel power."

**Scot McKnight,** professor of New Testament, Northern Seminary

"It's likely that most readers of this book will both possess more power than they realize and feel uncomfortable with the amount of it that they know they've got. This book holds keys to liberation. It illuminates that power is, foundationally, *good.* It offers 3D pictures of what power is for (flourishing) and what its right use looks like (creative image-bearing that expands our own and others' joyful 'meaning-making'). Crouch's Bible-saturated teaching frees us from guilt and guides us in the active, humble and, importantly, *essential* calling to steward our power, thus helping us avoid the equal dangers of abusing our power and neglecting it. *Playing God* is a wise, deeply insightful, imaginative work; by heeding its lessons, Christians will be far more fruitful in their efforts to advance Jesus' kingdom in our broken world."

**Amy L. Sherman,** author of *Kingdom Calling*

"This book plowed through my heart, leaving idol shards everywhere in its path. Andy Crouch, one of Christianity's most compelling visionaries on culture, examines power and the ways we should harness it for human flourishing and the glory of God. The book will prompt you to rethink assumptions and perhaps to reset priorities. It is a 'powerful' read, in the right sense of that word."

**Russell D. Moore,** president, Southern Baptist Convention
Ethics & Religious Liberty Commission

"Andy Crouch presents an essential treatise on one of the most important yet undiscussed topics for the promotion of justice in American Christianity—the issue of power. The work of God's justice in the world requires an understanding of the dynamics of power. Crouch shines the light of Scripture on what could be a divisive topic. *Playing God* should spark this long overdue conversation."

**Soong-Chan Rah,** Milton B. Engebretson Associate Professor of Church Growth and Evangelism, North Park Theological Seminary, and author of *The Next Evangelicalism*

"Perhaps no question with such urgent life-and-death consequences is more poorly understood among Christians in our era than the stewardship of power; but gloriously, in *Playing God*, Andy Crouch provides the clarity we need in this once-in-a-generation work of sweeping theological and sociological depth. It is fresh, rigorous, profoundly helpful and a delight to read."

**Gary A. Haugen,** president & CEO, International Justice Mission

# ANDY CROUCH

# PLAYING GOD

## REDEEMING THE GIFT OF POWER

IVP Books

An imprint of InterVarsity Press
Downers Grove, Illinois

*InterVarsity Press*
*P.O. Box 1400, Downers Grove, IL 60515-1426*
*World Wide Web: www.ivpress.com*
*E-mail: email@ivpress.com*

*InterVarsity Press® is the book-publishing division of InterVarsity Christian Fellowship/USA®, a movement of students and faculty active on campus at hundreds of universities, colleges and schools of nursing in the United States of America, and a member movement of the International Fellowship of Evangelical Students. For information about local and regional activities, write Public Relations Dept., InterVarsity Christian Fellowship/USA, 6400 Schroeder Rd., P.O. Box 7895, Madison, WI 53707-7895, or visit the IVCF website at <www.intervarsity.org>.*

*Scripture quotations, unless otherwise noted, are from the New Revised Standard Version of the Bible, copyright 1989 by the Division of Christian Education of the National Council of the Churches of Christ in the USA. Used by permission. All rights reserved.*

*While all stories in this book are true, some names and identifying information in this book have been changed to protect the privacy of the individuals involved.*

*Cover design: Cindy Kiple*
*Interior design: Beth Hagenberg*
*Images: © Pavel Khorenyan/iStockphoto*

*ISBN 978-0-8308-3765-6 (print)*
*ISBN 978-0-8308-8436-0 (digital)*

*Printed in Canada* ∞

**Library of Congress Cataloging-in-Publication Data**
*A catalog record for this book is available from the Library of Congress.*

| **P** | 20 | 19 | 18 | 17 | 16 | 15 | 14 | 13 | 12 | 11 | 10 | 9 | 8 | 7 | 6 | 5 | 4 | 3 | 2 | 1 |
|---|---|---|---|---|---|---|---|---|---|---|---|---|---|---|---|---|---|---|---|---|
| **Y** | 30 | 29 | 28 | 27 | 26 | 25 | 24 | 23 | 22 | 21 | 20 | 19 | 18 | 17 | 16 | 15 | 14 | 13 | | |

*for David Sacks*

*1968–2013*

*artist, warrior and friend*

# CONTENTS

## PART 3
Institutions and Creative Power: *From Generation to Generation*

## PART 4
The End of Power: *We Had to Celebrate*

# INTRODUCTION

**P**ower is a gift. That is this book's central, controversial idea.

It may be that you don't find that idea controversial, in which case you can happily skip this introduction and go straight on to the heart of the book. But I suspect most people have a hard time believing that power is a gift.

Gifts are good, and many people have a hard time thinking of power as good. Not long ago I was on a panel with a woman whose wisdom and insight I very much respect. During our discussion the topic of power came up. "I recognize that power is a reality," she said reluctantly, "but I think all we can do is contain it and limit the damage it causes." In her mind power always does damage. Yet she exercises great power, with much care and skill, in her work as a university professor.

Gifts also require a giver. Our use of power will always be disordered and destructive—will result in idolatry and injustice—unless we find a way to a restored relationship with the Giver of power. Even a great deal of Christian thinking regards power, as the apostle Paul said in another context, "from a worldly point of view." But while power is in some ways the most worldly thing of all, if we take our understanding of power from the world we will miss its promise and misjudge its dangers. To truly understand the gift and danger of power, we have to put it back in the context of the Christian story, with that story's audacious claims about the true beginning and end of the world we think we know. As we revisit that story, we may find it has much more to say about power than we have imagined, and that what it has to say is not what we expected.

Of course, many people would prefer not to think about power at all, and they sometimes use language borrowed from the Christian story to avoid thinking about it. A friend was speaking with the pastor of a multi-thousand-member megachurch, one whose name is instantly recognizable in the world of evangelical Christianity. "How do you handle the power that comes with your role as senior pastor?" my friend asked. "Oh, power is not a problem at our church," came the reply. "We are all servant leaders here." I believe it was a sincere answer—this leader's commitment to servant leadership is genuine. But I have been in rooms when he walked in and have felt the palpable change of atmosphere, as if someone had abruptly turned down the thermostat and shut off the background music. He is indeed a servant leader, but he is also a person with power.

Because of our discomfort with power, we employ a wide range of near synonyms that seem more comfortable. We speak of leadership, influence or authority. All these are important and beneficial forms of power. But these words can camouflage what is really at stake. The best word for it, with all its discomfort, is *power.*

There is, I should add at the outset, one group of people who talk about almost nothing but power. The academic world, especially the humanities, has been shaped in the last generation by a new attention to the power dynamics at work in human lives and institutions. Influenced recently by Michel Foucault, and perhaps most deeply by Friedrich Nietzsche, whole disciplines have reoriented themselves around excavating the hidden power lines in human endeavors.

I agree with the Foucauldians that power is everywhere. But in this book I am going to offer the outlines of a different way of seeing this reality. Underlying much of the academic fascination with power, it seems to me, is the presupposition that power is essentially about coercion—that even when power looks life-giving and creative, it actually cloaks a violent fist in a creative glove. I believe this is exactly backwards. I actually believe the deepest form of power is creation, and that when power takes the form of coercion and violence, that is actually a diminishment and distortion of what it was meant to be. Indeed, instead of creation being merely well-concealed coercion, violence is best seen as the result of misplaced and misdirected creation.

I have no hope, of course, of being as erudite or influential as Foucault himself. I am not a philosopher or a scholar of any sort; I am a journalist, and my job as a journalist is to do my best to make complicated things clear, quickly, for people who could be doing something else. Readers who want the real philosophical meat should turn to the book that first started me down this path, John Milbank's supremely difficult *Theology and Social Theory*. (I wish them a safe journey.) Oliver O'Donovan's life work, especially *Resurrection and Moral Order* and *The Desire of the Nations*, is a gift to those who want to think more deeply about the political implications of seeing power as creative love. A very different influence on me, years ago, was Marilyn French's feminist manifesto *Beyond Power*, which awakened one privileged male university sophomore to the interaction of power and gender, and also started a low-simmering dissatisfaction with the idea that we could ever get "beyond power" in the way she seemed to hope. When I started to seriously explore these topics, Janet Hagberg's wise and practical *Real Power* seemed much more helpful than French. None of these influences can be held responsible for anything I say here, except that they planted the seeds of a question: What if the Western intellectual tradition at least since Nietzsche (but further back, as Milbank shows, through Max Weber to the ancient Greeks) is mistaken about power? What if there is another way? If the gospel really is good news for all of creation, is it possible that the gospel is good news about power?

The truth is we need far more deeply Christian, deeply honest conversations about power than any one book can offer. My hope with this book is simply to get us talking about power, and talking about it in a new way, a way that goes to the heart of the good news and the One who alone is good.

There are four parts to this book. Each is punctuated by biblical explorations—looking at the themes of power in biblical texts from Genesis to John to Philemon to Revelation. The amazing thing about Scripture is that when we bring almost any serious question to it and begin reading and listening with that question in mind, we discover a richly textured, endlessly provocative way of seeing that question in the stories, poems, prayers, laments and prophecies of the Bible's witnesses. A book that tried

to treat "the biblical theology of power" would be a different and far
thicker book, but I hope these biblical explorations at least show us, like
geologists digging test wells in a newly discovered formation, just how
much treasure remains to be unearthed when we start asking the Bible to
form our imaginations about power.

The first part of this book makes the case that power is a gift—a gift that
has been diminished and distorted by sin, but a gift nonetheless. Power is
rooted in creation, the calling of something out of nothing and the fruitful,
multiplying abundance of our astonishing world. It is intimately tied to
image bearing: the unique role that human beings play in representing the
cosmos's Creator in the midst of creation.

You can't tell a biblical story about image bearing, however, without
talking about false images. The story of what has gone wrong with power
is the story of how the image bearers misused their gift of creativity. They
replaced the true image of the invisible God with all too tangible substitute images, false gods who bring nothing but diminishment and disappointment. The misuse and rejection of God's gift of image bearing takes
the form of idolatry and injustice, the two things God most hates. Understanding how these two distortions of image bearing relate to one another
is the key to understanding what has gone so tragically wrong with the gift
of power. Only when the true Image Bearer arrives do we begin to see how
the story of our idolatry and injustice may have, against all odds, the hap-
piest possible ending.

The second part of the book is about the very concrete ways that
idolatry and injustice creep into our use of power—the ways we are
tempted to play false gods. Like the man and woman in the Garden after
they ate the fruit, power, so present and visible in the very good creation,
now hides and seeks invisibility. It has gone underground and underfoot,
tripping us up and luring us into false dreams and foolish ventures. When
power resurfaces, it takes the form of coercion and violence, the most
visible and visceral distortion of what power was meant to be. But even
here we will see glimpses of a better way.

In the third part we will examine the way power is channeled over space
and through time in the form of institutions. These days it is fashionable
to be anti-institutional; around the world, people are losing trust in insti-

tutions and those who hold institutional office, whether prime ministers, company presidents or popes. But a closer look suggests that institutions are themselves a gift, indispensable for human flourishing and for the fulfillment of God's intention for his image bearers. Indeed, so deeply do institutions express the gift of power, when they go wrong they go wrong in the most spectacular and fearsome way, becoming the "principalities and powers" that transcend mere human existence and join forces with the spiritual powers at war with God in the heavenly places. And yet God's redemptive story is good news for institutions as well, and gives us a role to play in their taming and their thriving.

Finally, we will consider how to bring power, with all its gifts and all the ways it grips us, back under the lordship of the One before whom every knee will eventually bow, through the disciplines that put powerful people—like us!—in their proper place. The classical spiritual disciplines, along with disciplines as small as doing the dishes, humble us and open us to grace. They are capable of making us people who can truly bear the weight of the glory of the image of God, a life of true power. There is a way beyond power's grip, through the practices of sabbath and worship that bring power to its proper end.

Why is power a gift? Because power is for flourishing. When power is used well, people and the whole cosmos come more alive to what they were meant to be. And flourishing is the test of power. Writing a book is an act of creative power, with all the risks and uncertainties that come with any true act of creation. Reading a book is its own exercise of creative power, one that requires the investment and risk of time, attention, hope and a kind of love. I'm grateful that you have taken up this book. I pray that when you put it down, you will be one step closer to the flourishing for which you were created, and that as we, together, make something of the world, the cosmos itself would groan a bit less and sing a bit more, as the whole creation awaits the revealing of the children of God.

# THE DISCOVERY OF POWER

Last night in our neighborhood, the power went out.

Only for a few minutes, mind you. Not enough to wake us from sleep, though the fan in the bedroom window must have coasted to a halt before resuming its cooling and soothing whir. Just enough to disrupt our digital clocks—when I got up this morning three of them were blinking in confusion—and unsettle the family computer, which was dark and silent until I restarted it. Just enough to remind us that flowing through our home, our neighborhood, our town and our nation is a current of power that almost never fails us. Almost every morning the clocks know what time it is, the computer has completed its overnight backups, the milk in the refrigerator is cold, and the water in the shower is hot.

I live surrounded by power. It very nearly killed me.

The summer after we moved into our current house, I started noticing a strange popping sound when I opened and closed the garage door. Somehow, for several weeks I failed to connect that sound to a problem we were having with our air conditioner. Its circuit breaker was tripping at odd moments. We would go to the garage, reset the circuit breaker and the air conditioning would work again. One more gift of power—effortless comfort on hot summer days.

One morning I had put my bike in the garage after a good long ride. Closing the garage door, I heard the abrupt "pop" again. This time I also noticed, barely out of the corner of my eye, a flash of light.

I opened the door again. I heard another pop and saw a searing bright arc of light illuminating the garage. There is only one thing that makes light that bright: high-voltage electricity jumping a gap from somewhere it should be to somewhere it shouldn't. I jumped back in alarm, then gingerly crept under the half-opened door into the garage to investigate.

Our garage door, like most, was mounted on tracks and counter sprung with heavy coils of wire on each side that made it possible to raise and lower it easily. Some quick-working electrician, who had installed the air conditioning unit just outside the garage shortly before we moved in, had run the wire from the circuit breaker to the compressor right past one of those heavy metal springs. This was, shall we say, not exactly according to code. Over several months the travel of the spring back and forth had gradually rubbed off the insulation. Every successive opening or closing of the door dug deeper. Bare copper was waiting to make contact, and when it did the resulting arc of electricity was tripping the circuit breaker, making that popping sound and flash of light, and coming within moments and millimeters of finding its path to the ground through my hand on the door. There is no good reason, other than sheer luck, that I was never on the receiving end of 4,800 watts of power at the end of one of my morning bike rides.

The frayed cable is long since fixed, rerouted away from the door and protected by shielded conduit, by an electrician who swore under his breath when he saw the original job.

I still open that door a bit gingerly. I live surrounded by power.

## MAKING SOMETHING OF THE WORLD

Like the electric current that runs, with the rarest of interruptions, through my home, power is a fundamental feature of life. And as with electricity, those who have the most unfettered access to power are the ones who are likely to think about it the least—unless and until it suddenly disappears or violently appears. But that does not make it less important or dangerous or valuable. For power is all those things. It courses through our lives. When it is rightly used, it makes possible most of what makes us truly human. When it is misused, it puts all of us at tremendous risk. Like Narnia's Aslan, it is never safe, even when it is good. Unlike Aslan, it is not always good.

What, then, is power? May I begin with a deceptively simple definition: power is the ability to make something of the world. Here I am borrowing unabashedly, just as I did in an earlier book, from the journalist Ken Myers, whose simple and profound definition of culture will serve us so well: culture is what human beings make of the world, in both senses—the stuff we make from the raw material of nature, but also the meaning we make. This is our basic task, preoccupation and quest: to make something of a world that comes with no ready explanation yet has seemed to nearly every human being to throb with meaning.

Power is simply (and not so simply) the ability to participate in that stuff-making, sense-making process that is the most distinctive thing that human beings do.

Of course, when we define power this way we recognize that we human beings are not the only creatures that make something of the world. Chimpanzees do it, and (with less complexity and more methane out the back end) so do cows. At an elemental level all life exhibits power, transforming its surroundings. And all life requires power. The yeast that transforms my dough into bread requires the input of heat and the stored energy in the carbohydrates of the flour in the dough. The tree in our back yard, shading our home with the new green of spring leaves or covering our lawn with the yellow blanket of fall, draws its power from the sun itself, the ultimate source of almost all the power we or any other part of creation have yet learned to harvest. The same sun, indeed, once shone on eons of living creatures that then slowly decomposed in layers far beneath the ground, becoming the coal, gas and oil that make our lives so seemingly effortless in so many ways. In all these transactions, slow or speedy, local or global, power pulses wherever we find life. When power departs, as in some of the darkest corners of the oceans or in the final gasp of death, world making also ends and, dust, we return to the earth that for a little while we had the power to change.

So power, in this broadest sense of making something of the world, is a universal quality of life, from coral reefs to cellists. But only human beings, as far as we can tell, exercise power in the second sense that Myers calls our attention to, not just making stuff but making sense. It is the unique power of human beings to invest our creations with meaning, to interpret the world rather than just blunder through it. As singular as our human power has become to physically reshape the world into gardens and cities, dammed rivers and mushroom clouds, even more singular is our ability to pass on meaning to the next generation, to shape their horizons of possibility with interpretations of not just what the world is but what it is *for*.

And what is powerlessness? It is being cut off from these two kinds of world making. The powerlessness of death means that the world may act on us, but we will never again act on it. Such powerlessness, just as much as power, is a fundamental feature of human existence, a reality of which those in the prime of our lives probably need all the reminding we can bear. We began, not so long ago, quite unable to make anything of the world, and we will soon be, much sooner than we can truly grasp, once again at the mercy of others' power to sustain us. And a moment after that, as far as this world is concerned, we will be gone altogether. Our short interlude of power takes place between two infinitely long seasons of helplessness. The phrase "temporarily abled," sometimes used by advocates for the "disabled" to describe those of us who currently have command of our bodies' functions, is empirically, unassailably true.

Just as there is more to world making than just making stuff, however, there is more to powerlessness than being unable to bring about a tangible change in the world. The deeper and more debilitating form of powerlessness is to be cut off from making *meaning*. There are able-bodied people all over the world whose physical capacity to make something is undiminished (much less diminished, in fact, than my own body's after decades working at a screen), but who are denied any opportunity to make their own sense of the world. Perhaps they were denied this by being cut off from education, the process by which human beings gain the cultural fluency to participate in culture's ultimate task of meaning making. Perhaps they are denied by deeply ingrained assumptions about who matters in the world—excluded from the circle of meaning making by virtue of their skin color, gender or dialect. Their attempts at sorting out meaning, bestowing significance and telling truthful stories are ignored, mocked or worse. In an unsettling irony, millions of them make the very cultural artifacts that allow us to engage in meaning-making acts—within reach as I write are my smartphone, my laptop, my ebook reader, my widescreen monitor, all the essential tools that allow me to make something of the world in the deepest sense. But the voices and stories of those who made these tools remain unheard and untold, and the goods they manufacture arrive in our stores and homes sealed in supernaturally clean plastic, from which human fingerprints have been conscientiously removed.

This is not the way it was supposed to be. To be sure, not all powerlessness is bad. Some of our limits are themselves a gift. The things our human bodies cannot do far outnumber the things we can do; our ability to make sense of the world runs up against the world's many unfathomable mysteries. These limits often serve us well. But when powerlessness results from the exercise of power—when one person or group of people acts to deprive another of power, and especially when that pattern of exclusion persists from generation to generation—then something has gone fiercely wrong, and not just for the ones who directly suffer their disempowerment. Because the ability to make something of the world is in a real sense the source of human well-being, because true power multiplies capacity and wealth, when any human beings live in entrenched powerlessness, all of us are impoverished.

## MODERN-DAY SLAVES

Perhaps no statistic reminds us more graphically of the distortion of power in our world than this: there are twenty-one million slaves in the world today. They labor as brick makers, coffee harvesters, cigarette rollers and domestic servants. They are not free to leave. If they try, they are savagely beaten. Millions are serially raped in brothels—as young as nine years old—and even those not enslaved in the sex industry are liable to be sexually exploited at the whim of their masters. They are paid nothing beyond the barest amount for their subsistence, often ostensibly to pay off debts incurred by themselves or their parents, but in fact laboring under onerous interest rates that ensure that their debt will never be discharged.

One early summer morning I was on a train to meet some of these modern-day slaves. The train departed from the bustling station in Chennai, in southeastern India, rolling west through the lush fields where you never fail to see people, countless people, planting, harvesting, culti-

vating, working. I had come to Chennai to meet Jayakumar Christian, the
director of the Indian affiliate of the international humanitarian organization World Vision. I had asked for a few hours of his time for an interview
and had assumed we would meet at World Vision's headquarters. But
Jayakumar had emailed me a few weeks before my arrival, telling me to
expect a train trip. "I am taking you to Gudiyatham," he said when we met
just after dawn on an already-sweltering morning. "I need to visit our
program there, and I want you to come along."

In the Gudiyatham district, nine years before this visit, child slavery
had been rampant. In one small village of perhaps two hundred people,
twenty elementary-school-age children were enslaved: Prabhu worked in
a filthy motorcycle shop, Boobalan sat at a loom all day weaving, Ghanthi
rolled cigarettes, Suresh made matches. None went to school. The debts
they were theoretically paying back were for 2,000 to 4,000 rupees—in
US dollars, fifty to one hundred dollars. But everyone knew that those
debts would never be paid off.

The tiny amounts are significant and indicative of the new face of slavery
worldwide. In the era of the Anglo-American Atlantic slave trade, to purchase another human being could cost thousands of dollars. Slaves obtained
through the Atlantic trade were (as odious as it is even to write this phrase)
valuable property, as valuable as a horse or a mule. Today, it is not just India
where you can purchase a slave for one hundred dollars—in his 2008 book
*A Crime So Monstrous*, the journalist Benjamin Skinner describes negoti-
ating to purchase a twelve-year-old girl in Haiti, for the purpose of labor and
sex, for a grand total of fifty dollars. In the documentary film *At the End of
Slavery*, Ambassador Mark Lagon observes that this means that modern
slaves are in effect disposable, "like a styrofoam cup."

Such slavery is illegal in every country in the world, and few government officials are eager to admit that it is happening on their watch.
But it is happening, thanks to official complacency and, often, complicity.
(Not infrequently, Indian police are called to brick kilns that enslave
children, called, that is, by the owners of the kilns, to give the slaves a
beating and thus also to undermine any hope that the authorities care
about their captivity.) There is a cruel irony in the fact that two centuries
after the abolition of the Atlantic slave trade by the British Parliament,

one hundred and fifty years after the Union's victory in America's Civil War, more human beings are enslaved today than were trafficked across the Atlantic in two hundred years of chattel slavery.

If you want to understand power's dangers, slavery has one advantage: it is vivid and complete in its corruption. In enslavement one human being asserts unlimited power over another, an assertion that requires not just the inflation of the slave owner's power to unholy, godlike levels, but the eradication of the slave's power. Some masters may be relatively benevolent (as some were, at least in their own eyes, in the era of American slavery). But the master-slave relationship remains one of categorical lordship, and it is predicated on the owner's assertion of the right to take anything and everything from the slave, up to and including her life. Ultimately the owner owns everything; the slave owns nothing.

In this corrupted version of absolute power—very different from other kinds of power we will consider shortly—power is a finite resource, jealously hoarded. For a slave to gain power requires the master to lose power, which is part of the reason that full slavery includes a claim on the children of slaves, leading to the phenomenon, still common in parts of Southeast Asia today, of multiple generations enslaved by a single owner. A slave owner can never admit that the slave might create something outside of the owner's control, even a child. In a corrupted power relationship, *all* power must accrue to the powerful.

## "WE FREE SLAVES"

For time out of mind, this had been the reality of life in Gudiyatham. But when I met Prabhu, Boobalan, Ghanthi and Suresh, they were no longer slaves. For nine years World Vision staff had been patiently, steadily working in the district. They had started a women's association with an emphasis on financial literacy and pooled savings. The members told Jayakumar proudly that just a few months before they had walked into a local bank, something "we would never have had the courage to do before," and found that the bankers treated them with respect, thanks to the substantial sum they had set aside for a deposit account. World Vision had worked with local village councils, called *panchayats*, to address substandard housing and create job training programs. They had started a citizenship training program for former "untouchables" who had never before thought of themselves as having the rights of citizens. (A few weeks before my visit, local Hindu fundamentalists had attacked the World Vision office, claiming that the citizenship program was a covert effort to prose- lytize. Fortunately, village leaders rallied, persuading the local police that the program was entirely legal, and managed to avert mob violence.) At every step World Vision had educated the community about India's laws against bonded labor and the right of children to go to school.

So at lunchtime a dozen middle-school-age children filed shyly into the World Vision office, immaculately dressed in their school uniforms, and told Jayakumar and me their stories. Ghanthi, perhaps twelve years old, quickly warmed to Jayakumar's questions and gentle prompting, and told us that two years before she had given up hope for her future. Now she was in school. What did she want to do when she finished school, Jaya- kumar asked? "I will become a doctor and come back to this village," she answered without hesitation and with a twinkle in her eye. Was child slavery still a problem in her district, he asked? "There are a few children still in bonded labor. But we go to the slave owners and tell them, 'You need to stop this! You could go to jail!'" I wasn't sure I had heard correctly. Was she saying that former child slaves were confronting slave owners? "Yes, and we tell the children they have the right to leave. We have freed three children this month."

Perhaps the most astonishing moment of our visit was the "children's panchayat." At this weekly meeting the children could practice the skills of civic life, rehearsing roles they might eventually play as adults. Except they weren't just playing. With obvious delight and pride, fifty boys and girls sat on banana leaves in a small clearing and told us how they were ending slavery in their district. They presented fragrant garlands of honor to Jayakumar and me (feeling entirely unworthy), sang local songs for us, told stories of how life was changing in their village and then asked Jayakumar to address them.

Jayakumar is a man of a few well-chosen words. His face gleamed with perspiration and pride as he said, "There are three things I want you to remember when you grow up. Remember God. Remember your parents. And remember your community." It struck me that he was asking them to remember—and honor—parents who had handed them over to slave owners, and, for that matter, to remember God when many circumstances in their lives might seem to argue for God's distance or nonexistence, and to remain committed to a community that for many years had tolerated the most egregious forms of injustice.

Yet as I listened to Jayakumar's simple and gentle words I felt, and the children's intent faces suggested they too felt, that something essential was being restored to them. The liberation being accomplished in this district was not just individual release from bondage, the sum of the names posted on the wall at the World Vision community office. The lines of community, family and faith, fractured by exploitation, were being healed as well. What poverty and powerlessness had taken away, Jayakumar's colleagues were steadily, carefully restoring—or, actually, had already restored.

Indeed, there was nothing in the demeanor or manner of the children or their parents that would have caused me to think that they were either poor or powerless. They radiated confidence and pride, yet also humility and generosity. One ten-year-old handed me a coconut, its top freshly lopped off to give access to the cool, sweet water inside. She was the host, I was the guest; she was the expert, I was the student; she was, in the time-honored tradition of hospitality, honored in the act of honoring her visitor. I can still taste that coconut water, the sweet and fragrant taste of *shalom*.

On the train on the way back to Chennai, I said to Jayakumar, "It's odd. These people are still materially poor. But they don't *act* poor."

He smiled broadly. "That is how I know it is time for World Vision to leave this district. Our work is nearly done."

## A DIFFERENT KIND OF POWER

Jayakumar Christian is a powerful man. He has a PhD from an American institution and works for one of the world's largest multinational organizations. He is responsible for eight thousand employees across India, with connections to the highest levels of Indian government, business and religious leadership. "Poverty is the absence of linkages, the absence of connections with others," Jayakumar told me. By that measure, Jayakumar is the very opposite of poor.

But when Jayakumar picked me up for our trip to Chennai, he was wearing the same utterly plain long kurta, made of coarsely woven cloth, that my friends told me he wears every day. For our day-long trip he carried a small cell phone, a few bills of currency and nothing else. Most leaders at Jayakumar's level would be answering their phone or responding to email and text messages at every spare moment; Jayakumar's phone rang once the whole day. When I visited him at World Vision India's headquarters the next day, his desk in a small, simple office was entirely bare. Jayakumar lived a life of utterly intentional simplicity—a life that allowed him to give his full attention to one place and person at a time, and to be equally accessible to a peasant farmer or a prime minister.

Jayakumar's staff in Gudiyatham greeted him with undisguised affection and excitement. They had endured the late-night raid by Hindu fundamentalists a few weeks before; Jayakumar's motive for making this trip, it became clear, had been less about showing a Western journalist a successful project and much more about visiting members of his team who had been through a harrowing experience and still faced threats. Several of them had been in Gudiyatham for nearly a decade, raising families in a district far from their home. They were working across the grain of local patterns of power (probably another factor in the mob's assault on their office) yet also working alongside local officials who were willing to recognize the persistent pattern of child labor and work to end it.

In a place where power had been abused for generations, Jayakumar and his staff represented a very different kind of power. This power was actually giving life rather than constricting it. It occurred to me that none of the children, women or village leaders I met would likely have wanted the World Vision staff to give up their power, any more than they would have welcomed the thought of disbanding their village savings association or the children's panchayat. For this power was not like the slave owners': it was not a finite quantity that had to be hoarded but a multiplying resource, like life itself. When the village children gained power, that did not mean that Jayakumar or his colleagues lost it. Indeed, with Ghanthi on their side, they were making more progress than ever.

## POWER AT ITS BEST

Here is what we need to discover about power: it is both better and worse than we could imagine. Power at its best is the power exercised by

Jayakumar and his colleagues at World Vision, and perhaps even more by twelve-year-old Ghanthi, boldly confronting slave owners and planning to be a doctor. It is the one swift stroke of the machete that opens a coconut for the honored guest. It is a source of refreshment, laughter, joy and life—and of more power. Remove power and you cut off life, the possibility of creating something new and better in this rich and recalcitrant world. Life is power. Power is life. And flourishing power leads to flourishing life.

Of course, like life itself, power is nothing—worse than nothing—without love. But love without power is less than it was meant to be. Love without the capacity to make something of the world, without the ability to respond to and make room for the beloved's flourishing, is frustrated love.

This is why the love that is the heartbeat of the Christian story—the Father's love for the Son and, through the Son, for the world—is not simply a sentimental feeling or a distant, ethereal theological truth, but has been signed and sealed by the most audacious act of true power in the history of the world, the resurrection of the Son from the dead. Power at its best is resurrection to full life, to full humanity. Whenever human beings become what they were meant to be, when even death cannot finally hold its prisoners, then we can truly speak of power.

Yet it is the way of our world that the very thing that makes us fully human at our best is what most truly corrupts us at our worst. Power at its worst is the unmaker of humanity—breeding inhumanity in the hearts of those who wield power, denying and denouncing the humanity of the ones who suffer under power. This is the power exercised by the money lender, by the police who ignore or protect him, by the officials who would rather not confront him. This power ultimately will put everything around it to death rather than share abundant life with another. It is also the power of feigned or forced ignorance, the power of complacency and self-satisfaction with our small fiefdoms of comfort. Power, the truest servant of love, can also be its most implacable enemy.

Many people who have heard the subject of this book have urged me to choose a less abrupt and unsettling word than *power*. What about *authority* or *influence* or *leadership*? But these words are too safe, and they are too one-sided, too reassuringly benign. The word *power* has electric force, jolting us awake. Power at its worst should unsettle us, should shock us. But power at its best is also much more than these safer words can convey. It is the current of life. It is dangerously good.

I think this book really began on the train home from the Gudiyatham district, having looked into the eyes of children who had known literal slavery and real freedom, sitting next to Jayakumar as he dozed after a long and intense day of listening to and loving his staff, their communities, their neighbors. I remember thinking, I am inches from a saint.

These are the moments that have shaped my life: the moments when I see that the world is infinitely worse, and infinitely better, than it appears. And that is what I have come to believe about power.

**PART ONE**

# THE GIFT OF POWER

## IN THE BEGINNING IT WAS NOT SO

# EXPLORATION

## GENESIS 1–2—ORIGINAL POWER

All of us have a functional Bible within the Bible—the parts of the book that we read, rehearse and remember. With a library as sprawling and complex as the Christian Bible, it is inevitable and probably necessary that we pay attention to some parts more than others. But I've concluded there are four chapters missing from the working Bibles of all too many Christians, and these missing chapters are not some obscure ceremonial texts or dusty corners of the royal chronicles. Instead, they are the very bookends of Scripture: the first two chapters of Genesis and the last two chapters of Revelation.

And to miss these chapters—the first two about the creation, the second two about the new creation—is to miss the whole point of the biblical story. When these chapters drop out of our functional Bibles, our understanding of culture, power and salvation itself is badly weakened.

Of course, these chapters are not literally missing from our Bibles, and indeed both Genesis and Revelation have been the subject of more than a little misplaced attention throughout church history. Revelation has been mined for clues to the very thing Jesus explicitly told his disciples neither he nor they could know—the exact timing of the end of the world. Genesis, meanwhile, has in recent history been used to undermine what we *can* know about the development of the natural world from the discoveries of cosmology, paleontology and biology, rather than being read as a definitive, revealed account of divine creation that confronted polytheistic pagan cosmologies of conflict. *good for him*

But the potential for misunderstanding and misuse shouldn't deter us from granting these crucial chapters the authority they were meant to bear. Beginnings and endings matter. If we were to come upon a novel with the first and final chapters ripped out, in order to enjoy it or even understand it we would need to fill in those missing pages with our best guesses about the protagonist's and antagonist's origins and final destinies. Our guesses might be true to the author's intent, or they might be wildly off the mark, but they would be guesses all the same. And if the first or last pages revealed some essential information or crucial plot twist, we might well misread the whole book in between.

Indeed, if we have not fully absorbed the message of Genesis 1–2 and Revelation 21–22, we will surely supply some sort of beginning and ending to our own subcanonical versions of the biblical story. And in fact you could classify recent Christian movements by the alternative beginnings and endings they have supplied in place of the Bible's own. In the last century some liberal Protestants, finding Revelation a bit embarrassing, adopted a progressive eschatology in which the benign processes of human history would lead to ever greater harmony. This had little to do with John's dramatic and cataclysmic vision, but it fit well at a moment when Christianity aspired to be utterly at home in the world.

Evangelical Protestants, less at ease in the world (or at least less willing to admit it), took a different tack. Many evangelical tellings of the biblical story, especially those designed to deliver an evangelistic message, effectively began with Genesis 3: the fall of humanity. And they ended with Revelation 20: the casting of Satan and all his works into the lake of fire. Understood this way, the gospel runs an abbreviated gamut from original sin to final judgment. The original good creation and the glorious new creation are afterthoughts when they are mentioned at all.

This smaller story is true, as far as it goes. We really do live under the curse of the relentless and restless human declaration of independence from God, and under the reality of coming judgment. But there are serious problems with this truncated version of the biblical story. The first is that it doesn't seem to offer much good news—a story that starts with sin and ends with judgment is a bad-news-to-bad-news story. What is the good news in such a story? In all too many tellings the good news simply becomes the message that for those who believe in Jesus, it is possible to escape the story altogether, being plucked by a kind of divine skyhook into an eternal life outside the doomed story of the world. But of the world itself, especially its beauty and wonder, the truncated story of Genesis 3 to Revelation 20 has little to say.

There is a deeper problem with a gospel that runs from Genesis 3 to Revelation 20. Such a "gospel" in truth tells the world nothing that the world does not already know. Original sin, Reinhold Niebuhr liked to say, is the only Christian doctrine that is empirically verifiable. Our neighbors may not believe in a Fall, but they cannot deny that something is terribly out of joint in the human story. At the other end of history, modern science has made it clear that "progress" is not just a historical fantasy but a physical impossibility. Thanks to the Second Law of Thermodynamics, the total amount of disorder in the universe is increasing, and one distant day the universe's vast reserves of information, energy and order will be dissipated in a great and final sigh followed by an everlasting silence. True, this cosmic story ends not in fire but in ice (although some models leave open the possibility that the universe will collapse again upon itself in a final fiery burst of annihilation)— but the ultimate loss of all things is not in doubt. The vision of a sulfurous, consuming lake of fire is an eerily apt metaphor for the eradication of history and meaning that is assured in the world as we know it. That end may be unimaginably distant, but it is inexorably approaching as certainly as our own individual deaths.

So a story that begins in sin and ends in judgment doesn't just fail to be good news. It isn't news at all. It tells our neighbors nothing they cannot figure out on their own. But the Bible's story is a story of good news: both good *and* news, both unexpected and unexpectedly hopeful. It is good news about the end: the astonishing claim is that the world will not be forgotten or left to its own decay, but rescued and remade. It is good news about the beginning: this world does not simply originate in primordial conflict, whether the cosmic conflict of the *Enuma Elish* or the pitched struggle of Darwinistic competition, but in abundance and delight. And it is good news about power.

## FROM "MAKE IT SO" TO "LET THERE BE"

The first chapter of Genesis is full of the goodness and good results of creative power. Genesis begins not with violence but with breath and word. The Creator God does not need to wrest being out of chaos; instead, God calmly speaks the simple words "Let there be." These words, in what grammarians call the "jussive" form, are not direct imperatives. They are simultaneously more powerful and less controlling than that.

When we think of power, we often think in the imperative mood. I came of age during the televised command of Patrick Stewart's memorable character Jean-Luc Picard, captain of the rebuilt *USS Enterprise* in *Star Trek: The Next Generation*. Captain Picard would famously lift a finger and say, "Make it so." The imperative mood is suited to command. It leaves little room for independent reflection or action by the subordinate, and indeed in the heat of an encounter with a hostile Romulan warbird the last thing anyone needs is an indecisive captain giving vague suggestions, open to various interpretations, to a philosophically minded crew. In times of crisis clear imperatives can be the difference between life and death, something that is as true for parents of toddlers as for captains of starships.

But the creativity of Genesis 1 is not the result of crisis. So rather than ordering the primal elements around like lieutenants on red alert, God says, "Let there be," in many ways an even more powerful phrase than "Make it so."

"Let there be" does not have to assert power, it assumes it. It does not have to impose power, it indwells it. Yet "let there be" also suggests a multiplication of power that is not found in the peremptory phrase "Make it so." "Make it so" is a strictly limited and limiting command. The subordinates making it so are not expected to make anything *else* so—their job is to put into practice the precise decision arrived at on the bridge, no more and no less. But when the words *let there be* ring through the universe, they accomplish very literally what they describe—the creation of *being* where there was none before. New beings come into existence, each with their own capabilities, potential and sphere of influence. Indeed, "Let there be" bequeaths power to others, making room for more power.

By saying "Let there be," the Creator God makes room for more being, for more agents who could utter their own "let it be." And in response to that divine jussive, acting in the space opened up by God's creative power, they will engage in their own acts of creativity. On the successive days of Genesis's story, those empowered creatures will yield seed, bear fruit, rule the day and the night, fly, be fruitful, multiply, creep, and fill the earth.

And they will swarm.

> And God said, "Let the waters bring forth swarms of living creatures, and let birds fly above the earth across the dome of the sky." So God created the great sea monsters and every living creature that moves, of every kind, with which the waters swarm, and every winged bird of every kind. And God saw that it was good. God blessed them, saying, "Be fruitful and multiply and fill the waters in the seas, and let birds multiply on the earth." And there was evening and there was morning, the fifth day. (Genesis 1:20-23)

God's creative act brings forth not carefully regimented sets of creatures but "swarms" of them. Swarms are not well suited to the imperative mood. Anyone who has been too near a swarm of honeybees, gone scuba diving among schools of fish or seen a wheeling flock of sparrows over a grain field at sunset knows how awesomely unpredictable a swarm can be. Other translations use the word *teeming* for the animals of Genesis's fifth day, another word of incalculable and inestimable abundance. The Creator is not seeking a world full of pets, individually domesticated animals bred to be attentive to their human masters. He delights in wildness. Swarming and teeming are part of what make the world good—the overflow and excess of life. All of this actually gives greater glory to God, who has breathed into existence the vast spaces of earth, sky and sea where these creatures can teem, than would a meticulously tended back yard. The Creator loves teeming.

## FROM "LET THERE BE" TO "LET US MAKE"

And then, significantly, the voice changes and becomes more personal. Whereas the rest of creation is brought into being through the jussive "let it be," on the sixth day God speaks unexpectedly in the plural "cohortative" form, "Let us make humankind in our image, according to our likeness." Now God is personally invested and involved. This is no distant sovereign decree; it is an intensely personal decision to crown creation with the image bearers who will themselves be invited to share their Maker's fruitful dominion over the world.

Only after this personal decision do we hear an imperative addressed to the image bearers. And what are they commanded to do? To develop their own power: "Be fruitful and multiply, and fill the earth and subdue it; and have dominion over the fish of the sea and over the birds of the air and over every living thing that moves upon the earth" (Genesis 1:28). The command is to teem and become agents of teeming. These image bearers will become the kind of persons who can themselves say "Let there be" and "Let us make," not just deputies or functionaries in a heavenly bureaucracy of command and control, but agents of creativity in a universe designed to create more and more power.

Indeed, while you may never have thought of grammar as a particularly practical subject, this progression of verbs happens nearly every time human beings put their power to creative use. All creative work begins with the jussive "Let there be." As I was drafting this chapter, I was also drafting a proposal for a new project for my employer. My job was to lay out not just an accurate picture of the cultural and business environment, but to speak into being a picture of what should and could be, long before a single article was written or minute of video was shot. Every proposal, every business plan, and for that matter every architectural blueprint, culinary recipe, and Little League roster is an act of saying "Let there be." Let there be something rather than nothing. Let reality expand to include this possibility, let the world open up to this new way of seeing what is and what can be. Creativity begins in the jussive mood.

But if creativity begins with "let there be," it moves quickly to the cohortative: "Let us make." If even divine creativity requires a community, then any human creativity involves more than just an individual fiat—we gather with a circle of partners to define, refine and in many cases greatly improve the original vision. Just as the climax of creation, the introduction of God's own image bearers into the world, only happens in the context of the divine community, so we often find that our own creative vision does not reach its full potential until we bring others into the process. This is why the next stage of the project will involve meeting after meeting, as a core team begins to form and apply their own creativity toward asking what the ultimate, highest form of the original idea might become. In other words, we will apply our collective efforts to flourishing—to bringing the greatest possible result out of the early ideas and the initial forms. What will emerge from those conversations will almost certainly be more fruitful, creative, surprising and alive than what was envisioned in the pages of the original proposal.

Only after the jussive has given way to the cohortative and a group of image bearers have said "Let us make" together will we then use the imperative, and even then we will use hard-edged commands like "Make it so" quite sparingly. Mostly we will say "Be fruitful and multiply" to the people we employ and empower for the work. Fill the space created by our early vision with your own creativity. If we have done our job well, at this stage we will have surprisingly little to do because others will be taking up their own creative task. And if they do their task well, the creation will be enriched, more useful, more beautiful and more capacious for further creativity. This is power as it is meant to be.

## POWER IS FOR FLOURISHING

On the very first page of the Bible, then, power, flourishing and image bearing are connected. Power is for flourishing—teeming, fruitful, multiplying abundance. Power creates and shapes an environment where creatures can flourish, making room for the variety, diversity and unpredictability of coral reefs and tropical forests, but also the surprising biological richness of high deserts and ocean depths. And image bearing is for power—for it is the Creator's desire to fill the earth with representatives who will have the same kind of delighted dominion over the teeming creatures as their Maker. Which means image bearing is for flourishing. The image bearers do not exist for their own flourishing alone, but to bring the whole creation to its fulfillment.

Thousands of years after Genesis was written, we can see in a way its first readers could never have imagined just how much capacity these human image bearers had to fill the earth—just how much power was ultimately available to them, coiled in the physical elements' chemical and nuclear bonds, and emerging from the incredible complexity of the human mind and the fecundity of human culture. But we also know that on the very next page of our Bible is a tragic twist in the story. The original image bearers flaunt their freedom in the garden and abandon their original vocation. The result is diminishing, rather than flourishing, their own and the whole created order's, as dominion and delight turn to domination and exploitation. And here too today we see the inexpressible horror of the full playing out of this story in dimensions and at scales of which the first readers of Genesis were mercifully innocent. Image bearing has indeed turned out to be far better, and far worse, than anyone but the Creator could ever have imagined.

But as Christians we have the great privilege of reading this story from the perspective of its most decisive chapter, and we know that not all is lost. In the fullness of time two image bearers uttered their own "let it be" back to the Creator. A young woman called herself the handmaiden of the Lord, saying, "Let it be with me according to your word" (Luke 1:38), making room for the one true Image of the invisible God to take on visible flesh. And her son, in a garden on the night before his death, prayed, "Yet not my will but yours be done" (Luke 22:42). They returned to the humble power of the jussive, and there at the turning point of history, the promise of true image bearing, true flourishing and true power was restored.

# 2

# POWER IS A GIFT

**P**ower is for flourishing. This means power is a gift worth asking for, seeking and—should we receive it—stewarding.

This is not the only thing we need to know about power. We also need to know how power can go wrong—how it *has* gone wrong. But that is not where we should begin. There is a saying in the legal world: "Hard cases make bad law." There are plenty of hard cases with power. Sometimes, admittedly, it can seem that the whole history of power is one long story of perversion and betrayal. In fact, if I were not a follower of Jesus Christ I might believe that was the deepest truth about power. I might follow Nietzsche, Foucault and all their modern and postmodern disciples into the abyss of cynicism, seeing every human story as a power play.

I have come to believe, though, that the only way to understand power's abuse is to begin with its proper use. When we begin with the best kinds of power, we learn some important truths about power that we would never learn even from the most penetrating critique. Most of all, we learn something that criticism will never teach us: what to hope for. Hope is stronger than fear. If power is dangerous—and it is—our hearts will be most prepared to resist its dangers if they have been shaped by hope.

And that is why I started learning to play the cello.

## TEN THOUSAND HOURS

Catherine, my wife, had played violin since childhood; Amy, our daughter, was following in her footsteps. Timothy, after one brief detour into trumpet, had claimed the viola as his own and spent countless hours every week refining tone, timbre and texture to the point that I would hear music coming from his room and barely believe it was coming from my own son. The undeniable fact was that our family was just one cello short of a string quartet.

So I plucked up my courage and walked down the street to Dane Anderson's house. Dane makes most of his living as a luthier, building and repairing stringed instruments. He has seen every kind of damage a fourth-grader can inflict on a violin. But he is also a fine cellist, and rumor had it that he was occasionally willing to take on a student, even a forty-one-year-old with absolutely no experience.

"Will you teach me to play cello?" I said. "I've never touched a stringed instrument, but I promise to practice."

"We can give it a try," he said. He picked out a loaner cello from a coatroom overflowing with cases of every size. He offered some brusque instructions about how to protect it. (Borrowing a cello from Dane is like borrowing a Ferrari from the guy who owns a body shop; you can see him running through in his head all the possible ways this could go wrong.) He showed me some elementary bowing exercises, we set up a lesson time for the following week, and I was off.

Four years later, I am still a rank beginner. I have kept my word to Dane—when I'm not on the road, I practice an hour a day. When I'm in town on a Thursday morning, I trundle my cello over to Dane's house for a lesson. I sit down and begin warming up, Dane standing in front of me, watching keenly as I try to make it through a scale or a simple étude.

It's been years, fifteen years at least, since I had a teacher. Every time I carry my cello up the steps to Dane's front porch I feel a hint of anxiety. After all, I am going to spend the following hour failing, or at least flailing. A middle-aged guy trying to learn the cello is a squeaky, awkward affair for everyone involved.

To have power is, among many other things, to have control over one's body—to be able to dispose it in a way that brings honor rather than shame. In my cello lessons my body is frequently flatly uncooperative and the subject of unwelcome attention. One morning, as we are working on the extended left-hand position, where the index finger is supposed to reach up and back on the fret board, Dane gazes curiously at my long fingers (which, as a pianist, have been a source of pride) with just the slightest hint of impatience. "Huh. That's weird," he says. My hand simply will not contort into the direction every cellist needs their hand to go.

Dane steps behind me, places his hand on mine, and attempts to reposition my wrist, which keeps slipping in the wrong direction. We engage in a silent, cooperative struggle. At least I am *trying* to cooperate. My recalcitrant left hand just won't play its part. After several vain attempts, he laughs. "Well, we'll figure something out."

He sits back down in the chair a few feet from mine; the usual boundaries are once again in place. We move on, but that awkward struggle will stay with me for a long time: the feeling I had almost forgotten from adolescence of being all wrong angles and misplaced energy, the near blush of frustration at being unable to do something so seemingly simple that Dane can do without a second thought, and perhaps strangest of all, the physical intimacy of the teacher and student, a man's hand on mine, correcting and guiding me.

There is something undeniably quixotic about taking up the cello at age forty-one. Summarizing the research of Anders Ericsson, journalist Malcolm Gladwell has estimated that cultural mastery in pretty much any domain requires ten thousand hours of practice. At one hour a day, six days a week, fifty weeks a year, that comes to something like thirty-three years. Somehow I doubt that even at seventy-four I will be giving Yo-Yo Ma a run for his money.

I have already put in ten thousand hours on another instrument, the piano, and I get paid to play it. Best of all, I can use my skill on the piano to help thousands of people sing together in that fusion of heart, mind, soul and strength that the best music requires and delivers. It's unlikely I'll ever do anything like that with the cello. These hours will add nothing to my earning power, my cultural capital or my ability to impress girls. The only significant culture making that is likely to result will happen on Sunday afternoons when we gather up the music stands from the far corners of the house, open up Mozart's *Eine kleine Nachtmusik* or a hymnbook, and make music. And those afternoons of family music will be all too fleeting. Ten years from now our children will be off to college and beyond. The music we played will evaporate into the air, as does all music, that most insubstantial of art forms, bound to time and ever fading into the distance of memory. All these lessons, all this money, all this time, all this vulnerability—for what, exactly?

The best answer I can muster is that the goal of these ten thousand otherwise completely superfluous hours is flourishing.

I'm learning the cello to flourish as a father, and so my family will flourish. I want my children to hear and see me learning, growing, stretching (for that recalcitrant left hand, quite literally stretching), disciplining my body and mind to be able to create something I could not create before. I want our family to create together, not just to consume together.

I'm seeking to flourish as a disciple, a follower of Christ, the one through whom all things were created and in whom all things hold together: to explore another part of his endlessly abundant creation that I will only find on the other side of practice. Only on the other side of practice will I not just hear a cello's warmth and resonance, but be able to evoke it with my own heart, mind and strength. Studying the cello also requires me to humble myself, to go back to basics, to remind myself of how little I really know or have experienced. Without these constant forays beyond my own capacities, I would grow dangerously sure of myself. It's strange but true that the cello is teaching me about both praise and prayer, both of which begin when we allow ourselves to be made small.

I am also practicing the cello to wean myself from power and accomplishment, to place myself back in the posture of a learner, cultivator and creator. To become a bit like a child. To detoxify from the too-ready recognition and privilege that accompany even the most modest forms of success, to become available again for something surprising and new. Just as children flourish by growing up into adults, so adults flourish by cultivating childlikeness, avoiding the spiritual hardening of the arteries that comes with competence and experience.

In sum, I am studying the cello to acquire true power.

## THE MULTIPLICATION OF POWER

Learning cello is a weekly reminder that true power multiplies when it is shared.

The distribution of power between Dane and me is asymmetrical. Dane has power that I do not—the power to play the cello. I have some power of my own, of course: the ability to pay him a fair wage for his time. But the truth is that Dane was making a living before he took me on as a student. He does not depend on me for money in anything like the same way that I depend on him for instruction.

In fact, the exchange of money involved in cello lessons perfectly illustrates how different power is from money. After every cello lesson, I pay Dane fifty dollars. When I walk into his studio, I have fifty dollars in my pocket; after I walk out, I have fifty fewer dollars and Dane has fifty dollars more. This is what game theorists call a zero-sum transaction: Dane's wealth increases by precisely the amount my wealth decreases. The total amount of money in our little microeconomic system remains the same—only its distribution changes.

But the same thing is not true of power. At the beginning of the lesson, Dane has a (substantial) amount of power to play the cello, and I have a (small) amount. But in the course of the lesson, I acquire a bit more cello-playing power. And this increase in my power does no damage at all to Dane's power. This is what game theory calls a positive-sum transaction: at the end of the lesson, the total amount of power in the world to play the cello has increased.

As our teacher-student relationship continues, the asymmetry in our relationship will decrease, at least slightly. I will become more proficient, less dependent on Dane for the most basic level of instruction. Yet this increase in my power to play the cello will do no damage at all to Dane's power. Quite the reverse. There is an old canard, "Those who can't do, teach." But in a wide range of fields this isn't true at all. Teaching others, increasing their power, actually is a central part of developing one's own power. The most accomplished doctors almost always are found on the faculty of medical schools, training a new generation in both the essentials and the cutting-edge techniques of practice. (Teaching is so important to the highest ranks of the medical profession that Harvard Medical School,

*whoa*

with only 165 entering students each year, has 10,884 doctors attached to its faculty.) Likewise, the mechanic who services my car, a man of great skill and integrity with a flourishing business, has taken a series of young men under his wing as apprentices.

Excellence in these kinds of cultural disciplines requires not just excursions to the limits of ability but also a constant attention to the basics, frequently returning to the most elemental aspects of the field in order to maintain one's skills at the highest level. So even as Dane listens patiently and quizzically to my poor efforts at playing scales, he is reminding himself of fundamentals that he too has to practice every day. And of course he is growing in his power as a teacher, trying and learning new ways to teach just as I am trying and learning new ways to play.

Just because this power is positive-sum—generating more total power in the world—does not at all mean that it is easy or free. There is a kind of *suffering* required to enter into the virtuous circle of creative power, and the suffering is required of both student and teacher. I could, after all, remain in my home and never submit myself to cello lessons, never embarrass myself in front of my neighbor. I could remain secure in my other forms of power rather than voluntarily returning to the vulnerability of powerlessness. And as a teacher, Dane has his own vocation to suffering, the call to patience. He must be willing to welcome me into his studio, week after week, and listen (especially in those first years) to painfully bad cello playing. On the grand scale of human suffering, of course, this is not much—but then again, given how accomplished Dane is as a cellist and how bad I was and still am, it's probably worse than you might think. There is a reason many great performers are poor teachers—they are unwilling to suffer little children to come unto them. The true power that is available to us, the power that multiplies power, lies on the other side of the choice to empty ourselves of power.

Dane, after all, could spend the hour devoted to our lesson much more enjoyably by simply sitting down and playing his own cello. I could stay at home, put Yo-Yo Ma on my iPod and command him to play at the click of a button. In a moment, I would be surrounded by transcendent, effortless cello music. This is the power we are offered by consumer culture: the power to appropriate someone else's creativity and define ourselves by

*really good*

having the good sense to purchase it. This kind of power (later in the book we will refine our terms and call it *privilege*) requires no detour through humility, no apprenticeship, no risk. It is perfectly safe. It is also utterly inert, entirely detached from my real, embodied existence.

Every time I press play, Ma plays. Every time it is the same—the same music, the same intonation and expression and tempo. It is the same whether I am listening with utter concentration or with distracted inattention. In all its digital fidelity, Ma's recording will never deteriorate, even as Ma and I grow older and eventually die. It is always engaging and interesting; unlike me, Ma never fills the house with the sound of repetitive practicing, testing the limits of my family's patience. Ma's recording, as lovely and worthy as it is, is strangely disconnected from any real feature of my own life, completely unlike my own cello playing, which falters when I am tired, goes out of tune when the weather is cold or dry, and only intermittently rewards me with truly satisfying music.

The power to summon up such otherworldly, immutable beauty without commensurate effort is an example of what we once would have called *magic*. The dream of magic is to have power, the ability to make something of the world, without suffering, without relationship and without risk, which are all different ways of saying the same thing. We moderns think of magic as something premodern, superstitious and foreign. But in fact a technological age is devoted to magic. The truth is that we are far more dependent on seemingly effortless power than the most "primitive" society ever was. Even Yo-Yo Ma himself has given in to this kind of simulated power, when he appeared (and I mean "appeared" in both senses) to play a specially commissioned quartet by John Williams for the inauguration of Barack Obama on January 20, 2009. My son and I, watching live, marveled along with millions of others at the musicians' tenacity and skill, daring to play their instruments outdoors in the frigid weather. Then, later that week, the *New York Times* revealed it had all been recorded in a studio several days before. (A luxury that apparently was not extended to the brass players of the Marine band, but then again, they are Marines.) It was magical—but it was not real.

My cello lessons are not magical, but they are real. And they lead to real power. Both Dane and I leave our hour-long lessons a bit more able to create, a bit more able to pursue the excellence that we were made for. These days the lessons are not so painful for either of us. I've made a credible pass at Bach's first cello suite and am moving on to the second. Some days actual beauty emerges from my instrument. But, even when the lesson has been frustrating, when my bow has been squeaking and my left hand has been stubbornly out of tune, we almost always end smiling. We are both departing with more power.

## UNCORRUPTED POWER

Can this really be true? Is there such a thing as power that leads to flourishing—power that leads to more power? If it were true, it would be good news, both truly good and truly news. For this is not the way we have been trained to think of power. If there is one thing people think they know about power, it is Lord Acton's famous dictum, "Power tends to corrupt, and absolute power corrupts absolutely" (the words I have heard most often from others when they learned I was writing a book about power). Any claim that power can be a good thing is subject to intense suspicion, if not the settled prejudice of cynicism.

Lord Acton's dictum would not have achieved the status of a proverb if it did not capture something important and true. But if it were categorically true—true of all kinds of power, including all kinds of absolute power—there would be no one to read these words. For at one time all of us were subject to the absolute power of others, that is, power unconstrained by our own capacity to resist.

For each of us was once a baby.

Adults have tremendous power over babies. The millennia-long practice, more common in some cultures than others, of exposing unwanted babies to the elements, or aborting them before they are born, has probably always been by far the most common way human beings take other human beings' lives, and it certainly is today. According to the Alan Guttmacher Institute, which advocates for legal abortion, there were forty-two million induced abortions in 2003, the most recent year for which worldwide statistics have been compiled. That number approaches the fifty million killed in all of World War II.

Babies can be exposed or aborted because they cannot effectively resist. Adults' power over them is, in this sense, absolute, without any effectively opposing power. (Many mothers who undergo abortion, to be sure, would desperately prefer not to make that choice but are unable to resist the pressure from other powerful people and institutions.)

And yet, notwithstanding the absolute power they have over their children in the first days and months of life, the overwhelming majority of parents are *not* corrupted, certainly not absolutely corrupted, by it. No baby makes it to the fifth year of life without being the recipient of lavish amounts of attention, provision and love. In fact, so far from being absolutely corrupted by the absolute power parenthood confers over a new human being, many parents find themselves awakening to new capacities for resilience, sacrifice and servanthood that they did not know they had before.

And these capacities are called forth, remarkably enough, by the babies themselves; because though babies are helpless, they are not *powerless*. Not only do they have the power to breathe, eat and cry, anyone who has been in the room with a baby knows that babies command attention even when they are asleep. They have a compelling power over us, activating in us some of our most deeply rooted, most image-bearing capacities to enjoy, to marvel, to laugh and to care. There is something about realizing how utterly dependent this newborn image bearer is upon you that calls forth from both mothers and fathers a fierce commitment to become better stewards of our power.

Why are the vast majority of parents not corrupted by their tremendous power? Because they are overtaken by love. They find themselves viscerally committed to another. I remember looking at my son playing in his room one day in his first year of life and realizing with a jolt that if he were to run out in the street in front of a bus, and the only way to save him was to throw myself in front of the bus, pushing him out of the way, I would do it in a heartbeat, without even thinking. So deep, so instinctual, so total is my love for my son that I would give up all my powers so that he might survive and thrive. So would almost every parent, especially in those early days when our children are most dependent on us.

It is an almost precise inversion of Lord Acton's observation: the more power we have over our children, the more we are willing to sacrifice for them. Love transfigures power. Absolute love transfigures absolute power. And power transfigured by love is the power that made and saves the world.

## BIG ENOUGH FOR THE BOTH OF US

No one has expressed the cynical view of power more influentially than Friedrich Nietzsche. This brilliant, tortured figure, whose own will to finish his grand project demolishing Christian morality and advancing a pagan morality of the strong was laid waste by his descent into insanity, left behind a set of notes that his sister collected posthumously and was published in the volume *Will to Power*. Though Nietzsche is traditionally called a philosopher, readers of *Will to Power* discover that Nietzsche's writing is nothing like most philosophy before or since, much to the delight of most readers. In the place of painstakingly detailed and carefully hedged arguments, Nietzsche launches one rhetorical bombshell after another about the way the world really works, his words dripping with scorn and sarcasm.

While his approach is nothing like most of the rest of Western philosophy, Nietzsche is not only a supremely well-informed student of that tradition, he does exactly what philosophers attempt to do: go to the heart of the matters the rest of us take for granted, like existence and meaning. And for Nietzsche, the meaning of existence is power:

> My idea is that every specific body strives to become master over all space and to extend its force (its will to power) and to thrust back all that resists its extension. But it continually encounters similar efforts on the part of other bodies and ends by coming to an arrangement ("union") with those of them that are sufficiently related to it: thus they then conspire together for power. And the process goes on.

In Nietzsche's vision, all of us—"every specific body"—are on a quest for omnipotence, the ability to become "master over all space." We all would become not so much gods, plural, as god, singular, a single triumphant deity. The only problem is "other bodies," every-other-body, who all are engaged in exactly the same quest.

Nietzsche died in 1900, too soon to see the rise of the Western movie, which is a shame, because the early Westerns portray a Nietzschean world. In the 1932 film *The Western Code*, set in a small Texas town called Carabinas, the villainous foreman Nick Grindell declares to Tim Barrett, the virtuous lawman (played by Tim McCoy, who played no less than fifty

Texas Rangers named "Tim" in the 1930s), "I'm getting tired of your med-
dling. This town ain't big enough for the both of us and I'm going to give
you twenty-four hours to get out. If I see you in Carabinas by this time
tomorrow, it's you or me." There, in vivid language, is Nietzsche's idea in a
nutshell—"it's you or me." Grindell's challenge is met by the Ranger's la-
conic reply, "I'll see you at this time tomorrow," and followed by the inevitable and decisive gun battle.

The world of Westerns is a world over the horizon of conventional morality. In these small Texas towns, beyond the reach of the rule of law that
can be taken for granted on the civilized Eastern seaboard, the only right
that matters is might. Fortunately, the Texas Ranger named Tim rides into
town just in the nick of time, wielding his moral force against the villain's
immoral force. But make no mistake: what counts in this world is force,
not goodness. The power that matters is the one that is quickest to the
draw. We root for Tim because he is good, not because he is powerful, but
Tim wins the battle because he is powerful, not because he is good.

The premise of the Western, as with the Nietzschean strain in literature
from *Lord of the Flies* to *The Hunger Games*, is that when you strip away the
trappings of civilization, you will find raw, primal conflict, bodies in competition to occupy all space. All that good people, and the good itself, can
rely on is the hope that a good Übermensch—Nietzsche's "Superman"
who rises above the petty constraints of petit-bourgeois morality (and, in
Westerns, often sits rather loose in the saddle with respect even to the law
of the land)—will arrive in time to triumph over the evil Übermensch.
But this contest is, to borrow another of Nietzsche's famous phrases, actually "beyond good and evil." It is not a contest of morals but a contest
of wills. And the careful reader of Nietzsche will realize that "good" and
"evil" are not fixed and absolute categories, but simply names to justify
convenient alliances between those bodies who are "sufficiently related"
to one another, "conspiring together for power."

For Nietzsche even the most seemingly sympathetic and moral of communities is, just under the surface, a temporary and expedient set of alliances based on sufficient similarity to justify working together, for the
moment, to defeat those "other bodies" who are seeking to dominate all
space and time. But this "union" is in fact just a holding pattern, a mo-

mentary alliance until the threat from the others can be quelled. The moment that one "body" sees the opportunity, it will dissolve previous alliances and seize the opportunity to take over, even from its own closest relations. Ultimately, to borrow from another quasi-Nietzschean artifact of popular culture, "the world is not enough" for the godlike ones who will win this struggle for control. They must be like gods, extending their mastery further and further until eventually there will be nothing left but their own, absolute supremacy.

## WAITING FOR SUPERMAN

Ultimately we all have to make a choice about how to resolve the mystery, or contradiction, at the heart of human experience: the bewildering mixture in this world of violence and beauty, extinction and flourishing, betrayal and generosity. What is the deepest truth about the world? Is the deepest truth a struggle for mastery and domination? Or is the deepest truth collaboration, cooperation and ultimately love? Since Nietzsche, the deck has been stacked decisively against the second answer. To suggest that the ultimate truth of the world is love sounds laughably and dangerously naive. Suggesting that the world is a pitched battle for dominance, on the other hand, sounds admirably grown-up, sophisticated and, above all, realistic.

It is not much of an exaggeration to say that nearly an entire generation of students of literature and culture, under the influence of Nietzsche's intellectual descendant Michel Foucault, devoted tremendous intellectual energies to exposing the Nietzschean underbelly of domination in precisely the domains that were once thought to represent a refuge from the will to power—in art and architecture, in family and friendship, and not least in religion. In all of these places they claimed to find the naked quest for domination and the will to destroy any other body that stood in the way.

It is not just out-and-out nihilists who embrace the Nietzschean vision. Two dramatic political movements of the early twenty-first century in the United States, each motivated by a keen sense of social concern and righteous grievance, had a distinctive Nietzschean flavor to their activism. One was called Occupy, the loose assortment of protests that emerged in city centers in the wake of the 2008–2009 financial crisis, most notably in

shallow critique

downtown Manhattan's Zucotti Park. This movement's central strategy, taking over symbolic public spaces near the centers of financial power with semi-permanent encampments, was designed to "master space" in exactly the way Nietzsche described, in hopes of dislodging those who were seen as dominating the space of American business and finance from their perches in nearby skyscrapers. Though the Occupy movement also employed marches and other kinds of demonstrations, the central language and practice of "occupying" space was deeply Nietzschean in its static quality.

Occupying a park is very different from, say, marching down a street. A march has a destination and a goal, passing through space and time and then disbanding, leaving space before and after for others to flow into. And because marches flow through space and time, they can grow, including more and more people in their train; they can ebb and adjust to the shape and capacity of the spaces they pass through, and (unless marred by opportunistic or deliberate violence) they can coexist with other uses of space in ways that an "occupation" cannot. To "occupy" a space is to completely master and dominate its use, and to do so in a way that cannot easily scale or grow beyond that space's fixed capacity. Of course, the core conviction of the Occupy movement was that this kind of occupation was exactly what the holders of privilege and status had done on Wall Street. The protest methods mirrored the vision of reality being protested: a limited space that is being "occupied" by unjust holders. Such a contest is zero-sum—two people, or two groups, cannot "occupy" the same space in the way that they can join together in one march. To march is to embody hope—hope that others will join, that a momentary demonstration can lead to enduring change, that there is a symbolic goal we are moving toward. To occupy is to take a much grimmer view, planting oneself in determined and static resistance to implacable forces on the other side, and to hope that one's cause will triumph in a kind of metastasis, driving out the others.

But Occupy was not the only political movement driven by a sense of implacable conflict at the heart of politics. It had an ideological mirror image, the Tea Party movement that sought fiscal restraint and limited powers for the federal government in the United States. The Tea Party's members relied more on occasional protests than prolonged occupation, but their political vision was comparably Nietzschean. The first Tea Party was a nocturnal overthrow of existing powers that destroyed goods in order to win freedom from oppression. Chief Justice John Marshall's words in 1819, "the power to tax involves the power to destroy," could be the motto of both the original Tea Party and its twenty-first-century namesake. Such a motto reflects a deeply Nietzschean assessment of the power of government, in which taxes are oppressive extensions of power that undercut life and liberty.

By aiming squarely at electoral politics, the Tea Party movement almost inevitably committed itself to a zero-sum vision of power. Elections in majority-vote systems like the United States' are zero-sum events. Only one candidate and party triumph in any single contest, and they do so by removing their opponent from power (however slim the margin of victory), at least until the next election. The Tea Party aimed, with mixed success, at "occupying" the seats of power with their representatives in the Republican Party primaries, dislodging even those representatives who had previously been considered quite conservative. The Tea Party's determinedly anti-hierarchical, anti-establishment approach to political organization, refusing to name leaders or work within party systems, was another sign of its suspicion of structures and individuals that might acquire too much power. Anyone currently "occupying" positions of leadership was likely on a quest to expand their influence at the expense of ordinary people.

Even those who do not identify with dramatic movements like Occupy and the Tea Party can embrace a basically Nietzschean vision in which our society is like the small Texas town in an old-fashioned Western, where the only hope for God-fearing good people is the arrival of someone who will wield decisive power to drive out the forces of disorder. A Nietzschean worldview can easily coexist with deeply held moral beliefs—all one has to believe is that might is the only hope for the right, and place one's hope in someone sufficiently strong to conquer on behalf of the truth. In a Nietzschean world we are all reduced to waiting for Superman— or, just perhaps, acquiring enough power that we ourselves can thrust back all that resists us, achieving the domination we believe is necessary for the triumph of the good.

## ANOTHER POSSIBILITY FOR POWER

"From the beginning it was not so" (Matthew 19:8). With these words about marriage Jesus rebuked the casual and casuistic toleration of divorce, hearkening back to a time when God's image bearers, male and female, were created to cleave to one another and demonstrate the power of covenant love. Jesus' words should also bring us up short when we are tempted to give in to Nietzsche's vision of power. A vision as pessimistic as Nietzsche's is, frankly, conducive to insanity. It would not have been so influential if it were not so plausible in our fallen world. But Jesus holds out another possibility for power—that the story of beginnings told in Genesis still matters east of Eden. Could it be that the creative power of Genesis 1–2 is still real, living and active in the world? What would it look like to paint an alternative to Nietzsche's dark vision of bodies in competition?

Here is my idea.

*All true being strives to create room for more being and to expend its power in the creation of flourishing environments for variety and life, and to thrust back the chaos that limits true being. In doing so it creates other bodies and invites them into mutual creation and tending of the world, building relationships where there had been none: thus they then cooperate together in creating more power for more creation. And the process goes on.*

In writing this paragraph I admit I have allowed my words, very much like Nietzsche's "specific bodies," to crowd out and overwrite Nietzsche's own words. (Though his words are still there a few pages back in this book, offering their cynical testimony.) I want to argue that Nietzsche's "idea" can be countered, point by point, with a very different vision of ultimate reality.

Do all bodies strive to become master over all space? Is space actually a finite resource? Not so: there is a kind of being that delights in sharing space and a deeper, truer being that is able to create more than enough space—room for more being.

Is power primarily good for thrusting back opposition? Not so: there is a deeper, better power that actually creates the environments where many more beings could exist and thrive.

Are other beings basically a problem to be tolerated and ultimately solved by domination? Not so: the existence of "other bodies" actually is the deepest desire of any true body or being.

Is any cooperation between bodies a temporary, expedient conspiracy that will end as soon as one of them can seize all power? Not so: beings were always meant to work together to cultivate and create. The worst fate one could wish for would be to end up alone with one's power, for then there would be no one left with whom one could tend and shape the world.

Is cooperation based only on being "sufficiently similar," those who have something to gain from one another? Not so: there is a power at work in the world that can actually reconcile those who seem most different from one another.

Is the result of cooperation the seizing of power? Not so: cooperation mysteriously creates more power than there was before, so that the more we work together the more power we discover is available to us.

Yes, in the world we have Nietzsche's words ring with awful truth. But *from the beginning it was not so.* Indeed, in the very good world created by a Creator God who delights in teeming, there was one thing that was "not good": "It is not good that the man should be alone" (Genesis 2:18). One body is not enough. Being was never meant to be by itself. True being seeks more being—and seeks relationship, connectedness and mutual dependence. The power to love, and in loving, to create together, is the true power that hums at the heart of the world. The power to conspire, dominate and eventually become a single, isolated, lonely god is lifeless and ultimately powerless. True power comes from the very creativity and love that Nietzschean power would extinguish.

## TRIUMPH OVER THE POWERS

It's crucial that we meet Nietzsche's scorching criticism of Christianity directly. The quest to become Superman does *not* produce strength adequate to master reality—it undermines it. For in his commitment to power as godlike domination over all space and over all other beings, Nietzsche commits the most basic human mistake. The biblical name for it is idolatry. And as we will see, even when idolatry seems to work, it is radically unstable. Idols may not fail immediately, but they do fail, and usually sooner rather than later. Idols disappoint their worshipers, and the injustice that flows from idolatry ultimately ruins not just its victims but its perpetrators.

This is one reason both the Old and New Testaments are simply packed with power language. Israel and the first few astonished followers of Jesus experienced incomparable power. Real power, not just passive-aggressive coexistence but the power to turn the page of history, to deliver the poor, reconcile the lost, and raise the dead. The followers of Jesus, witnesses of his rescue from the very grip of hell, could say, then, that he had triumphed over "the powers"—all the idols and entrenched systems of injustice with their shrill claims of telling the truth about the world and providing the only path to overcoming the world. In the resurrection the original power of creative love displaced sin and death. Indeed, sin and death turn out to be the only things that will ultimately be truly defeated and destroyed in the Nietzschean sense. Sin and death are the two things that cannot abide the teeming, flourishing world of creative love.

The only Nietzschean defeat is for those perversions of power that cannot tolerate anything but Nietzschean victory. Sin and death, and the twin systems they create, idolatry and injustice, are already unmasked and have lost the crucial battle. Creative love was always stronger and more real—and in the community of the resurrection, the first and latest followers of Jesus find that reality living, breathing and working powerfully through us. We are in the world to declare, "In the beginning it was not so," and to anticipate the end where all idols and injustice will fail and be forgotten, and where true power will thrive.

# IDOLATRY

The real news about power—the new news, if you will, the news we haven't yet heard or have largely forgotten—is the good news about power. Power is meant for image bearing, and image bearing is meant for flourishing. But to understand just how good this news is, we also must understand the old and sad news about power's distortion.

When we think about distorted and damaging power, we quickly think of the starkest forms of power's abuse. What comes to mind, all too often through painful personal experience, is the strong imposing their will upon the weak, resorting deliberately or casually to acts of violence and exploitation. This, we have every reason to think, is power at its worst. And we are tempted to think with Nietzsche that power at its worst is the true face of power, and that even the more apparently benign forms of power are simply Nietzschean quests for dominance cloaked, for the time being, in a velvet glove.

But reading deeply into Scripture and the Christian tradition leads us deeper than this. Genesis suggests that creative power is the deepest form of power. Jussive "let there be" power leads to cohortative "let us make" power, in all its relational and communal joy. Imperative "make it so" power is a kind of third derivative that is always dependent on prior creativity and relationship.

But if this is true, our understanding of the bad news about power will also need to change. It is not just the highest and best uses of power that will be creative and relational. The worst distortions of power will also be creative and relational—albeit in a distorted way. Ultimately, violence and domination, which we tend to think of as the worst abuses of power, are actually symptoms of its abuse. They are signs of a deeper sickness, a sickness that strikes at the heart of our deepest created goodness. And the biblical words for that sickness are *idolatry* and *injustice*.

## IDOLATRY

Idolatry is the biblical name for the human capacity for creative power run amok. Human beings are vested by their Creator with the ability to make something of the world, both to fashion tangible artifacts out of the fruitful material of creation and to give voice to the meaning of creation. These are the "stuff" and the "sense" of our cultural calling, and every human act of making involves making both stuff and sense. There is no material cultural good that does not participate in some project of meaning making, and there is no human venture of meaning making that does not result in the creating and sustaining of material things. All of this is the very good calling of God's image bearers in the world. Our most fundamental task is to unfold the world's abundant possibilities and deep meaningfulness—to cultivate and create in such a way that the true God's identity and ways are named and praised.

In idolatry, however, this capacity for making something of the world is misdirected. An idol is a cultural artifact that embodies a false claim about the world's ultimate meaning. The word *ultimate* is crucial here. All sorts of cultural goods can reflect misunderstandings about the true meaning of the world. Bloodletting with leeches, for example, was a practice of early "medicine" based on a mistaken understanding of illness and health. Bloodletting did little or no good, and probably a lot of harm, but it did not embody any ultimate beliefs about the world. It was mistaken, but in a relatively superficial way.

An idol is a special kind of human creation, one that is not just mistaken in a superficial way. Rather, it advances a claim about the ultimate nature of reality that is ultimately mistaken. And since the Creator God is the ultimate meaning of the world, an idol is a representation of a false god. Implicitly or explicitly, all idols represent a challenge and counterclaim to the identity and character of the true Creator God. Like the serpent in the Garden, they all raise the question of the Creator God's truthfulness and goodness, subtly or directly suggesting that the Creator God is neither true nor good.

What is this ultimate claim that idols make? It turns out that there is a clear pattern to idolatry. In fact, idols turn out to be depressingly consistent in the way they misrepresent the world—distorted creativity turns out to be boringly uncreative. All idols begin by offering great things for a very small price. All idols then fail, more and more consistently, to deliver on their original promises, while ratcheting up their demands, which initially seemed so reasonable, for worship and sacrifice. In the end they fail completely, even as they make categorical demands. In the memorable phrase of the psychiatrist Jeffrey Satinover, idols ask for more and more, while giving less and less, until eventually they demand everything and give nothing.

## FROM GOOD TO GREAT

A cultural artifact does not have to be a figurine in the shape of a deity to serve the function of an idol; it just has to offer transcendent benefits and demand ultimate allegiance. In modern, secular societies perhaps the clearest example of idolatry is the pattern we call addiction. Addictions begin with essentially good, created stuff; even the chemicals that become addictive drugs are part of God's good creation and often have beneficial uses in the right context. But in the throes of addiction, we invest that created stuff with transcendent expectations. It begins to hold out the promise of becoming like a god. The most powerfully addictive substances, like crystal meth, are the ones that can deliver the most dramatic sensations of godlike freedom, confidence and abundance—in other words, power. A behavior like gambling promises to give us a sense of mastery over the random forces of nature and the ability to bring something out of nothing, to create wealth without having to work. Pornography promises intimacy without risk, commitment and the limitations of our often awkward and vulnerable bodies.

The first move of all idolatry is from good to great—more precisely, from created goodness to unrealistic greatness. We start with a good,

like most consumer goods in our advertising based society

created thing, but then we ask it to be great. We seek not to enjoy the created good's own proper goodness, within its intended limits, but to use it to free us from limits and usher us into an elevated kind of life. We invest it with our deepest hopes and look to it to address our deepest fears.

Initially, all idols seem to deliver exactly this escape from mere goodness into transcendent greatness. Consider the weather. In our scientific age, amidst the technological achievements of modernity, we have lost much of our reverence for and sense of helpless dependence on the weather. But imagine the sense of mastery and awe that must have overwhelmed the first people who pounded out an exuberant and desperate dance, in hopes of cajoling the sky god into bringing rain, when they were rewarded by an unexpected cloudburst an hour or a day later. Or the sense of awed gratitude and newfound power when a libation poured out on the ground seemed to deliver an abundant harvest. There must have been some such moments—how else would the rituals have become credible?

At the heart of primal idolatries, but also at the heart of many of our most closely held addictions, is the belief that we have found a way to bring a recalcitrant and unpredictable part of the world under our control. Are human beings, meaning-seekers that we are, just innocently fooled by the apparent functioning of idols? The biblical worldview is not so benign. Behind the "functioning" of idol worship, biblical people glimpsed an ancient and supernatural struggle, the work of demonic powers that set out to deceive and destroy God's image bearers with facsimiles of divine power. Jesus himself encounters such a tempter in the desert, a malign personality who appears at Jesus' most human moment of hungry vulnerability and promises him magical results in exchange for worship.

Far from putting such idols behind us, seeing them for the demonic deceptions that they are, we make them the objects of our devotion and studied attention. And the short-term results are extraordinary. Suddenly in an arena where we felt dependent and vulnerable—whether ancient people waiting for rain or a modern man looking for love—now we feel potent and free. The dance and the libation, the rain and the harvest, were and are good things, even very good things. But they became idols when they elevated priests and people to an illusion of greatness, extraordinary and transcendent power. The same is true for our addictions. Wine, games of chance, even the visual depiction of love, eros and bodies, are all part of a very good world. But we are not satisfied with very good. When we use them as fuel for our journey to greatness, they become our idols.

And for a while idols and addictions deliver exactly what they promise. Indeed, the most powerful idols seem to work for quite a long while. On the scale of potential idolatries, crystal meth, for all its destructive power, is a fairly minor deity. Its only power is in the crushing brilliance of its early highs; its baleful effects show up much too rapidly. The more effective idols deliver more measured doses. In the "success phase" of idolatry, you will never convince an idolater that his addiction is not working. It *is* working—it is rescuing him from his human vulnerability and giving him an intoxicating taste of invulnerable ecstasy.

But whether quickly or slowly, all idols begin to work less effectively or predictably. The dances that once seemed to reliably move the rain god now work only intermittently. The surefire system for predicting the lottery numbers begins to sputter. It is actually in this intermediate stage, when the rewards of idolatry are unpredictable, that idols consolidate their control over their worshipers. Intermittent reinforcement, as psychologists know, is by far the most habit-forming kind of reward. Give a mouse a tasty pellet every time it pushes a lever, and it will eventually become satiated and lose interest. But give a mouse a pellet *sometimes* when it pushes the lever, with no rhyme or reason beyond the experimenter's whim, and the mouse will keep pushing whether it is hungry or not. Establish the rule of intermittent reinforcement strongly enough and mice will push levers without any reward until they collapse from exhaustion.

Likewise, idols really gain traction when they cease to work consistently—when they work just often enough to keep alive the great hopes we initially placed in them. And idols can be as small as a line of powder or as massive as a global system of thought. In his slim and sly 1992 book *If You're So Smart: The Narrative of Economic Expertise*, the economist Donald McCloskey suggested that much economics is actually more akin to magic than to science. Magic, the close cousin of idolatry, promises great control over hidden forces, if only you know the right incantations. When the magic fails, there is always a story ready to hand that convinces you that *you* are the problem, not the magic. The incantation was not said correctly, or the priest was not properly purified, or it was the wrong phase of the moon: there is always a way to excuse the magic from working and keep alive its promise. Of course, this pattern of justification gradually ratchets up the demands on magicians and their customers, demanding more and more, even if the magic seems to be delivering less and less.

This, McCloskey suggests, is the way economists work too. Promising power over the fiendishly complicated workings of human transactions, they end up mostly explaining after the fact why their formulas didn't work the last time but will definitely work the next time. The problem is not economics, nor economists, nor the human economy of creativity and commerce, all of which are in fact very good things. The problem is expecting ultimate things from them, expecting them to give us godlike control when all of us, economists included, are never more—and sadly, sometimes less—than very good image bearers who cannot even know what we cannot know. "Great" economics presupposes rational actors and pristine mathematical models. "Very good" economics would acknowledge the vast potential scope for human error, fallibility and frailty. If we are fortunate, the twenty-first century could be the age of "very good" economics—often called behavioral economics—that has more modest claims for its powers and a more chastened understanding of human nature. If we are not so fortunate, the idol of omnicompetent central bankers, like the idol of godlike Soviet economic planners before it, will eventually fall flat on its face in the temples of commerce, but not before demanding a great deal from its worshipers. Idols do not give up their power without extracting an exit fee.

## THE IMAGE BEARER AND THE IDOL

Steve Jobs, the cofounder and CEO of Apple until his death in 2011, was an image bearer—in some ways *the* iconic image bearer of our age. He played a central role in two of the most innovative commercial enterprises of the late twentieth and early twenty-first centuries, not just Apple but also the movie studio Pixar. There are thousands of founders and tens of thousands of CEOs, but what made Steve Jobs such a uniquely powerful figure was the way his companies' products responded deeply to the image-bearing qualities of humanity.

Jobs is remembered above all for Apple, but Pixar is an equally extraordinary cultural achievement. Pixar's stories, almost without exception (sorry, *Cars 2* fans), probe the deepest questions about what it is to be human, to be relational beings set in the midst of friendship and family. In *WALL•E* and *Ratatouille*, nonhuman characters mirror our human callings to cultivate and create faithfully and excellently in the world. *Finding Nemo* is about a father's fierce and persistent love, while *The Incredibles* portrays a family overcoming evil, not as isolated "superheroes" but together, dependent on one another's gifts. *Up* portrays marriage and intergenerational friendship, while *Toy Story 3*'s climactic vision is of a community of friends who hold on to one another even at the gates of hell.

Pixar began as a technology company, selling its RenderMan software to other animation companies, but under Jobs's stewardship it quickly put that technological capability to use in the hands of some of the world's great storytellers. And when great storytellers came to work for Pixar, they became even better. Michael Arndt's pre-Pixar work included a fine and funny screenplay called *Little Miss Sunshine*, which was well above average for commercial cinema. But his first screenplay after joining Pixar was the far more powerful (while still fine and funny) *Toy Story 3*.

What both Pixar and Apple had in common was their uncommon ability to take technology—computer-generated imagery and computers themselves—and put them at the service of something more important, human beings' quest for relationship and beauty. In film after film Pixar transcended the previous limits of its genre to offer a genuinely compelling, multifaceted vision of human flourishing. And what Pixar did for the previously two-dimensional genre of children's films, Apple did for the world of technological devices. Personal computers in the 1980s and cell phones in the 2000s were merely useful and often maddeningly unresponsive to the needs and instincts of ordinary, nontechnically minded human beings. But Apple, starting with the simplicity of its "A is for Apple" corporate name, created products that answered a hunger deeper than mere technical wizardry. In fact, to the frustration of many techies, they did their best to conceal their technological underpinnings altogether. Instead of making their users adapt to them, Apple devices are exquisitely designed around the capabilities and limits of the human body, and frequently optimized for the things that human beings find most compelling—music, visual beauty and a sense of connection to other persons.

Of course, neither Pixar's nor Apple's success was solely Steve Jobs's doing. But it's hard to imagine anyone else who could have more effectively instilled in two major corporations the primacy of excellence and responsiveness to human experience—as Jobs put it in an interview, the marriage of engineering and the liberal arts. As an image bearer, Jobs created countless opportunities for others to flourish. Jobs could famously be an unforgiving and capricious leader who was more than capable of playing god in the worst sense. But without a deep reservoir of image bearing, his dominating and mercurial management style alone would never have had a chance of producing the kinds of excellence that emerged from Pixar and Apple in the 1990s and 2000s.

And strikingly, Jobs seemed to instinctively recognize the need to hire leaders who tempered his own god playing. Notwithstanding his own perfectionism and impatience, his top lieutenants were remarkably patient and empathetic, none more than Tim Cook, his appointed successor as CEO at Apple. Even more surprising given Jobs's Eastern spirituality and this-worldly-mindedness, not to mention the companies' location in secular northern California, Pixar's and Apple's top executives were surprisingly often people of Christian faith. Pixar is certainly the only movie studio where Christians like Andrew Stanton (writer and director of *Finding Nemo* and *WALL·E*) have consistently been given so much creative responsibility. Steve Jobs's quest for excellence led him to invest power in leaders whose temperament and faith commitments were so different from his own.

In so many ways, then, Steve Jobs was an exemplary image bearer.

But he also had an idol.

## BITTER FRUIT

Strangely, Jobs's idol was not technology. Jobs's genius for design and marketing may have contributed to more than a few people coming perilously close to worshiping their iDevices, but a close reading of Walter Isaacson's authorized biography suggests that Jobs himself had a much healthier relationship to technology than the average Starbucks patron.

Instead, Steve Jobs's idol was food.

This is perhaps the most surprising and wrenching revelation of Isaacson's admiring book: from early in his life, Steve Jobs was obsessed with food in ways that increasingly dominated his attention, distorted his relationships and affected his decisions. The teenage Jobs began experimenting with unusual diets as part of a broader exploration of Eastern spirituality. At one point he and a friend went for two weeks eating only apples. (Fruit turns out to be central to Jobs's story in more ways than one.) According to Isaacson, the various diets, often based on raw food and almost always vegetarian or vegan, gave Jobs an exhilarating and ecstatic sense of energy and control. They set a pattern that would last Jobs's whole life: scattered through the biography are instances of Jobs refusing to eat food prepared even by master chefs, storming out of restaurants as quickly as he had stormed in, and skipping meals with his family.

In short, Jobs had an eating disorder, a phrase Isaacson does not hesitate to use. Or perhaps Jobs had several eating disorders at different points in his life. Like all idols, his obsession with food worked at first. It was part of Jobs's larger project of attaining to superhuman amounts of control over his surroundings and other people—intimately linked with his perfectionism in other areas of life.

But the picture that emerges in the course of Isaacson's biography is of an addiction that gradually demanded more and more, while benefiting Jobs less and less, and cost him dearly in his relationships with his family and his own health. Indeed, Jobs's idolatrous relationship to food may very well have cost him his life.

In October 2003, when a routine scan turned up evidence of cancer in Jobs's pancreas, Jobs's doctors had every reason to expect the worst. Pancreatic cancer, at any age, is normally a swift death sentence. But when Jobs's doctors saw the results of an initial biopsy, tears of joy came to their eyes. Jobs had islet cell cancer, a rare version of pancreatic cancer that is slow-growing and consequently almost always curable with prompt surgery to remove the pancreas.

And at this moment Jobs's idol—food as a method of control—failed him. As Isaacson writes:

To the horror of his friends and wife, Jobs decided not to have surgery to remove the tumor, which was the only accepted medical approach. "I really didn't want them to open up my body, so I tried to see if a few other things would work," he told me years later with a hint of regret. Specifically, he kept to a strict vegan diet, with large quantities of fresh carrot and fruit juices. To that regimen he added acupuncture, a variety of herbal remedies, and occasionally a few other treatments he found on the Internet or by consulting people around the country, including a psychic. For a while he was under the sway of a doctor who operated a natural healing clinic in southern California that stressed the use of organic herbs, juice fasts, frequent bowel cleansings, hydrotherapy, and the expression of all negative feelings.

For nine months, as his friends and family pleaded with him to have the surgery, Jobs refused. Not until July of the next year did he consent to the "modified Whipple procedure" to remove part of his pancreas. During the surgery, doctors found that the cancer had spread to the liver. Jobs would never again be free of cancer, and just over eight years later he was dead at age fifty-six.

Isaacson attributes Jobs's failure to promptly acquiesce to surgery—against the advice even of health-food gurus like Dean Ornish—to "the dark side of his reality distortion field," his unwillingness to engage with hard realities when he didn't want to. But this is an odd thing to say. In fact, according to Isaacson himself Jobs was deeply engaged, pursuing the wide range of outlandish "treatments" that Isaacson recounts. He was in the terminal stage, not of cancer, but of idolatry, when the idol ceases entirely to deliver but exacts its full demands for unwavering worship. Even after Jobs's surgery, according to Isaacson, his unwillingness to modify his diet to include reasonable amounts of protein almost certainly complicated his recovery and ability to benefit from chemotherapy. When the general public became aware that Jobs was increasingly gaunt, commentators rightly suspected that Jobs's disease had come back with a vengeance. What few knew or suspected was that his exiguous frame was not just the result of his cancer and treatment but his own dependence on control through food.

If Jobs had had surgery immediately in October 2003, would he have lived a long life, cancer free? No one will ever know for sure. What we do know is that he substantially diminished his chances of a successful recovery by pursuing the central obsession of his life, against all the counsel of his family, friends and physicians. And we know that far earlier than the biblical span of threescore and ten years, his capacity to bear the image of God was cut off, leaving his children fatherless and the wider world bereft of his creative power.

## EVERY IDOL'S PROMISE

Every idol makes two simple and extravagant promises.

"You shall not surely die."

"You shall be like God."

These are the two promises, when whispered at the right moment by a cunning adversary, that can wind their way around the human heart and bind it to any created thing. They are, of course, the words of the serpent in the Garden in Genesis 3, as he lures the woman and man into taking a bite of the single fruit they are forbidden to eat. In this context "You shall not surely die" does not refer only to human beings' creaturely mortality. It is always important to remember that in the Genesis story, as consistently throughout the Bible, there is no idea of "immortal" creatures or eternally existent souls. To be a creature is to be mortal, and men and women, image bearers though they are, are formed of dust, like every other creature.

But up to this point in the story of the Garden, the mortality that comes with being made of matter has been kept at bay through the gift of the Tree of Life. Along with that gift has come a warning: should God's image bearers defy their Maker and eat from the one reserved tree (the tree of the knowledge of good and evil), the gift of life will be withdrawn. This, the serpent implies, is a lie—the image bearers are not as dependent on God as they have been led to believe. "You shall not surely die" is a promise of *life apart from God*, life that does not require relationship with God to be sustained.

Every idol intimates that life apart from God is within reach, within our grasp, available for our control. This is the first lie of power, and the clanging irony is that we can only indulge in this fantasy at all because of God's own continuous gift of power—the life and breath that are sustained moment by moment by God's creative Spirit—and because God continually tempers his own power in order to make room for his creatures' teeming and flourishing.

Idolatry is, in fact, the result of a curious hybrid of power and powerlessness. On the one hand, idolatry is only possible because of the unique capacities of image bearers; no other creature would be subject to this temptation nor able to follow through with such audacious and misplaced works of imagination. On the other hand, idolatry results from the extraordinary vulnerability—the powerlessness or sense of powerlessness—these image bearers feel. The other creatures in the creation accounts go about their teeming and flourishing with abandon, but the man and woman, made in the image of God though they are, need to be placed in a Garden, a protected environment with special resources devoted to their flourishing.

Without the Garden, without the freely accessible Tree of Life, the man and woman would quickly be overcome by their creatureliness. The creatures on whom God bestows the unique capacity to bear, reflect and refract the divine image into the created world are in many ways the most vulnerable of all creatures. No other creature comes into the world as ill-suited to survival as a human being. Every other creature has an ecological niche to which it is adapted, often exquisitely so, but human beings' natural adaptation is ill-fitting to say the least. Far slower than the fastest predators; duller of sight, hearing and every other sense than countless other animals; equipped with a digestive system that is a jack of all trades but master of none (it lacks various useful enzymes that other animals, even our near evolutionary relatives, can take for granted)—*Homo sapiens* would be thought a colossal failure of natural selection if not for one thing. We are able to adapt not biologically but *culturally*, through cooperation and creativity, to nearly any environment where we find ourselves. It is into these uniquely culturally agile but also uniquely biologically vulnerable creatures that God breathes his Spirit—and it is in response to that vulnerability and dependence that they put their creative capacities, the very gift of the Spirit, to work making substitute images, conjuring up the impossible promise "You shall not surely die."

In the heat of the day, surrounded by the protective abundance of the Garden but with the Gardener apparently absent, the serpent is able to imply that vulnerability and dependence are unnecessary for human flourishing. More than that, "You shall be like God"—not only will the woman and the man be rescued from their creaturely vulnerability, they will transcend creatureliness altogether. If the first promise addresses the anxieties of vulnerable creatures, the second addresses the aspirations of image bearers. There is simply no other creature in the world that harbors the ambition to "be like God," except for image bearers. Next time you are at the zoo, try approaching an elephant, cheetah or crocodile and whispering to them, "You shall be like God." Not only will they regard you with indifference (or possibly faint stirrings of hunger), you will have a hard time not laughing. For all their grandeur and power, the world's creatures just do not give the faintest evidence of wanting to be something other than a well-fed version of what they already are. (I will admit there is a partial exception—cats. But cats give every sign of *already* considering themselves equal to God, and thus they are supremely, serenely free of petty human traits like ambition.)

Yet whisper in a human being's ear "You shall be like God," and every one will inwardly tingle with an inescapable recognition that this is, somehow, what we were made for. Absurdly for such frail, vulnerable creatures, we resonate with both the promise of lasting life and the promise of godlikeness. Absurdly, but also fittingly. The vulnerable are meant to exercise dominion; the corruptible is meant to put on incorruption. In the strictest sense the idol promises nothing we are not made for.

But the idol's promise introduces a dissonant phrase into that harmonious resonance: you will have life and you will be like God *apart from God*. Every idol demands a separation and differentiation from the Creator. The Garden had been the Creator's model of a teeming, flourishing environment where his own image bearers could dwell in full being alongside other creatures and the Creator himself, but the serpent introduces a Nietzschean note of zero-sum competition. Idols do not know how to share being; they know nothing of teeming or flourishing. Instead, what they know is conquest and displacement. For the man and the woman to grasp at life apart from God and godlikeness apart from God, they will have to step away from God and replace God. In the serpent's world there is no room for life or godlikeness with God and for God; only without God and against God.

## THE END OF IDOLATRY

At the end, idols completely fail. They not only fail to deliver the godlikeness and immortality they promised at first, they rob their worshipers of even the most minimal human dignity and agency. Of all the charges the biblical prophets file against idols, the most damning is this: "Those who make them become like them." The very human creativity that was able to fashion a god substitute is undermined and eventually eradicated by idolatry. The idol maker, originally an image bearer, becomes as inanimate and mute as a statue, no longer able to move, feel, care or love. The idol, originally invested with all the human hopes for power, ends up robbing human beings of their power.

And in the end idolatry does not only rob image bearers, the culmination of creation, of their dignity; it robs the whole creation of its goodness. Wine is a very good part of creation, an effervescent mixture of natural and cultural processes that generate boundless complexity and beauty. But to the idolater of wine all that very goodness is lost. Wine becomes prized only for its drug content. In that sense the "alcoholic" is perfectly named, because for an alcoholic there is no such thing as wine, only alcohol—a delivery system for ersatz godlikeness that requires higher and higher doses to be effective. A lover of wine can sip from a glass of fine wine for hours, treasuring the way it unfolds its aroma and flavors, the delight it gives to every sense, but to an alcoholic it is just a drug. Indeed, because every good thing can become a god, even someone who never becomes an alcoholic can make the beauty of wine itself an idol, seeking transcendence in ever more expensive and exclusive experiences of oenophilia. That idol too will fail, after consuming vast resources, draining away creativity, and ultimately separating its worshiper from true and rightly ordered loves. Every such god ultimately becomes less than what it was meant to be, dragging image bearers down with it into a dull ditch of disappointment.

Power is all about image bearing—reflecting and refracting the creative power of the world's Maker into the very good creation. And image bearing is for flourishing. But as idolatry fills the world with false images, and as those false images proliferate, the image bearers lose their capacity to bear the true image. The more the image bearers lose this capacity, the more creation itself is diminished, reduced to utilitarian means to bitter ends. Idolatry is the true failure of power.

# INJUSTICE

In the first chapter of this book I mentioned my train trip with Jayakumar Christian, the director of World Vision India, to a district in southern India where child slavery—often known by the more technical and less ugly term "bonded labor"—had been endemic for generations. On that trip Jayakumar said something to me that was destined to change the way I saw power and poverty, and has ended up transforming the way I read the Bible and think about power.

"The poor are poor," Jayakumar said to me, "because someone else is trying to play God in their lives."

For Jayakumar the root of poverty was not the lack or misdistribution of money. Nor was it the lack or misdistribution of power, the ability to make something of the world. Of course Jayakumar would be the first to say that both of these are real and pressing problems, but he saw them as symptoms of something much deeper and fundamental. Poverty and persistent injustice were signs that some person or group of people had played god in the life of another person or group of people.

Playing god—it's a disturbing phrase, and Jayakumar meant it to be disturbing. And as I learned more about the peculiar institution of bonded labor, it came to me to seem a very apt description. The moneylender played god in the lives of families too poor to repay their debts. Like some kind of local deity, he offered benefits unobtainable elsewhere, with disproportionate amounts of money at his command. The benefits, of course, came at a price, and the price was not just financial but also extracted in the currency of cringing respect and humiliating homage to the great man's status. Still, the benefits were essential and the terms apparently reasonable—a loan of much-needed cash, paid out from a pile of bills that would seem unimaginably abundant to a poor family, for an amount of interest that would sound usurious to us but that paled beside the immediate need.

But over time the benefits the moneylender offered would quickly evaporate, while the demands escalated. The money was quickly spent on necessities or perhaps, people being what they are, unnecessities; whatever the case, it was soon entirely gone. Soon henchmen were at the door, demanding repayment of the debt with interest. But the initially reasonable interest was now compounding with every failure to pay. All too soon it would become clear to the family that they would never be able to pay the exponentially increasing debt. And then would come the demand that was the real secret of the moneylender's success, the henchmen peering beyond the door of the home to spot the young child in the corner.

The debt could only be paid by someone working every day. That girl was strong enough, and what was she contributing to the household anyway? It was time for her to earn her keep. And bundled off to the moneylender's back lot, she did indeed earn a great deal for the money-lender, but never quite enough to cover the still-escalating interest. In the meantime, which for all anyone could see stretched into the endless future, she would become not just his employee but his slave, available for use and abuse without recourse, taken out of school, kept in line with threats of violence, exploited in unthinkable ways at whim, always dirty with the dust and grime of the shop floor.

In this grim sequence of events two images are altered. The image of the moneylender, who might otherwise have been simply a marginally prosperous small businessman, is step by step inflated and enhanced. He is powerful; he is in control; he possesses singular resources. But not just that, he demands to be recognized as beneficent; his status is carefully guarded by assorted hangers-on and accomplices; and eventually he is manifestly above the law. To whom do the local representatives of government authority defer, if not to someone whose image demands reverence far beyond that due to the government? In the small world over which he holds sway, the moneylender is not good. He is great, and greatly to be feared. He is the successful god player.

But it is not just the moneylender's image that is altered. As his image is inflated and magnified by a series of transactions, another set of images are being marred beyond recognition. The parents exploited by the god player, who otherwise might have been simply poor but dignified residents of the village, see their own image begin to degrade and be defaced. They lose their sense of agency and power; they find themselves drawn into a vortex of need that far exceeds even the original debt that prompted their request for a loan; now they are not simply poor but desperate. They cease to believe that they have any real capacity to affect their own situation; they become helpless. And in every social interaction they are increasingly reminded of their marginal and scorned status; they stop looking their neighbors in the eye; they carry all too visible marks of shame. All the more so for their child, who becomes a cog in another person's money-making machine and the object of another's whims, separated from the family that gave her a name and identity. Who in this village believes that the child or the parents are of infinite worth, the very good subjects of their Creator's delight and the agents of God's abundance in the world? The image of God in them is effaced if not erased.

The dynamics of god playing in this community go far beyond a single microeconomic transaction. There is a whole history of god playing: certain families, clans and ethnic groups grasping or being granted the privilege of playing god. There is a whole litany of exaltations of some and humiliations of others, and deeply rooted beliefs that often justify it all. These beliefs seem justified by the empirical reality that some have godlike capacities and others seem barely human in their desperation and abasement.

And this, in turn, is not just the case in a few villages in South Asia. For everywhere we look, we find some people who play god all too successfully, while others, ground under the heel of injustice, come to seem to themselves and others not only far from image bearers but barely human. This is the story, one way or another, of every broken human community—which is to say, every human community we have ever known.

## INJUSTICE = IDOLATRY

You will already have grasped what is going on in this all-too-real tableau of injustice. It is no more and no less than idolatry. The moneylender, who delivers less and less while demanding more and more until eventually he gives nothing and demands everything, is a false god. His victims may not literally worship him—though the reverence demanded by false god players often does border on worship—but they are ultimately in thrall to him. God making and god playing are the same thing.

Amidst the Bible's many declarations of God's love, faithfulness, patience and kindness, there are two things that God repeatedly is said to hate, two things that draw God's wrath and the ire of the prophets who speak in God's name. They are idolatry and injustice. The Hebrew prophets can turn on a dime from one of these topics to the other, in ways that can seem odd to our modern sensibilities. Isn't injustice a political matter and idolatry a religious matter? It is true, but not adequate, to say that ancient Israelites did not make the clean distinction between politics and religion that secular Western societies do. That is an accurate superficial description, but it does not explain *why* Israel's prophets and priests made such a deep connection between the two. Why would idolatry and injustice be the two topics that the prophets return to over and over with fierce conviction?

To put it another way, does God hate injustice and idolatry in the way that I hate licorice and Brussels sprouts? I do happen to dislike both of those foods, but I dislike them for independent reasons. Does God just dislike it when human beings are mean to one another, and also happen to dislike it when human beings create false gods?

No. God hates injustice and idolatry *because they are the same thing*: the introduction into God's very good world of false images, images that destroy the true images God himself has placed in the world to declare his character and voice his praise. Whether making false gods (idolatry) or playing false gods (injustice) the result is identical—the true image of God is lost, and not just lost but replaced by something that purports, often very persuasively, to represent the ultimate truth about reality. The truth about God, and the truth about God's very good world, is exchanged for a lie. This happens in the very same way whether through god making or god playing, which is why the true God hates god making and god playing in the very same way. What God hates is the eradication of his image in a world that is meant to be full of his image bearers.

The startling fact is that the Hebrew word used for the crowning achievement of the Creator God on the sixth day, the creation of creatures made "in his image" (Genesis 1:26), is a word we translate elsewhere as "idol" (the Hebrew *tselem*). It sounds extremely odd to our ears, but God's intention all along was that the world be full of idols—full of images. *icons?*
More exactly, the world was meant to be full of representatives of its Maker. And the only adequate representatives of the Creator are *image bearers*, not lifeless images, since only persons can adequately reflect the image of a relational, personal Creator. Indeed, one distinctive loss of idolatry is that it ascribes to nonpersons—figurines or totems, drugs or devices—qualities that only persons can actually bear, which is why the prophets scorn idols for their inability to speak or act on their own. No graven image can fully represent the true Image; only an image *bearer* can do that.

But the loss of the image caused by injustice is equally devastating. On the one hand, the image born by the god player ceases to resemble the true Creator God and begins to bear false witness. This false image is all the more devastating because it is accompanied by acts of violence and domination that seem to ratify the claim to represent true power in the world. Far worse than this hypertrophied false image, however, is the effacing or even eradication of the image-bearing capacities of the poor who cease to believe that they bear any image at all. At least the god player is still exercising some capacity for agency and activity, however distorted, but the equally valued image bearers among the poor come to believe they have no capacity whatsoever. Their unique contributions as image bearers, the individual dignity they each bear as an irreplaceable refraction of the true Image, are lost to the world, eclipsed by the strutting false images.

*excellent*

What God hates, ultimately, is the loss of the true Image, the Image that can only be contained in image bearers. He hates the way idolatry diminishes the capacity of human beings to bear the image until eventually "those who make them become like them," losing the qualities of personal power that were theirs by gift and design. He hates that the poor, who have infinite value as image bearers in their own right, become devalued and commodi-

*perhaps not as many "victims" feel this way as he thinks? They are still trying to act, but are rebuffed by the more powerful.*

God

tized, pawns in the self-inflating schemes of the god players. And he hates
that all that remains is a world of broken images, a world where you could
readily believe that the final truth is domination, demanding more and
more while offering less and less until eventually the absolute winner and
wielder of power has everything and needs to give nothing. This is idolatry,
this is injustice, and God hates them because they are the same thing.

## THE BENEVOLENT GODS

There was a further insight lurking in Jayakumar's words. When we think of
injustice, we think of a god player like the moneylender, a malevolent and
rapacious presence in the lives of the poor. But there is another way to play
god, not malevolently but benevolently, in the name of helping the poor.

On the train home from Gudiyatham, Jayakumar and I talked about
what we had seen. "One of my great fears is that in the very process of
breaking the human tendency to play God, I can begin to play God," he
said. "As much as the poor are in need of transformation, World Vision is
in need of real, desperate transformation: in our understanding of power,
our tendency to play God, our tendency to become the spectacular 'savior.'
We need to be continuously confronted with those brutal facts."

Here was a subtle and dangerous kind of god playing I had not considered. Not the god playing of the ill-intentioned, but the well-intentioned.
Not the god playing of obvious abuse and violence, but the god playing of
provision and protection. Yet the more I have reflected on Jayakumar's
words, the more convinced I have become that benevolent god playing can
be even more destructive than malevolent god playing.

Benevolent god playing happens when we use the needs of the poor to
make our own move from good to great—to revel in the superior power
of our technology and the moral excellence of our willingness to help. Benevolent god playing makes us, not those we are serving, the heroes of the
story. It happens whenever technological and financial resources are de-
ployed in such overwhelming force, and with so little real trust building or
relationship, that we maintain a safe distance between ourselves and the
recipients of our largesse.

Consider how these qualities can play out in one of the great benevolent god-playing enterprises of our time, charity and development work.

among the materially poor and politically powerless. The goodness of this
kind of work goes almost unquestioned in an age of celebrity fundraisers,
earnest philanthropists and media-savvy charities. But among the "brutal
facts" Jayakumar might have had in mind are the ways global charity work
takes up the classical qualities of divinity: omnipresence, omniscience
and omnipotence.

   *Omnipresence:* air travel and Land Cruisers can transport us at great
speed from one place to the next in climate-controlled ease. This experience, unavailable to any human being until a century ago, is generally
out of reach for the people we believe we are serving. They still must rely
on their own two feet to carry them from place to place, while we harness
fossil fuels and engines to transport us like Helios in his winged chariot
from one end of the sky to another. Equally amazing, we can project our
images and voices using the tools of telecommunications and the Internet,
showing up in places where we have no physical presence.

   All this leads to the simulation of *omniscience.* I am able to know a great
deal about others while allowing them to know very little about me. In my
own home I can observe others in the midst of the tremendous vulnerability of tragedy and disaster, while they see nothing except the lidless eye
of a video camera held by a Western crew. I will never forget a short piece
of tape that played right after the massive earthquake in Haiti in January
2010. For a few hours it was almost the only video available from the country,
so it was played incessantly to satisfy television's demand for vivid images
while anchors in American studios rehearsed the little we knew about the
unfolding events. It showed a young mother, clad only in her underwear,
clutching her crying toddler and wandering through the devastated streets.

   Amidst the many tragedies of that day, this was one more: the prying
eye of the camera, catching her in her grief, confusion and disarray. She
would never see *me* disoriented and undressed. Indeed, she would never
see me at all. But I and millions of others could see her, in a state that no
human would choose to be seen in, with godlike access to this most vulnerable moment of her and her child's life.

   As if omnipresence and omniscience were not enough, the technological resources at the disposal of my society's corporations and government can give us a sense of *omnipotence.* Compared with the mate-

rially poor, we seem to ourselves to be able to get things done with
supernatural levels of efficacy and efficiency. Our machines can outwork
any mere creature; our organizational techniques can coordinate action
on a massive scale. We begin to believe that the only thing lacking in a
needy world is our own will—that if we choose, we can end poverty and
provide water and stop slavery and cure disease. In a world of omnipotence, with our ability to change the world taken for granted, charity
becomes a matter of marketing, simply persuading the powerful to use
their godlike powers for good.

All this god playing can take place with the best of intentions, with
every hope of helping and with real "results" at the end: wells dug, structures built, children immunized, perpetrators arrested. And the materially
poor may well be grateful for the concrete assistance provided by benevolent god players, and glad to be out from under the thumb of malevolent
god players. But even at its very best, such god playing does nothing to
alter, let alone transform, the most basic reality of poverty, which is the
presence of irresistibly powerful god substitutes in the life of the poor.
Whether those god substitutes are malevolent or benevolent makes less
difference than you might suppose. Their presence makes no room for the
possibility that the poor themselves bear the image of God and could be
agents of their own transformation. Nor does such god playing address
the hearts of the benevolent themselves—our tendency to exaggerate our
own capabilities and minimize our own folly, our use of power to conceal
and protect ourselves from exposure and vulnerability. Benevolent god
playing may remedy the most obvious symptoms of injustice, but it leaves
the underlying disease untreated.

## SHORT-TERM GODS

There may be no better example of benevolent god playing than the phenomenon of short-term missions, in which volunteers from affluent countries travel to needy parts of the world for one- or two-week ventures in
compassion. The United States alone sends some two million short-term
"missionaries" beyond its borders each year (not counting the many more
who take similar trips within the country). Travel to nearly any developing
country, especially one with a relatively temperate climate and convenient

flights to a Western gateway airport, and you are likely to see a group en
route or returning from such a trip, often clad in matching T-shirts.

Short-term missions are rife with opportunities for god playing of the
worst sort. Sometimes it is explicitly Christian: the Latin American theologian Ruth Padilla DeBorst told me of arriving at the Tegucigalpa airport
with a Honduran friend to meet an arriving passenger. Before their friend
emerged from the customs and immigration hall, a boisterous group of
Americans burst through the doors wearing T-shirts that proclaimed (in
English), "Bringing Jesus to Honduras." Ruth's friend turned to her, dis-
mayed, and asked, "Do they think Jesus is not already here?"

Even when our T-shirts do not proclaim our ability to "bring" the Son
of God to a country, as if he could be packed along with our cameras and
other possessions in our bulging backpacks, such fleeting visits only reinforce the godlike powers of those who take them. Who, after all, but a
person of tremendous affluence has the ability to interrupt their daily
lives for a week or two to visit a faraway place? Meanwhile, any interaction
with the image bearers they may encounter, while often enjoyable and
memorable, is in a real sense optional. Time is tight, after all, so these
groups often arrive self-contained, with all the resources they need to
survive for their short visit, including the social resources of people who
know their names, speak their language and understand their needs.

*me =
evil*

Western missionaries once sought to learn the language of the people
they served, a process which requires dependence on local knowledge and
reinforces the value of local culture. Indeed, mission historians like Lamin
Sanneh argue that Western missionaries have been among the most important agents of the preservation of indigenous culture and language. They
stayed for years or decades (some, famously, shipping their possessions to
their destination in their own coffin), ensuring some level of relationship
with and reliance upon their new, lifelong neighbors. And they went as individuals or single family units, not gregarious groups of a dozen or more.

To be sure, the history of long-term Western missions is also rife with
god playing (alongside extraordinary acts of service and sacrifice), and
even today one can encounter Westerners, long-time residents in developing countries, who play god in little fiefdoms, lording it over their dependents in ways they never would have been able to do at home. And it is also

true that some short trips are embedded in long-term relationships of real mutuality, partnership and trust. They can help the privileged gain valuable first-hand experiences of the profound realities of idolatry and injustice in a world of vast disparities—as indeed happened on my own one-day trip with Jayakumar to Gudiyatham—while empowering and encouraging local leaders among the poor who often feel harried and forgotten. But without careful and intentional planning, a short trip with a large group is likely to reinforce the patterns of god playing already in place.

As the anthropologist Brian Howell describes in his fascinating ethnography *Short-Term Mission*, short-term trips almost always fall into a fixed pattern. Before the trip the dominant focus is on preparing for concrete acts of service to "the people who have so little." Afterward, participants consistently report the discovery that "we came to serve, but we received so much more than we gave," and their astonishment that people they visited "had so little, but they had so much joy." On the surface, then, it could seem like these trips, which many participants remember as transformative experiences in their lives, have made a real difference in how powerful North Americans see the poor. But if these trips were truly so transformative, surely after two decades of short-term trips the script would have begun to change. We would have begun to see ourselves as pilgrims and witnesses, not activists and missionaries. We would go seeking to understand and empower, not help and fix. But that would require us to ask deeper questions that, Howell observes, short-term missions rarely seem designed to probe: why poverty remains entrenched, what role Western military, commercial or agricultural policies have had in shaping the situations short-term visitors encounter, and how the same dynamics visible in such dramatic forms overseas may be playing themselves out in our own communities. Perhaps this is why studies by the sociologist Kurt Ver Beek have found that no matter how "life-changing" participants say short-term trips were, there is no statistically significant effect on financial giving or volunteering a year after the trip.

This is one sign that the gods we play in the name of benevolence are not the true Creator God. When the true God acts in history, no one and nothing is left unchanged. But false gods leave everything the way it was—or worse—even while they flatter us with fleeting sensations of emotional and spiritual elevation. The true God takes even small offerings and produces abundant results; false gods take huge offerings of money, time, energy and talent, and give little or nothing in return. Is image bearing in the world flourishing in proportion to the billions of dollars that Western Christians have spent on short-term missions? If not, it is a sign that for all our best intentions we have failed to challenge the idolatries and injustices that keep the image of the true God hidden among the faces of the poor.

## BEHOLD THE MAN

There is another way. The true Image Bearer arrived in history to deal decisively with idolatry and injustice. And yet he came with none of the obvious trappings of divinity. Instead he arrived in the world the way all image bearers arrive, an utterly dependent child. In an image-conscious age it is striking that we have not a single jot of information about his actual appearance, aside from the prophecy that he would have nothing in his appearance to make us desire him. His most remarkable deeds of power were hidden from all but a few close friends; his extraordinary knowledge and insight were camouflaged in parables, questions and, on more than one occasion, silence. Far from winging his way around the globe, he spent nearly his entire life traveling at the speed a man can walk (with a few excursions on boats and donkeys). In the ultimate showdown with injustice, betrayed by a friend, indicted by perjurers, and condemned by religious and political god players, it seemed that he conclusively lost.

And yet in fact what was set in motion by the incarnation, crucifixion and resurrection was the restoration of true image bearing. In one of the Bible's finest moments of mistaken identity, John tells us of Mary Magdalene meeting the risen Jesus in the garden by the open tomb and mistaking him for the gardener. Of course, she is wrong, and of course, she is quite right—here in this garden we have again a woman and a man inaugurating a new chapter in history, this time not the sober and sad loss of the image but the glad recovery and restoration of it.

Just pause, though, to observe that at the very moment when the power of God to overcome death was made manifest, the one who was borne up by that power could be mistaken for a most ordinary man. If we are to play the true God, it seems, we will have to be gloriously, ordinarily, ourselves.

*excellent.*

# A NOTE

## Evangelism and Social Action

Somewhere along the way, this intimate connection between idolatry and injustice was lost. We began to believe that one was a "religious" question, the other a "political" question. And the Christian world began to separate into two camps, sometimes pitched against one another—one stressing "evangelism," the other "social action," one pursuing religious conversion, the other pursuing social justice.

Or, to borrow terms the influential evangelical pastor John Piper used in an address to the Cape Town Congress in 2010, one group was concerned about present-day suffering while the other was concerned about "eternal suffering."

The lines are not so hard and fast today as they were when modernist Protestants talked exclusively about a "social gospel" and fundamentalist Protestants devoted their lives to "saving souls." There are scarcely any Christians today, from any tradition, who insist on maintaining a lopsided focus on justice without evangelism or evangelism without justice. Of course they still have their emphases and preferences—it is hard to weigh "present suffering" and "eternal suffering" on the same scale. "Eternal suffering," being of infinite duration and depth, sounds vastly more consequential than the sufferings of this life, with obvious implications for where the church's energies ought to be directed. But even this loaded language was used in the context of affirming that of course Christians care about relieving suffering here and now, an affirmation that once would have earned even the most evangelistically energetic preacher the suspicion of supporting the social gospel.

What both sides have gradually (and sometimes grudgingly) realized is that "care for the poor and oppressed," and proclamation of the good news of salvation through Jesus, simply are both essential biblical themes. But what has remained surprisingly muddy is the fundamental question of how social action and evangelism are related. Most often, perhaps, they are presented in terms of the two great commandments of loving God and loving neighbor. But this still leaves the question of why loving God and loving our neighbor are more than just two distantly related things that we are supposed to do. Why did Jesus single out those two commandments when asked to name the greatest *commandment*—singular? Why do the biblical writers from beginning to end seem to weave themes of justice and worship, injustice and idolatry, proclamation and demonstration?

But if the whole story is about restoring the image of God, filling the world with fruitful image bearers who represent the world's Creator by cultivating and creating, then there is no gap at all between evangelism and doing justice, just as there is no gap between idolatry and injustice. Neither can exist in any serious way without the other. Both are about restoring the image.

Evangelism is not an end in itself. It is the means to an end: restoring the image bearers' capacity for relationship and worship, where the true Creator God is named, known and blessed. Evangelism gives us the name of the God who made us, the Son who redeemed us and the Spirit who empowers us to be reborn in the image of the Son. Without evangelism, Eve's and Adam's descendants after Eden will never know the full story; they will never know the identity of the true Image Bearer. Just as important, apart from the redeeming and empowering gift of salvation, they will never be fully able to bear the image themselves. They will remain captive to idols, false gods that can never deliver what they promise, rather than coming to know and imitate the true God who gives abundance and gave himself to fulfill his promises.

And doing justice is likewise the means to an end—*shalom,* that rich Hebrew word for peace, describing the conditions where every creature can be fully, truly, gloriously itself, most of all where God's own image bearers bear that image in all its fullness, variety and capacity. The work of justice is to restore the conditions that make image bearing possible. Without justice, without the kind of restoration that reopens the way to dignified, delighted image bearing, it is much less likely that the good news about the true Image Bearer will be believed even if it is proclaimed. And even if Adam's and Eve's children have heard and believed the story of restored image bearing, without the work of justice they will not be able to participate in it. They will be prevented from the dominion and tending of the world they were made for. And the world, and their fellow image bearers, will continue to groan under exploitation and diminishment, defying the will of God for his own creation.

The result of both real evangelism and real doing of justice is the restoration of the image of the only true God in the world. The image cannot be restored without naming the name and telling the story of the one true Creator God; so all serious efforts for justice must be connected to evangelism. And that image cannot be restored without God's own image bearers taking up their true identity and calling and having the capacity to fulfill that calling; so all evangelism must be connected to efforts to create the conditions where every image bearer can experience full dignity and agency.

Some who emphasize evangelism ask, Won't the world always be full of broken, imperfect systems until Jesus returns? So what good is it to work for justice and shalom in this world, when we know any human efforts will fall short? Shouldn't our greatest effort be devoted to giving people the hope of an eternal kingdom that will never pass away, rather than trying to improve conditions in this world that is passing away?

Of course, these faithful evangelists have no problem presenting the gospel to people knowing that only some will repent and turn to Christ in this life. We could equally ask, What good is it to evangelize when we know only some people will come to faith? The obvious answers are, first, that we cannot know ahead of time who may hear and respond; second, that even if only a few come to salvation they are still of infinite worth; third, that even those who will not respond deserve to hear that they are loved this deeply by God; and fourth, that we are not accountable ultimately for the results—only God can bring the fruit we seek—but for our faithfulness.

But all these are the reasons that we should work for justice, even knowing we will never see perfect shalom this side of the new Jerusalem. We cannot know ahead of time what efforts for justice, restoring the conditions that lead to image bearing, will bear astonishing fruit. In my own lifetime we have seen the sudden, peaceful end of apartheid in South Africa; the collapse of totalitarianism in the Soviet Union; and closer to my home, the election of an American of African descent to the highest office in the land. None of these could reasonably have been foreseen a generation before they happened. Each has been a victory for the restoration of image bearing. To be sure, there are still countless other places where injustice reigns, and in each of these situations the victories have been partial at best. But not to work for justice because of those hard realities would be as odd as refusing to evangelize because some will not believe.

As for the question of why we should work for justice in a world that is passing away—well, the world *is* passing away. Our work for justice should no more be based on the idea that humanity will somehow progress on its own merits to utopia than proclaiming the good news about eternal life should be based on the idea that someone who accepts Jesus into their heart will never die. The Christian hope is not for a gradually improving world any more than it is for a fountain of youth. But Christian hope overcomes the forces of despair and decay in the midst of this world, and provides foretastes of the coming kingdom where anyone who will receive the Lamb's sacrifice will be raised to life, and where the glory and honor of the nations will be presented as offerings to the King of kings. Hope for a life beyond this life, and a world of shalom beyond this world of injustice, is the greatest resource for the work of justice here and now. Christian hope for a world made new is not an alternative to doing justice—it is the most essential resource for it.

But let me admit my true concern in taking this little excursion. These days I do not often meet Christians so passionate about evangelism that they question the need for doing justice. I am much more likely to meet Christians so passionate about justice that they question the need for evangelism.

Meeting the physical needs of the poor wins attention and affirmation from a watching world. Naming the spiritual poverty of a world enthralled to false gods provokes defensiveness and derision from those who do not even believe there is a god. Disaster relief and economic development seem like achievable goals that bring people together; religious claims to know the one true God seem like divisive mysteries that drive people apart. Our secular neighbors care, many like never before, about relieving human need—and more of them than ever before are indifferent or hostile to the idea that Jesus is the way, the truth, the life and the one who meets the deepest human need.

In short, working for justice is cool. Proclaiming the gospel is not.

Inevitably, then, as Christians recover a calling to justice and receive the affirmation of neighbors who do not believe in a world beyond this one, we can begin to wonder whether evangelism is really necessary after all. To put it another way, our vision of "justice" owes less and less to the rich biblical concept of shalom, interwoven as it is with the story of the Creator God and his yearning for restored relationship with his people. More and more it conforms to the necessary but thin language of human rights and international humanitarian efforts. Justice becomes simply a name for improving certain, often fairly superficial, social conditions, without probing very deeply into the roots of those conditions.

In short, we do not truly believe that the gods of the nations are idols. Our vision of justice has become secularized; we have lost the biblical conviction that God alone is good. In a sense, John Piper captures this thin conception of justice in his reduction of the work of justice to addressing "suffering." You do not have to believe in the Creator God to want to alleviate suffering. But justice is about much more than relieving suffering—it is about a vision of human flourishing. And the audacious biblical claim is that even good things that seem to contribute to flourishing become idols when they become our ultimate ends. Even the laudable goals of economic development, political freedom and human rights are only ultimately good when they are put in the context of something more ultimate than themselves. When we try to establish justice apart from worship of the true God, at best we will, as Jayakumar reminded me, simply replace one set of god players with another. What will never be addressed by these thin, secular conceptions of justice is the heart of the biblical understanding of justice: the restoration of the human capacity to bear the image in all its fullness.

This does not mean that Christians cannot work in secular societies to secure relatively limited forms of justice. Indeed, we can value the religious freedom and diversity that secular societies provide. Image bearing, from its very beginnings in the Garden of Genesis 2, included the capacity to turn away from the Creator. In some mysterious way this is part of the dignity that God grants Adam and Eve: the apparent absence of their Maker who only walks in the Garden "in the cool of the day" and leaves them to their tending, and their temptation, at other times. When we secure for our neighbors the right to worship other gods or to convince themselves that they believe in no god at all (something we, who know too well the human heart's incurable bent toward god making and god playing, will never actually agree that they have managed to do), we are actually securing one of the fundamental freedoms of image bearers.

But Christians who truly want to seek justice cannot afford to let "justice" be reduced to the lowest common denominator we may be able to agree on with our neighbors. To do that would be to surrender to gods that are not real gods—to assent to the serpent's promise that apart from relationship with God we can be like God, knowing good and evil. We can work for common goals for uncommon reasons. Because we believe every one of our neighbors is an image bearer, however broken their relationship with the One whose image they bear, we will find much common ground for working for justice and freedom. The things our neighbors seek are good; they are just not ultimate goods. We can work alongside them for the good while worshiping the One who alone is good.

Ultimately the reason for both the work of evangelism and the work of justice is not simply the relief of suffering, whether present or eternal. It is the restoration of God's true image in the world, made known in the one true Image and Icon, Jesus Christ, and refracted and reflected in fruitful, multiplying image bearers set free by his death and resurrection to reclaim their true calling. Our mission is not primarily driven by a calculation of which suffering, present or eternal, we need to relieve most urgently; it is the fruit of glorious promises that call us into a new kingdom where the world is full of truth-bearing images. No image bearer can fully return to their true calling without finding themselves rescued and redeemed by the true Image Bearer, so no serious Christian witness in the world can fail to call people to put their trust in Jesus and the true God he makes known. And no image bearer can bear full witness to the glory of the Creator without the conditions for flourishing that are summed up in the rich biblical conception of justice. "He comes to make his blessings flow / far as the curse is found." Because idolatry and injustice are the twin fruits of the curse, the work of evangelism and the work of justice are one.

# 5

# ICONS

We know of just one time when Jesus himself specifically used the language of the image of God—and it was at exactly the moment when he was confronted with a question of power.

Mark, Matthew and Luke all record an encounter with the Pharisees and Herodians, who seek to trap Jesus in a question of ultimate allegiance. "Teacher, we know that you are a man of integrity," they say accurately and completely insincerely. "You aren't swayed by others, because you pay no attention to who they are; but you teach the way of God in accordance with the truth. Is it right to pay the imperial tax to Caesar or not? Should we pay or shouldn't we?" Jesus asks for a denarius, the imperial coin—"Bring me a denarius and let me look at it"—a sly way of implying that not only does he not handle Caesar's money himself, but can't even quite remember what it looks like. When one is brought forward, it is not Jesus who inspects the coin but his questioners: "'Whose image is this? And whose inscription?' 'Caesar's,' they replied. Then Jesus said to them, 'Give back to Caesar what is Caesar's and to God what is God's" (Mark 12:13-17 NIV).

Jesus' opponents and Jesus himself know that this is not a conversation about money. To Jesus' opponents, it is a conversation about power. The "trap" in the question is between two powers that are locked in a zero-sum competition—the oppressed and the oppressor, Jesus' Israelite followers and their Roman rulers, and the Herodians and the Pharisees themselves, one group willing to compromise with Roman rule and the other seeking

to escape entanglement with it. By pressing Jesus for a decision that will
infuriate one side or the other, they seek to undermine his power and
increase their own.

But Jesus knows that the real contest here is between two competing
images. Jesus' world, unlike our own, was not full of pictures. Images of
human beings were rare and powerful things. And no image was more
powerful than the precious coins that circulated throughout the empire
bearing the image of Caesar, reinforcing his rule and bringing his symbolic
presence to every corner of the known world. Along with that rule came
the demand to give this far-off quasi-god a share in every commercial transaction, even if you were at the edges of empire where Roman rule meant
mostly subjugation and brought little flourishing. Imagine the power of
every celebrity, dictator and central banker in our world rolled into one
human being, and you have some idea of what the image of Caesar meant.

In the Roman empire, as in empires before and since, image making
and god playing went together on a vast scale. The Roman rulers, who,
generation after generation, ascended closer and closer to divine status
even as the benefits of their rule diminished, justified injustice with
idolatry and were driven by idolatry to injustice. They were not the last to
put their images on currency, stamping their claim on every transaction—
indeed, a rough guide to the political health of contemporary nations is
how many different images appear on their money. The more, the better. If
every coin and bill shows always and only the same face, and if images of
that face are required by law in every office and shop, you have a clue to
the patterns of god playing in that society. In Caesar's Rome, there was
ultimately only one image, before which every other had to bow. That is
what it meant to say "Caesar is Lord."

Jesus' response to this vast, idolatrous empire demonstrates the truth of
his opponents' feigned praise: "You aren't swayed by others, because you
pay no attention to who they are." He dismisses Caesar's powerful image
with the Greek word *apodote*—"give it back." Caesar has made this graven
image. Give it back to him. His answer is astonishing because in a world
where Caesar is worshiped as all-powerful, the most radical response to
Caesar is indifference, dismissing Caesar's coins with a simple "return to
sender" and treating Caesar himself as simply one more human being.

*but there is a tie between the economic system of the coin and the idolatrous image on it.*

What matters to Jesus, it seems, is not what is done with the lifeless coins on which Caesar has placed his stamp, but another image—the image of God in living image bearers. The image of God is found in human beings, and the real demonic power of Caesar is to demand not the sacrifice of coins but of people, not money but lives. The bearers of God's image must offer themselves in allegiance and worship only to the Creator God, not to human usurpers.

So much Jesus' hearers might have understood. But only the readers of the Gospels are in a position to understand the deeper significance of Jesus' words. For the Pharisees and Herodians were trying to entrap not just one more troublesome teacher, but the one true Image Bearer, the one who had come into the world to restore the divine image that had been lost in a world of idols. Having failed to trap him in their own zero-sum game, they would themselves render him to Caesar, turning over the anointed representative of the Creator, the world's true Lord, to the Roman procurator who was the representative of Caesar and the enforcer of his claim to lordship. The petty matter of the imperial tax was nothing compared to the sacrifice they were about to make, turning God's Son over to the powers of idolatry and injustice to do their worst.

## THE RESURRECTED IMAGE

I implore my readers to stick with me—the next few pages will get pretty theological. But that is exactly what happened when the politically savvy pundits of his day tried to lure Jesus into pronouncing on a thorny political issue. If Jesus could turn a question about taxes into a conversation about the image of God, we too will have to think in new, deeper and different ways if we really want to understand the gift of power. We need our imaginations, so diminished by millennia of idolatry and injustice, to be reconsecrated.

We need to rejoin the thought world of the early church, gobsmacked by Good Friday, Easter, Ascension and Pentecost.

We will never have the slightest hope of comprehending the gift of power until we come to believe what they came to believe: We were created image bearers—but we are meant, by grace, to be icons.

For the writers of the Hebrew Scriptures, the question was never whether there would be idols—divine images—in the world. The world would be full of images one way or another. The question was whether human beings would serve as living, breathing representations of the living God who breathed creation into existence, or whether, in breathlessly running after lifeless parodies of that true God, they themselves would cease to fulfill their original vocation.

And for the writers of the New Testament, the good news is that after human beings, and even God's chosen people, chose the path of false god making and god playing, Christ came as "the image of the invisible God" (Colossians 1:15). The Greek word here is again *eikōn*, the ordinary word for image or likeness that Jesus used in his dispute with the Herodians and Pharisees. But it has come into the English language as the word *icon*. And an icon is no ordinary image. An icon is an image freighted with divine significance that is nonetheless not an idol. Like an idol, an icon is an image that claims to present ultimate truth. But unlike an idol, an icon tells the truth about ultimate reality. And unlike an idol, an icon can be trusted. An icon is a trustworthy image.

Jesus was the Icon of God—the trustworthy Image Bearer. Unlike all false images, in everything he did and said, the way he lived and died, Jesus showed us what the true God is like. The true God is nothing like the false gods of the nations, nothing like Caesar who claims to be lord. And when the Image of this true God enters the human story, not only does he arouse the anger of the forces of idolatry and injustice in their many guises, but he triumphs over them even as he suffers the death that every idol eventually deals. The good news is that even when the Image of God was rendered to Caesar, Caesar did not become Lord. Indeed, because Jesus suffered the worst that Caesar could do, humbling himself even to the point of death on Caesar's cross,

> God also highly exalted him
> > and gave him the name
> > that is above every name,
> so that at the name of Jesus
> > every knee should bend,
> > in heaven and on earth and under the earth,
> and every tongue should confess
> > that Jesus Christ is Lord,
> > to the glory of God the Father. (Philippians 2:9-11)

Jesus died, rose and was glorified to show what true lordship is, and to forever unmask the power of idols and the injustice that comes in their train.

The resurrection conclusively vindicated the most unbelievable yet unavoidable part of Jesus' teaching—his teaching about himself. No one in the history of Jewish monotheism had so unabashedly referred to God as Father, claimed the messianic title "Son of Man," or dared to refer to himself as "the Lord." Yet in the wake of Jesus' resurrection the first Christians became convinced that this exalted intimacy and authority belonged rightfully to Jesus; that, indeed, the only way to do full justice to Jesus' relationship with God was to acknowledge that he shared God's very being as an only-begotten Son. He was both fully divine and fully human, a perfect image bearer, the icon of the invisible God.

But early Christians quickly recognized that this extraordinary claim about Jesus had implications not just for Jesus alone but for every human being. The earthquake of the resurrection was followed quickly by two massive aftershocks that would forever alter Christians' vision of what true humanity means. First there was the ascension, in which the exalted but still very human body of Jesus was taken in some mysterious but undeniable way into "heaven," understood then and by careful Christian thinkers today not as "up in the sky" but as the realm of God's unlimited being and authority. The Word who had existed before anything was created, "very God of very God" in the words of the creed, now was present to the Creator God with the body of the *very human* Jesus of Nazareth. Humanity itself had been ushered into the heavenly life of the Trinity.

But this aftershock was followed days later by an equally extraordinary event, when Jesus' all-too-human followers, gathered together in Jerusalem on the day of Pentecost, received what Jesus had promised at his ascension: "You will receive power when the Holy Spirit has come upon you; and you will be my witnesses in Jerusalem, in all Judea and Samaria, and to the ends of the earth" (Acts 1:8). Until Pentecost the followers and friends of Jesus were bystanders, occasionally brave and mostly bumbling, as this extraordinary Son of Man went about his works of power, his final passage of suffering and his unexpected return in fullness of life. But at Pentecost, just as Jesus had promised, the 120 first disciples were filled with power. What was the power they were filled with? It was a power not primarily military (as many of the followers had expected), economic or even cultural; instead it was the power of restored image bearers. At Pentecost the curse of Babel, the culmination of the frustration of idolatry and injustice, was spectacularly reversed. What was unleashed at Pentecost was the power of true image bearing, the long-awaited pouring out of God's own Spirit upon "all flesh," as Peter makes explicit in his sermon in Acts 2: young and old, male and female, free and slaves—the imparting of God's own agency to those in whom that image had become tarnished and dim.

In the wake of Easter, Ascension and Pentecost, the church began to nourish hopes that would have seemed fantastical to even the most pious and hopeful member of Israel. Could it be that Jesus had come not just to wash away the worst effects of human sin and rebellion, but to usher humanity itself into a greater and grander calling? Could it be that God's image bearers would one day not simply reflect God's glory as in a dim mirror but actually participate in that glory? That is precisely what the first Christians, overcome with the power of God manifest in the resurrection and in their own experience of the overpowering and empowering Spirit, began to believe. "Do you not know," Paul asks the Corinthians in the mid-60s, using a formula that strongly suggests they had heard these ideas many times before, "that we are to judge angels?" (1 Corinthians 6:3). "I endure everything for the sake of the elect," Paul says in 2 Timothy many decades later, "so that they may also obtain the salvation that is in Christ Jesus, with eternal glory." (What is waiting for us is not just salvation, not just rescue from sin, but glory.) He continues, again with a phrase that marks a firmly established and familiar tradition:

> The saying is sure:
> If we have died with him, we will also live with him;
> if we endure, we will also reign with him. (2 Timothy 2:10-12)

These and many other New Testament texts can only reflect the very earliest Christians' stunned absorbing of the full implications of what they had witnessed and experienced—that in Christ human beings were not just being restored to their original caretaking role over creation but ushered beyond it into the very authority and power of the creative Word himself.

Perhaps the most striking expression of all comes in 2 Peter 1:3-4:

> His divine power has given us everything needed for life and godliness, through the knowledge of him who called us by his own glory and goodness. Thus he has given us, through these things, his precious and very great promises, so that through them you may escape from the corruption that is in the world because of lust, and may become participants of the divine nature.

*Participants of the divine nature*—this is the ultimate goal of the "divine power" unleashed through the glory and goodness of God.

## A HUMAN BEING FULLY ALIVE

There is a marvelous phrase from the early Christian bishop Irenaeus, *Gloria dei vivens homo.* This phrase is often translated today, "The glory of God is a human being fully alive." Literally, the phrase simply means, "The glory of God is a living human being." "Fully alive" is an embellishment of sorts. Now, Irenaeus is hardly speaking of human beings in general. What could Irenaeus, or anyone in the first centuries of the church, have meant by *vivens homo* if not *the* living Son of Man? In the original context of this phrase (Irenaeus's treatise *Against Heresies*), Irenaeus is arguing against the heretical idea that God must be invisible and unknowable. Of course God is invisible and beyond our comprehension, Irenaeus replies, but always with the invisible and unknowable Father has been the Word, the Wisdom of God, through whom everything was created, and the entire purpose of creation was to make God known in his image bearers.

But Irenaeus goes farther than that in this (admittedly run-on) statement:

> Now this is His Word, our Lord Jesus Christ, who in the last times was made a man among men, that He might join the end to the beginning, that is, man to God. Wherefore the prophets, receiving the prophetic gift from the same Word, announced His advent according to the flesh, by which the blending and communion of God and man took place according to the good pleasure of the Father, the Word of God foretelling from the beginning that God should be seen by men, and hold converse with them upon earth, should confer with them, and should be present with His own creation, saving it, and becoming capable of being perceived by it, and

freeing us from the hands of all that hate us, that is, from every spirit of wickedness; and causing us to serve Him in holiness and righteousness all our days, in order that man, having embraced the Spirit of God, might pass into the glory of the Father.

Irenaeus's language here is breathtaking, and stated in multiple ways to make sure we (and the heretics) do not miss the point. The point of the Word becoming flesh was to "join the end to the beginning, that is, man to God"; the result of that incarnation was "the blending and communion of God and man"; all this "in order that man . . . might pass into the glory of the Father."

So when Irenaeus speaks, two paragraphs later, about the *vivens homo*, the living human being, he has in mind this expansive vision of human life: the resurrected, ascended life of the truly Human One who has now poured out his Spirit on us and invites us into nothing less than God's own glory. Indeed, those who enthusiastically quote the first half of Irenaeus's wonderful sentence often do not realize that it has a second clause in which he defines what it is to be fully alive: *vita autem hominis visio Dei*— "moreover, the life of man consists in beholding God." For Irenaeus, being "fully alive" is only possible in the full presence of the only One who *is* fully alive—the eternally living Creator, his Son brought back to life, and the life-giving Holy Spirit. The only reason, in Irenaeus's view, that we are alive at all is that God has already revealed himself through creation, which even now is sustained by the Holy Spirit, without whom the world would vanish in a moment. But the Christian hope is for a much more comprehensive life in the very presence and fullness of the Creator, whom we now glimpse only in the mirror, as it were, of his creation and his creatures.

We can go further. The world is abundant and alive precisely because in the beginning God dared—or was delighted—to do exactly that thing that the Second Commandment forbade to human beings: make an image of himself. The world without image bearers was good, but it was not very good. But the early church began to believe that as very good as the completed creation was, the new creation would be even better. God's final plan for creation was not *just* restored images, not just reflections, however accurate and complete, of the glory of the Creator. Instead, leaders like Irenaeus began to teach that the goal of creation was that the images would "pass into the glory of the Father," taking part in the exalted life already known by the risen Christ, seated at the Father's right hand. Just as with the original creation, so with the new creation. What human beings never should do—take created things and treat them as divine—is exactly what the love of God intends to do.

All this may seem impossibly esoteric. What relevance can these speculations about human beings sharing in God's glory have to do with our daily use of the power we have and our response to the power others have? Are there any practical implications at all to these grand words about glory and exaltation? Indeed, one cannot read the early fathers and mothers of the church without sensing that their publishing priorities were rather different from most Protestant church leaders today. No books on leadership, on excellence, on practical tools for faithful living? Wouldn't Irenaeus be better off writing a book about the five marks of organizational excellence than a treatise on the true meaning of the invisibility of God?

The only possible Christian answer to these questions is that these seemingly esoteric and eschatological teachings are intensely practical—are, in fact, the most practical things in the world. They are practical in exactly the way that the resurrected body of Jesus is practical, that is, hard to recognize, impossible to control, marked by suffering, ineffably glorious, and categorically the most real thing in all of creation.

To the practical men who led the Roman Empire, collected its imperial taxes, or administered the religious life of Jerusalem and its surrounding territory, the cross and the guarded tomb were eminently practical, and apparently successful, solutions to pressing social problems. By all the available evidence, even a resurrected body, however momentarily inconvenient, caused no great concern for either the Roman or Jewish leaders in its neighborhood in the first century: for them the practical matters were much nearer at hand. But within a generation the fragile ceasefire these practical men had tried to secure had turned into a conflagration of rebellion and repression, and another generation later Jerusalem was a burned-out husk of a city—fulfilling Jesus' tearful prophecy that its residents and leaders did not know the things that made for peace.

But within a few more generations, the news of Jesus' resurrection had indeed "turned the world upside down," just as the alarmed early reports from Thessalonica suggested (Acts 17:6). The proclamation that the true Image Bearer had lived, had not been vanquished by the powers of idolatry and injustice but had risen victorious over them, and had now poured out his Spirit on flesh, turned out to be the pivot point of history, the hinge on which the whole story turned. The promise that human beings were not destined to be ground under the dust of idols and god players like Caesar, but to rule and rise to participation in the divine nature, set in motion the most wide-ranging social movement in history. It is no accident that the New Testament is so saturated with talk of power, even though its writers follow Jesus in showing minimal interest in directly combating the powers of their day with revolution or radicalism. Their sights were already fixed on something far more glorious and, strangely, of greater practical import than any merely political movement. They had discovered the true, divine gift of power.

## ICONS OF WHO WE CAN BECOME

One icon has accompanied me for nearly twenty years now. In my early twenties I found my way to the Monastery of St. John on the island of Patmos in the Aegean Sea. In the monastery's dim and austere galleries one unusual icon caught my eye. Most icons are square or rectangular; this one was in the shape of an oval. Most icons show one saint; this one showed two, Saints Peter and Paul. And they were embracing. Indeed, they were nearly kissing; their faces were pressed up against one another in an intimate greeting, presumably something like the "holy kiss" that Paul refers to in his letters. The traditional circular halos behind their heads overlapped, forming a kind of heart shape. The icon was a series of symmetries from top to bottom—their halos, their hands on one another's shoulders and forearms, their overlapping garments of deep green, crimson, blue and gold all combining in a moment of balanced but dynamic harmony.

I ended up paying several visits to the icon during my week on Patmos, drawn back to it by the tension between its harmonious beauty and the complicated historical moment it portrays. The icon, as a visiting Greek scholar did his best to explain to me using his limited English one day as we stood in the dry cool air of the gallery, shows the moment when Peter and Paul meet for the first time. "*Synaspismos,*" he said emphatically. "Ah yes, *synaspismos,*" I responded, pretending that my four years of classical Greek were not wasted. For many years I thought he was telling me the name of the icon; only later did I learn that the word refers to an ancient battle practice of advancing with shields overlapping one another, just as the saints overlap in this moment of greeting. It is a word for shared strength, comradeship and partnership—the sharing of power that enabled both Peter and Paul to fulfill their vocations as ambassadors of the gospel across the Roman Empire.

But while Peter and Paul are indeed greeting one another with a holy kiss, fellow warriors lending one another their strength and blessing, the longer I looked at the icon the more I suspected that Peter and Paul's feelings about this meeting were, well, complicated. The expression on each of their faces is somber, even a bit suspicious. Indeed, as they embrace they are quite conspicuously not looking one another in the eyes the way I do when I meet a long-lost friend; they gaze across and out of the frame of the icon, each looking at something beyond the other. These are not old friends reunited after a long journey. They are, in fact, very recent enemies meeting shortly after Paul's conversion from persecutor of the church to energetic defender of the Way of Jesus. And they would soon become rivals of sorts, divided at least for a time on some of the most basic questions facing the early church, leading to the public dispute Paul reports in Galatians.

Peter and Paul were alike in some ways. Both seem to have been bold if not brash, both were evangelists, both seem to have had an instinct for seeking out and training young leaders like Mark and Timothy. Yet they were also undeniably different. Paul, the cosmopolitan Pharisee and student of Gamaliel; Peter, the fisherman with the Galilean accent. Oddly, the Galilean outsider became a leading figure in the Jerusalem church and ultimately was thought of as the apostle to the Jews; the Pharisee insider ultimately made his greatest contribution to Christian history by embracing a mission to the Gentiles. The iconography of the Synaspismos icon plays up their differences even as it brings them together in their embrace—Peter with his traditional bushy head of hair, Paul darker in complexion and already balding (the iconographer thoughtfully gives him a little tuft of hair on top of his head—fortunately, the combover seems to have been a later

invention). It also emphasizes, if not exaggerates, the difference in age between the two men: Peter is portrayed with gray hair and beard, so that Paul,
in spite of his premature balding, looks like the younger man.

So the Synaspismos icon has become for me a picture of fellowship,
partnership and community, and also of difference, distance and difficulty.
Ultimately they are all part of the same thing. It is perhaps the best por-
trayal I have seen of the reality that love is as much an act of the will as an
impulse of the heart. In the Synaspismos we witness two strong leaders
willing to submit to one another—to embrace the gifts the other brings
and to join together, shields overlapping, in a shared mission. The icon is
all about Peter and Paul, and it is also all about something much greater
than Peter and Paul. Precisely because of their differences, both the differences we see portrayed and the differences we know about from the New
Testament, the icon invites us to ponder what could bring two men together in this way. What—or who—would be powerful enough to draw
them together in this greeting, to hold them together across all of their
barely concealed discomfort?

Icons are not meant primarily to be looked *at*; they are meant to be
looked *through*. The Synaspismos icon is of some real interest on its own.
But it is not, and is not meant to be, primarily a captivating work of art in
its own right. Its golden background reminds us of an incomparably
greater reality that shimmers behind the somewhat flattened and stylized
figures in the foreground. The real purpose of the icon is to draw us not
into contemplation, let alone worship, of the icon itself or the persons it
depicts, but to invite us into a relationship with the One who drew Peter
and Paul together, held them in fellowship in spite of themselves, and
through them began to build one holy, catholic and apostolic church. It is
not just a picture of a human embrace; it invites us to ponder the mystery
of reconciliation, the idea that we ourselves will be welcomed into a
greeting by one who is both so like and so unlike us. And it ultimately asks
us to consider the great mystery of God himself, not one solitary person
but a fellowship of persons distinct from one another yet completely one,
in whom difference is not so much a challenge to be overcome but the essential condition of love. All this is possible because Peter and Paul, with
all their particular stories, sometimes prickly personalities and human

faults, were image bearers. They are icons of who we, too, could become—who we, thanks to God's grace, already are.

Orthodox churches are crowded with icons, but no more crowded than the world. Thanks to the activity of Jesus' Spirit in the world, almost anywhere we look we can see, even if only through a glass darkly, true image bearers, true God players. We see them even, or perhaps especially, in the midst of the most entrenched systems of idolatry and false god playing. In the midst of the colossal, arrogant idolatry of National Socialism we find Dietrich Bonhoeffer and Oskar Schindler; in the gulags of Stalin we find Aleksandr Isayevich Solzhenitsyn; amidst the bitter, dead-end violence of apartheid we find Nelson Mandela and Desmond Tutu; in precisely the states where Jim Crow was most entrenched, Rosa Parks sits down and Martin Luther King Jr. rises up. In each of these places, as well, are countless image bearers who do not achieve celebrity, whose names we do not remember but who kept alive the reality of the true image in their time and place and indeed made it possible for these celebrated figures to emerge and triumph.

Image bearers, as this list makes clear, do not have to name the name of Jesus Christ to play the true God—because image bearing, true God playing, is not a vocation only for Christians. It is a vocation for every human being, and whenever a human being manages to refract into the world something of the true character of the Creator God, even when they do so imperfectly and incompletely, we who are Christians recognize the unmistakable sign of God's original grace in creation, his continuing grace in sustaining goodness in a world gone wrong, and his ultimate intentions for the cosmos. What is amazing about the world, after all, is not that it is full of false images, but that after ages of sin and rebellion it still so often gives us a glimpse of the true image.

So the question is not actually whether we are playing God. We are playing *some* god, without a doubt. The question is, which god are we playing? And if we wanted to be extra cheeky, we would add that the question is not whether we are involved with idolatry. The question is whether we are *making* idols—investing created things with ultimate significance—or whether we are *being* "idols" in the sense of Genesis 1:26, images and signs of the ultimate truth about the world. Whether we are idol makers or icons.

## MY GLORY I GIVE TO NO OTHER

Isn't there something dangerous about believing that we mere creatures will eventually "pass into the glory of the Father," in Irenaeus's words? Didn't God say, "I am the LORD, that is my name; my glory I give to no other" in Isaiah 42:8? But this question itself shows how zero-sum our understanding of power and glory remains.

Read out of context, God's words in Isaiah can sound like God is jealously hoarding glory, which is apparently a scarce resource under threat. We can fall into speaking of God's passion for his own glory as if "his own" meant what we would mean by "my own"—something exclusively belonging to God and held, like private property, for God's benefit alone. Indeed, the word *alone* has become a touchstone of certain Christians' vocabulary: for God's glory alone, for God and God alone. This may well serve as a useful caution against the all-too-common tendency to treat God as a friendly therapist for our own needs, a supporting actor in our own supremely interesting personal dramas, or even as our own private magical idol.

Yet when we turn to one of the great image-bearing psalms, Psalm 8, we get a radically different picture of God's relationship with his image bearers. It begins with an unequivocal statement of the glory of God: "how majestic is your name in all the earth! You have set your glory above the heavens." This is a God who needs no regular offerings from dutiful worshipers to top up his supply of glory. Indeed, so secure is this God in his majesty that his recourse against his enemies is "the praise of children and infants." The smallest members of the community give God enough praise "to silence the enemy and the avenger."

But then the psalmist turns to a crucial question. If the Creator God, unlike false gods, does not require human effort and sacrifice to sustain his glory, why should this glorious God care about mere mortals at all? One of the delights of our idols, after all, is that they assure us that we play a central role in the world. Every idolatry and every injustice begins with elevating someone out of mere goodness to greatness, and both idolatry and injustice are sustained by insisting on the necessity of sacrifice and submission. But what to make of an infinitely great God who is beyond the heavens, needing nothing from us—how does this God offer us any reassurance in the face of the vastness of the cosmos? "What are human beings that you are mindful of them?"

Yet this is precisely what the psalmist celebrates. "You have made them a little lower than God, and crowned them with glory and honor." And God has given his image bearers the responsibility for ruling over "the works of your hands," directly echoing the creation story of Genesis 1:

> you have put all things under their feet,
> all sheep and oxen,
>> and also the beasts of the field,
> the birds of the air, and the fish of the sea,
>> whatever passes along the paths of the seas. (Psalm 8:6-8)

In its original context this can hardly have meant domination in any usual sense of the word. How could the birds in the sky or the creatures swimming in the paths of the sea be under any ancient person's feet? This is metaphor just as surely as the image of God's glory being set "above the heavens"; it reflects neither physical nor technological control over the teeming world, but the same kind of rule that God exercises. It is the rule of beings who do not need to fearfully extract resources from a recalcitrant world, but who can be mindful of even the smallest thing in creation, dignifying the whole creation through their careful tending and keeping.

The psalm leaves its central question—what are we human beings that God cares for us?—unanswered. Its unanswerability is the very thing that prompts worship. There is no explanation for this lavish gift of dignity to creatures formed from the dust; there is no ulterior motive or rationale, unlike the gods of the Babylonian myths who order the creation of human beings to ensure constant sacrifices of worship. Rather, the gift of glory and honor, like the gift of power and rule, is simply the reflection of true being, the character of the Creator God who always seeks more being, not less, and is glorified by the multiplication and distribution of glory, not by the guarding and hoarding of glory.

So what does God mean when he says, "My glory I give to no other" in Isaiah 42:8? The answer is in the second phrase of the poetic couplet, "nor my praise to idols." God is unwilling to give his glory *to other would-be gods*. What makes the Creator God jealous is precisely those false gods that share none of their glory, that rob image bearers of their intended glory and do-minion over God's very good world, and that remake God's image bearers in their own image, turning us into greedy exploiters of one another and the whole creation for our doomed projects of self-glorification. These false gods are nothing like the true Creator God, who intended from the beginning to pour out glory and honor on his own image bearers. In fact, what distinguishes the true God from every idol is precisely his generosity with glory; for it is this Creator's desire that the earth be filled with glory, refracted through the dominion of his image bearers, fruitful and multi-plying until there is nowhere where the true God is not named and known.

## THE EMPEROR'S NEW CLOTHES

Perhaps no other detail in the Genesis creation account so captures the fragility and dignity of image bearing: "And the man and his wife were both naked, and were not ashamed" (Genesis 2:25). *Naked* is a fascinating word (and not just because we find nakedness itself fascinating). It applies only to human beings. No other creature comes into the world naked. God clothes the lilies of the field, Jesus observed, and God will also clothe us, but the lilies of the field bear their raiment from the day they burst forth until the day they die, whereas we return regularly, most of us daily, to an unclothed state, "naked as the day we were born." Only human beings require clothes, because only human beings can be naked.

Nakedness is the subject of one of the most famous folk parables of power: Hans Christian Andersen's tale "The Emperor's New Clothes." A vain emperor is visited by two "weavers" who promise that their fabric is not only exquisitely beautiful but also, shall we say, revealing: "clothes made of this cloth had a wonderful way of becoming invisible to anyone who was unfit for his office, or who was unusually stupid." Spotting a chance to both acquire a new set of clothes and discover which of his sub-jects and ministers are unfit, the emperor commissions a magnificent set of clothes from the swindlers. One after another, beginning with an "honest old minister" sent to check up on the work in progress, the em-peror's most trusted advisers, and then the emperor himself, visit the weavers. Seeing nothing at all on the loom, and stricken with the thought that their foolishness and unfitness might be revealed if they admit they cannot see the cloth, all of them, right up to the emperor himself, carry on with the pretense right up to its logical and ridiculous conclusion:

> Then the minister of public processions announced: "Your Majesty's canopy is waiting outside."
>
>   "Well, I'm supposed to be ready," the Emperor said, and turned again for one last look in the mirror. "It is a remarkable fit, isn't it?"

The waiting crowds, too, go along with this awkward game, until a little child says, "But he hasn't got anything on!" Soon the whole town is crying out, "But he hasn't got anything on!" And in folk memory, or at least the way I most often have heard the story told, that little child's inconvenient truth telling puts the foolish pageant to an end. But not in Andersen's own version, which ends rather differently:

> The Emperor shivered, for he suspected they were right. But he thought, "This procession has got to go on." So he walked more proudly than ever, as his noblemen held high the train that wasn't there at all.

Andersen's story is a veritable catalog of insights about power and the human condition. Power, even up to the absolute power of an emperor, is invested in ordinary human beings (the word *invested* comes, of course, from a Latin root for clothing), who underneath even the most exquisite trappings, or for that matter armed with the most fearsome technology, are naked mortals. The maintenance of power, then, comes not from any extraordinary quality in the powerful themselves, but from the consent and continual reaffirmation of those around them. That affirmation is a frail thing, subject (at least in the world of fairy tales) to disruption even by the voice of a single child.

And at a deeper level, this story is about how unfit any of us is for power. It is not just the emperor but his entire retinue and all his subjects who are revealed by the swindlers' magical fabric to be "unfit" and "foolish"; they are all, indeed, unworthy of the roles they play and beset by anxiety that their unfitness and foolishness will be exposed. "It is a remarkable fit, isn't it?" turns out to be the perfect description—the only robes of power that are really suited to this foolish Everyman are invisible ones, ones that would show him, and us, as we really are. But beset by the anxious thought that our nakedness would be revealed, we give ourselves over to swindlers, colluding in our own deception rather than confront our own vanity.

The emperor is undone by his own desire for godlikeness, for that is the right phrase for his foolish eagerness to acquire the magical ability to see beneath the surface of his ministers and subjects to discern who is worthy and who is unworthy. There is poetic justice here—the one who wants to see what is hidden ends up being the one who is seen by everyone else— but there is also the negative-sum results of idolatry and injustice, which leave everyone involved worse off than they were before. The emperor's shortcut to omniscience breaks trust rather than securing it (and sends a couple of clever swindlers off with their purses full of imperial coin). And the story ends, in Andersen's unsentimental way, with everyone involved only more resolved to keep the procession going, "more proudly than ever." At the end of the story, we doubt whether this emperor will ever gain the wisdom to truly understand who is false and who is true, who is foolish and who is fit to serve. Too much depends on this game of god playing for it ever to end with true image bearing.

The paradoxical nakedness of image bearers—the vulnerability and de- pendence on God that seems so at odds with the promise of godlike do- minion and rule, the fear of shame juxtaposed with the gift of dignity—is at the heart of our temptation to replace image bearing with image making and god playing. It was not meant to be this way. In the primordial moment of blessedness, in unbroken relationship with the Creator, the vice regents of creation were unashamed in their nakedness. Vulnerability and dignity were not opposed to one another, and neither were dependence and dominion.

Yet it may also be that our first state was never meant to be our final state. The language of nakedness and clothing takes a remarkable turn in the pages of the New Testament. In a passage rich and dense with metaphor, Paul writes of Christians' resurrection hope:

> We know that if the earthly tent we live in is destroyed, we have a building from God, a house not made with hands, eternal in the heavens. For in this tent we groan, longing to be clothed with our heavenly dwelling—if indeed, when we have taken it off we will not be found naked. For while we are still in this tent, we groan under our burden, because we wish not to be un- clothed but to be further clothed, so that what is mortal may be swallowed up by life. (2 Corinthians 5:1-4)

In the early church Paul's imagery of nakedness and clothing would have made immediate sense. Converts were often baptized naked—naked as the day they were born, and as the day of their death, since baptism was both a death and a birth—and then vested with a white robe upon emerging from the water. Paul wants the Corinthians to understand that our destiny is not the "unclothed" life of a disembodied soul but the life of a embodied person, and he also suggests that the resurrection will not return us to the Garden's nakedness but usher us onward to the fuller life of the City's martyrs, clothed according to Revelation in robes of white and vested with the symbols of reign and power.

Indeed, I once heard the New Testament theologian N. T. Wright suggest, in an offhand way, that the very essence of clothing and fashion is to signal our destiny: resurrection bodies that will have beauty, power and glory far beyond our current "tent." We adorn ourselves in anticipation; *we wish not to be unclothed but to be further clothed.* In the immediate aftermath of the primordial act of idolatry, the man and woman seek to provide entirely inadequate protection for themselves, and their Maker graciously provides more adequate garments for life east of Eden. But one day all of our anxieties about being seen and known for what we truly are, and all our idolatrous desire to wrap ourselves in the garments of power while simultaneously unveiling the secrets of others, will be brought before God's merciful but piercing judgment. Then we will be provided with garments that never wear out. After taking off this mortal and inadequate body, we will put on a body suited to all of our deepest dreams.

The story of the emperor's new clothes, then, is both a diagnosis of our shared condition at our worst and an ever so subtle hint about our future. But it also echoes the great upside down story in which the world's true Ruler and only true Image Bearer was stripped of his clothes and paraded before his own people, none of whom was able to see that he was at that moment most fully the King he claimed to be.

He became naked so that we might be clothed; he who was truly fit to rule took all our dishonesty and unfitness to rule upon himself; he rose from the utter dependence of death with an imperishable body, "more fully clothed," so that we, too, clothed in his merciful robe, might be fully knowing and fully known in love's full embrace. Like God. As we were meant to be.

# EXPLORATION

## JOHN 2—THE WEDDING WINE

The grand pattern of creation is good, to very good, to glory.

Creation begins good—as we already saw, that is the radical claim of Genesis 1, in spite of all the conflict and trouble we see in the world around us. "In the beginning it was not so." The first truth about the world is that it is good.

And once God's image bearers are present in the creation, then and only then the world is declared "very good." For the essential function of the image bearers is, through tilling and tending, attention and intentionality, to cultivate the world in a way that unfolds its potential.

Nature is good. Culture—human beings acting with creativity and care upon the good gifts of the natural world—is very good.

Grain is good. It grows by the grace of God laid down over eons of evolution, the accumulation of nutrients in the soil and the cycle of water from ocean to cloud to ground to river. Grains were growing long before human beings were here. But then human beings arrive and begin to cultivate the grain. They harvest and thresh it, separating the nutritious germ from the tough chaff. They grind it and mix it with water, yeast and a bit of salt, and bake it, and the result is bread.

Grain is good—but bread is very good.

This is the essential pattern of all culture at its best. Eggs are good, omelets are very good. Trees are good, a beautifully wrought wooden chair is very good. Sound is good, music is very good. When human beings do what they were created to do, the latent possibilities in creation come to fruition, a flourishing reality that would never exist without the application of human intelligence and intentionality. This is what image bearing is for.

And from time to time human culture is so carefully tended and developed that the artifacts that emerge are something even more than very good. They approach something we could call *glory*. Glory is the magnificence of true being, the captivating beauty of something that is so rich in realization that it leaves us in awe and close to worship.

So there is the goodness of sound, the whisper or roar of the wind, the chirps of crickets, and the babble of brooks—such sound is good. Then there is the very-goodness of music, the skillful tending and tuning of sound that is found in every human culture.

But from time to time, you hear music—whether Tuvan throat singing, a Beethoven symphony, a Bach chorale, a black gospel chorus—that shakes you to the core and leaves you both utterly satisfied and hungrier than you have ever been for true life. That is glorious music. The best of culture has this quality of transcendent excellence, the ability to be utterly itself and to speak of something far greater than itself.

There are not many human cultural achievements that embody this pattern better than the cultivation of the grape. Grapes are good. But when the grapes are harvested after countless hours of laborious tending, when they are crushed underfoot or in a press and then placed in vats to release their sugars and feed the little creatures we call yeast, and when this whole process is superintended by someone with great skill and discernment, you get wine. (Certain of my Christian brothers and sisters will have to make what follows apply to grape juice.) Wine, with its layers of flavors, its color and aroma, and initial burst of taste and lingering finish, its hint of the *terroir* where it was grown, its effervescence and sweetness and tannic tension. Grapes are good—wine is very good. And the best wine? The best wine, for someone prepared by years of observing and tasting and swirling (for all glory requires preparation and skill to be fully recognized), is among the most glorious experiences of which the human senses of sight, taste and smell are capable. The odd truth is that the most glorious things are the ones that begin as the simplest. A bundle of grapes—the right grapes, at the right time, in the right hands—can become the glory and honor of the nations.

This is the pattern of creation: good, to very good, verging on glory. The best of culture anticipates the time when all things are made new, when the glory of the Lord will cover the earth like the waters cover the sea.

## PARABLES OF POWER

Into the unfolding story of creation, from time to time, burst miracles. And nothing upends our assumptions about power as much as miracles. Miracles, by definition, do not work the way the world works. They obey neither the physical laws of conservation of energy nor the cultural laws of appropriate agency and timing. Miracles happen outside the framework of expected power, serving as a sign that we do not know what is really going on; they are a warning as much as a gift, and fully capable of producing just as many unhappy, unsettled bystanders as grateful beneficiaries. Miracles seem to happen in odd, unpredictable ways that leave onlookers in some combination of awe, disbelief, confusion and even hostility.

Certainly this is the case for the two central miracles of Scripture, the exodus of the Hebrews and the resurrection of Jesus. Far from being unambiguous manifestations of divine power, both exodus and resurrection were resisted, questioned and ultimately denied by the holders of political power (among them Pharaoh, Caesar's representatives and the Sanhedrin), and both produced doubt, confusion and even disbelief in those closest to them—the Hebrews in the desert and the disciples of Jesus in that first tumultuous week after the Passover. The biblical accounts make it clear that how you ultimately interpret a miracle, or whether you see one at all, depends very much on where you stand and who you are. Miracles are parables of power, charged events that disclose what otherwise would be hidden: unexpected faith among unlikely people, unexpected resistance among the putatively pious, previously unperceived vested interests, and ultimately the ongoing presence in the world of a seemingly absent, and certainly invisible, God.

While all the Gospels place Jesus' miracles in a central place, the Gospel of John is especially purposeful in its use of miracles to unfold the meaning of Jesus' mission. And the very first miracle in John's Gospel is packed with insights into the true meaning of power. "On the third day there was a wedding in Cana of Galilee, and the mother of Jesus was there. Jesus and his disciples had also been invited to the wedding" (John 2:1-2).

Just below the surface of this story are the hidden, taken-for-granted patterns of life in first-century Palestine—the obligations, roles and expectations that shape human choices. Behind the three-part statement of the guests ("the mother of Jesus," Jesus himself and Jesus' disciples) we can glimpse the obligation of a wedding host to include not just the nearest friend of the family (presumably Jesus' mother) but that friend's family members, and—in the case of a prominent rabbi—what we would today call his "entourage." Some years ago I had the privilege of attending a wedding in India of the daughter of a prominent business and civic leader. At this wedding the guest list was not so much a list as a phone book, as local friends, clients, associates and admirers of the family all assumed they were invited, over a thousand in all. We can picture something similar happening here, and can quickly grasp how ruinously expensive a wedding could become as the number of guests expanded exponentially. It is not hard to imagine the initial order of wine, which seemed so generous at first, beginning to seem positively skimpy as more and more extended circles of guests arrived and began to enjoy themselves.

At a feast like this there are established roles. The servants report to the chief steward, who in turn is responsible to the bridegroom for executing the plan for the feast. These lines of authority are also paralleled by a literal layout of space: the bridegroom at the center of the festivities, with a figurative spotlight on him at all times, the chief steward just at the edge of that spotlight, the servants hidden in the darkness at the edge of the feast. There, at the edge, are also some prosaic jars of water.

The ensuing predicament, and then miracle, turns every single one of these familiar lines of power topsy-turvy (and, fittingly enough, leaves everyone tipsy). When power is in its accustomed place, the wine flows without anyone really noticing; no sooner is an empty glass held up than a servant appears to replenish it. But that festive confidence is fraying; the servants are becoming slow to appear, the wine glasses are remaining empty. It may be dawning on the guests that the natural order of the party is about to be disrupted, leaving everyone, most of all the hosts, in an awkward position. The power of the hosts to provide a rollicking good time, and the power of the guests to enjoy one, is about to come to a most unpleasant end, leaving everyone at a loss.

So Mary (though she is never called by name in this Gospel) steps in to activate, you might say, the power she knows her son has to avert social disaster. One of the delightful features of this story is how indirectly Mary goes about urging Jesus to act. In her indirectness ("They have no wine") she is asserting her own authority as his mother, with the backing of the divine commandment to honor mother and father. Mary is confident enough in her power, and her son's, that she does not need to request, let alone command, that Jesus act. Instead she employs what is in fact a more powerful approach than either request or command, a simple statement of fact.

With this background we may be able to better understand Jesus' brusque reply, "Woman, what concern is that to you and to me? My hour has not yet come" (John 2:4). In a few words Jesus signals that a host of existing assumptions of power and authority no longer apply. He will not act simply out of filial responsibility to his mother, and the impending social disaster that prompts her request is not enough to motivate him. Jesus is not present to simply maintain and reinforce the customary structures of authority. Instead, he answers to a different and higher power, his Father who has called him to a singularly important mission.

And yet, in another odd and humorous moment in this story, Mary's only recorded response to Jesus is to say to the servants, "Do whatever he tells you." And Jesus, in a few words, does in fact do exactly what Mary had requested at the beginning. "Fill the jars with water," he says, then, "Now draw some out, and take it to the chief steward" (vv. 7-8). There are no incantations of hocus-pocus, flashes of lightning or peals of thunder. Mary and Jesus both display power here—Mary in her serene confidence in Jesus' knowledge and capacity to act, Jesus in his calm and collected, but utterly effective, transformation of the water in the jars.

As the wine is drawn from the last place anyone would expect, the standing arrangements of power become confused. The chief steward, who is supposed to be the one with masterful knowledge and authority over every aspect of the feast, is completely in the dark, while "the servants who had drawn the water" realize what has really taken place. The steward, unable to imagine such abundance coming from another source, assumes that the bridegroom has arranged for excellent wine to be served toward the end of the feast. The normal way to deal with such a large number of guests, and their prodigious demand for wine, was a kind of sleight of hand—serve good wine first, then, as guests become drunk, bring out the cheap stuff, preserving the appearance of abundance even as you start tightening your belt. This is, of course, the way of substitute gods; make sure you look good at first, then gradually withdraw the benefits you had promised. It is a subtle, if socially acceptable, form of diminishing, not flourishing. The steward marvels that this bridegroom is taking the other path, pouring out more and more abundance the longer the guests dine and drink.

But we, along with the servants and Jesus' disciples, know that the bridegroom has had nothing to do with it. Or rather, we know that an unexpected Bridegroom is at this feast, sitting for now at its edges, responsible for all the brilliant wine being poured by the newly animated servants. It appears that the feast is going on just as planned, yet what has actually happened is a top-to-bottom rearrangement of the ordinary into the extraordinary, of which the miraculous rearrangement of water into wine is just the merest beginning.

We learn several things about power, Jesus-style, in this quite literally marvelous story.

*Jesus' power does not flow through predictable channels.* Jesus is bound by neither the laws of physics and chemistry nor the laws of social obligation and custom. Jesus' only obligation is to the mission of his Father—a mission that will withstand even the ultimate powerlessness of death. Yet here at Cana, Jesus' act of power, the sign of his ultimate mission, deeply affirms, indeed enriches with intoxicating abundance, the patterns of social life: marriage, hospitality, celebration and honoring parents. Certainly, at other points in his ministry Jesus' miracles and teaching will have a more dramatic, revolutionary effect. They will disrupt the dominance of legions of demons and unsettle the easy hypocrisy of priests and procurators. But here, in this "the first of his signs," Jesus' power restores family and feasting. It is too facile to say that Jesus' power was "radical" if by *radical* we mean overturning all existing social arrangements and tradition. Rather, at Cana Jesus' power restores the originally good patterns of life to their original blessedness: the honoring of parents, hospitality to guests, the venerable art of viniculture, even the presiding role of the chief steward, who in his blessed ignorance is saved from career-ending embarrassment and allowed to be the first to taste the new and best wine.

*Jesus' power reveals glory.* That freighted word *glory* is John's own summary of the sign: "Jesus did this, the first of his signs, in Cana of Galilee, and revealed his glory; and his disciples believed in him" (John 2:11). What does it mean to say that this miracle reveals Jesus' glory? He is not transfigured into a figure of dazzling brilliance. He never becomes the center of attention, continuing to recline at the outskirts of the newly revived feast. Rather, the glory revealed here is Jesus' true identity—the magnificence of true being. What is revealed for the first time at Cana is the ultimate truth of his mission: to make all things new, to bring all things to the glory for which they were made.

Just as a glorious glass of wine is one that is truly, deeply, completely itself, so this miracle shows the disciples and servants what Jesus is truly like: not just a good teacher but the restorer of all life; not just a dutiful son but the perfectly obedient Son of the Father; not just the fixer of our little cares and problems but the one who provides the best wine just when we would expect the worst. True power reveals glory, unfolding the abundant possibilities and realities of created things. And this revelation of glory happens at a wedding. A wedding, too, is a moment of glory, unveiling as it does two human beings, male and female, created very good in the image of God, reunited across the gap opened up between men and women by the Fall and sin, resplendent in the glory of their wedding garments, a sign of the magnificence of love.

And so *Jesus' power leads to overflow, abundance and excellence, that is, to flourishing.* The wine Jesus provides is, by far, surplus to requirements. (Six stone water jars, holding twenty to thirty gallons each, would amount to more than 750 present-day wine bottles.) This is a recurring theme in the parables of Jesus, the stories that so often turn on an unexpected abundance revealed only at the end of a story—the beggar Lazarus, comforted in the arms of Abraham; the workers hired late in the day, receiving a full day's wages; the son slinking home to apologize, smothered in his father's embrace.

There is one last notable feature of power in this story: its hiddenness. *Jesus' power is hidden even as it is revealed.* True, the servants and the disciples—and we the readers—are in on the secret. But as far as we can tell, for most of the guests, the chief steward and the wedded couple themselves, the miracle stays unnoticed. The event that reveals Jesus' glory thus spills over, you might say, blessing even those who neither know nor believe that God's own Son is at the party. The true power at work in the world may often be invisible, even as its effects are seen, celebrated and perhaps attributed to a completely spurious source. The bridegroom gets the credit, but Jesus gets the glory, a glory that, like his power, is hidden even as it is revealed.

Ultimately, of course, this story is not just about water, wine or weddings. It is a story of a *sign*—something that points beyond itself to a deeper well of meaning. And the story of the sign begins with an unmistakable signpost, the chronological note at the beginning of John 2:1. "*On the third day* there was a wedding." For John, for his first readers and for us, "the third day" is a signpost to the greatest of all signs. This first miracle, where Jesus' glory is revealed, is a foreshadowing and foretaste of the ultimate miracle and revelation of his glory. With power this glorious loose in the world, why would we settle for anything less?

## PART TWO

# THE GRIP OF POWER

**IT WILL NOT BE SO AMONG YOU**

# EXPLORATION

## EXODUS 20—THE TEN WORDS

What we know as the Ten Commandments, the Jewish people and the Hebrew Bible know as the Ten Words (*aseret hadevarim*). Some of these "words" are indeed straightforward commandments— "You shall not steal"—but most are more complicated. The first word, for example, begins not with a commandment but with a declaration. "I am the LORD your God, who brought you out of the land of Egypt, out of the house of slavery" (Exodus 20:2).

Whether they are commands or something more complex, each of the Ten Words is a word about power.

The Ten Words begin with the name of God and end with the word *neighbor*, thus encompassing what Jesus called the two great commandments—loving God and loving neighbor. And from beginning to end they are commandments about power, not just how to avoid its abuse but how to rightly order its use. It's especially fitting, then, that at their heart are two Words that are not phrased as negative "thou shalt nots" but as fundamentally positive "thou shalts." And these two words go to the heart of what it means to be an image bearer of the creating and liberating God. They describe the central practices that will order the use of power among God's people—work and rest, and honoring of parents—and that are at the heart of loving God and loving one another.

## REMEMBERING REST

The fourth word begins, "Remember the sabbath day, and keep it holy. Six days you shall labor and do all your work. But the seventh day is a sabbath to the LORD your God." There is not just one positive command, but two—not just the command to rest but the command to work. Both rest and work are faithful activities for image bearers. In work we apply our energy to making something of the world; in rest we echo God's satisfied declaration "Behold, it was good," and renew our strength by acknowledging our dependence on God rather than ourselves.

In fact, only with both rest and work can we be faithful. Rest without work is sloth; work without rest is, well, what is the right word? Busyness? But busyness tends to sound like a good thing. We have a host of negative words for resting without working, but almost none for working without resting (aside from the recent, ungainly coinage *workaholism*). And this lack of a proper name for restless work is a clue to the idolatry that the fourth word is meant to address.

Sloth, idleness, laziness are indeed failures in our human calling, the failure to take up our image-bearing responsibility to make something of the world. But busyness and restlessness are the deeper temptations. Busy, restless, sabbath-less people are idolaters. They have displaced the Creator God, who both worked and rested, with a god who is no true god, the god of relentless productivity who can never stop to enjoy, celebrate or—to use the commandment's resonant word—*remember*. Without remembering the sabbath, we cease to remember the Creator God who made the world and called it good; we cease to remember the one who brought us out of Egypt; we cease to remember the Eighth Day when God defeated death. We also cease to remember our future: that the end of the human story is a gift rather than an achievement. Sabbath requires us to "mark time," to stand still and pay attention to the unearned and infinite grace that is our origin and destiny.

It's fitting, then, that remembering the sabbath is the culmination of the "first table" of the Ten Words, the ones that deal directly with our relationship with the true God and our tendency to create false gods. Sabbathlessness is idolatry. Instead of remembering, enjoying and celebrating the goodness of the true God, we make ourselves gods, pressing ourselves to ever greater feats of self-sufficiency, and doubtless lapsing, exhausted, into slothfulness when our busyness overwhelms us. All idolatries, left unchecked, end up consuming us. A sabbathless life ends up with neither true work nor true rest, but with frantic and ineffective activity punctuated by couch-potato lethargy.

Remembering the sabbath, then, is one of the basic disciplines of power. Only sabbath keepers can be trusted with the work of image bearing. And notably, this word (along with the last word about covetousness, which we'll consider later) is the one that explicitly addresses the differentiated power that exists in every human community. It is not just "you" who are addressed as a potential sabbath keeper or sabbath breaker; you are also addressed as a parent ("you, your son or your daughter"), master ("your male or female slave"), farmer ("your livestock"), and citizen ("or the alien resident in your towns"). We will know we are keeping sabbath—we will know we are being true image bearers—when not just we ourselves have a day of fruitful and joyful rest, but when every other human being and every other part of creation over whom we exercise authority also experiences that same rest, that same remembering.

Keeping sabbath can be very hard to remember indeed, and not just because we live in an always-on and always-connected society that has largely forgotten the sabbath. Sabbath has been a core discipline of my own life since my undergraduate days, when I dutifully (and, to tell the truth, somewhat legalistically and pridefully) avoided studying for exams or writing papers on Sundays. But personal sabbath keeping, as difficult and rarely practiced as it is, is one thing—what is more revealing is whether we make room for sabbath when others are under our power.

In 2003 our family moved to a new home in Pennsylvania, a house that had been renovated top to bottom by a contractor named Ken. At least, it had mostly been renovated. As so often happens, the work was not quite on schedule when we arrived to sign the purchase and sale agreement, our moving van just a few hours behind us. A walk through the house yielded a long punch list of work that remained to be done. So we sat down in our real estate agent's office to write a rider to the purchase agreement, spelling out the deadlines and dollars involved in finishing the job.

As we sat there, something prompted me to add, "We need to make sure they work every possible day." Our agent duly wrote into the agreement that work would continue every day including Sundays, and Ken (who was just as eager as we were to have the job finished) made no complaint. I had just voluntarily, contractually obligated Ken to forget the sabbath. And on reflection, it became clear to me that my insistence on Sunday work was not just a matter of anxiety about getting unpacked and getting the construction workers out of our home. It had been a power play. Sitting in that office, about to exchange hundreds of thousands of dollars for someone else's labor and property, I was under the influence of an ever-so-slight but unmistakably intoxicating sense of control and importance. (The fact that most of those dollars were borrowed was, as any credit card user can tell you, no impediment to the sense of power they conferred.) I insisted that Ken and his crew work on Sundays not because we couldn't live with the consequences of a few days' delay in painting the final walls and woodwork, but simply because I could insist on it and get away with it.

So a few days later, I sheepishly asked Ken not to work on Sundays after all. To this day I'm not sure which this skilled, hard-working man resented more, being obligated to work on Sundays or being obligated not to work. But for several quiet Sundays, surrounded by the dust of unfinished construction, I was vividly reminded that I was most tempted to forget the sabbath when I was most in a position of power.

## HONOR YOUR FATHER AND YOUR MOTHER

The fifth commandment, the next word, is the other unambiguously positive command. The fourth word is the culmination of a life that has no gods other than the true God of meaningful work and grateful, glad rest. By emphasizing that our responsibility for remembering sabbath extends to every part of creation over which we may exercise rule, it reminds us that proper image bearing has profound implications for how we treat our fellow image bearers. The fifth word turns toward considering how true image bearing will affect our relationships, and it begins with the most unambiguously asymmetrical of all human relationships of power, that between parents and children.

Parenthood, as we've already noted, is the purest example of absolute power, at least at first. But the central drama of parenthood is the gradual handing over of power. From the day children begin to walk on their own to the day when "a man will leave his father and mother and be united to his wife," they are growing into their own capacity to make something of the world. Parents' power is not permanently absolute but must decrease as their children's power increases if their children are to fully flourish. And with aging come natural limits on the parents' ability to make something of the world, just as their children are reaching the prime of their own natural power. Like Isaac on his bed, blind and infirm with age, reaching out his hands to give a blessing to his son, at some point many of us will be dependent on our children for the kind of care we gave them as infants. Long before that point, we start losing ground to the children we raised: the boy I once hoisted on my shoulders now can do twice as many pull-ups as I can.

Perhaps this explains the intriguing form of the fifth word. It is not addressed to parents but to children—because it is precisely as we come into adulthood, with our own proper sense of our capacities, that we must choose to continue respecting those on whom we once had the most absolute dependence. And as our parents enter their old age and become deeply dependent on us, we face the same choice that they did when we were infants—to let absolute power summon us to greater reverence for the life that is entrusted to our care.

To be sure, *some* parents need to be reminded to love their children (and all need to be reminded to love them well, that is, not to make idols of them or play false gods in their lives). But *all* children need to be reminded to honor their parents, because being a child (at whatever age) exposes and challenges our pride. Pride is wounded by asymmetries of power, even or especially when that power is the result of a gift. Pride chafes at gifts. The fact that our parents knew us and cared for us when we were powerless can be a source of profound thanksgiving, or it can prick at our pride and prompt outbursts of god playing. And what better opportunity for god playing than the moments later in life when the asymmetry is reversed and we are the ones who can decide whether to care for or neglect those who are now under our power? At these moments the fifth word addresses us most intently.

Honoring of parents is not, shall we say, one of the strengths of Western culture. Other societies have much more effectively sustained respectful, if not reverential, relationships between generations. Indeed, some cultures can tend toward idolatry of parents or ancestors just as Western culture tends toward idolatry of youth and the self. The truth is that neither parents nor children make good gods. Neither dependence nor independence is at the heart of human flourishing. But the fifth word clearly suggests that Western culture's cult of autonomy is the more pressing temptation—to allow our growing power apart from, and eventually over, our own parents to be curdled by pride into disregard and contempt.

This danger is neither theoretical nor merely psychological. Even as many cultures throughout history have tolerated the exposure of infants by their parents, very few have tolerated the exposure of elders by their children. Neither does our own culture—yet. But the power of a culture of youth, combined with medicine's capacity to prolong old age in the face of infirmities, have placed euthanasia inside the realm of morally acceptable possibility in a new way in our time. Euthanasia of elders is a question of power at its most elemental. Its force, like all true questions of power, lies not so much in the direct decision about which treatments to administer or withhold, but in the deeper assumptions that lie beneath those decisions. What makes a life "worth living"? Independence, autonomy, freedom from need for others' care? What makes a life of suffering livable? The prospect of eventual relief or loving companions who suffer with us even when our condition may never improve in this life? Is real flourishing found in avoiding entanglements with suffering as much as possible, whether others' or our own, or is it found, as parents often find with their own children, in paradoxical places that both demand seemingly superhuman strength but where we also find unexpected grace?

The questions raised by honoring our parents, especially in the extremities of old age and infirmity, are ultimately questions about where our hope lies. But that is also true of many of the most consequential questions of power. When power is used in the context of genuine and durable hope, it is more often than not creative. When it is used in the absence of hope, when we are overcome by fear, it turns down the path toward exploitation and violence. So it is not surprising that the fifth word is the "only Word with a promise": "so that your days may be long in the land that the LORD your God is giving you." The right use of power toward our parents—using our adult capacities to bring them honor, reverence and care—comes with the promise that pouring out our power on their behalf will not rob us of our own hopes for our lives. To the contrary, as we give ourselves for their good, we will live long and well. In this most intimate and fraught of all relationships of power, the fifth word both commands and promises that power can be a gift.

## THE FIRST AND LAST WORD

Idolatry and injustice are intertwined in the Ten Words. To murder is to seize for myself godlike powers to take the life that only the true God can give or take away. To commit adultery is to scorn the boundaries of commitment that limit my creaturely intimacy, to be a kind of sexually omnipresent being who can take and know at will. To steal is to appropriate what I want for myself without negotiation or compromise with another image bearer. To bear false witness is to stand outside and above the law rather than trusting the justice of the law and the sufficiency of the truth. In all these cases I take on myself an exaggerated image of superlative greatness, and in all these cases the god I play is nothing like the true God. And in all these cases, my distorted image making undermines the image of the true God in my neighbor. As the tenth word makes crystal clear, the real issue is not the sinful activities but cultivating the heart of a false god player rather than an image bearer.

The Ten Words begin and end with matters of the heart. The sweeping, intangible command "You shall have no other gods before me" comes before the tangible instructions about graven images, misusing the divine Name, and sabbath. Likewise, the second tablet ends not with the tangible actions of murder, adultery, theft or false witness, but with an entirely inward disposition, covetousness. To covet is not just to take; it is to desire—to long for a godlike mastery over parts of creation I have not been given to steward. If the first word is about having no gods other than the true God, the last word is about playing no part other than the image-bearing role I have personally been given to play. The Ten Words begin by addressing the disposition that leads to idolatry; they end by addressing the disposition that leads to injustice. And both idolatry and injustice, ultimately, are about what we love and long to become. Power at its worst and best is a matter of the heart.

# 6

# THE HIDDENNESS OF POWER

The painfully hilarious TV series *The Office* features a boss (named Michael Scott in the U.S. version, played by Steve Carell) whose chief feature is a pathological lack of self-awareness. Perhaps no TV show has ever turned so much on nonverbal reactions. After Scott has once again made a stunningly inappropriate comment or given a deadly would-be motivational speech, the camera pans quickly to some member of the beleaguered staff, slack-jawed in mute confusion or disdain. Yet Scott is able to continue blundering along in his self-satisfied confidence, happily adjusting the figurine of a triumphant manager on his desk—because he is in a position of power.

Scott's clueless isolation from his colleagues at Dunder Mifflin takes on physical form in his own office-within-The-Office, the private redoubt that is at once the symbol of his power and the embodiment of his failure. His office is equipped with blinds, which are intended to be their own sign of power: the power to be concealed at will. In Scott's case, however, the blinds are most often pried apart with a furtive finger as he peeps through, trying to gauge the mood in the open space beyond. The blinds represent Scott's own blindness—just as he is unable to truly grasp or anticipate the needs of any human being other than himself, he has no real under-standing of what is happening outside his own office. When he emerges, having peered quickly through his blinds to check that the time is right, his exhortations and questions consistently misfire. Jesus said to some powerful people of his own day, "If you were blind, you would not have sin. But now that you say 'We see,' your guilt remains" (John 9:41). Michael Scott's problem is not that he shares with all human beings (and all managers!) limited insight and understanding; he is guilty, and hilariously so, because he does not know he is blind.

It is a strange fact that power, which so often is prominently displayed—whether with private offices and reserved parking spaces, turreted castles and tanks, or entourages and tour buses—very often also blinds us to features of the world that are blindingly obvious to others. The powerful have a hard time seeing their own power and its effects. We do not see when our exercise of power is cutting off life and possibility for others; we do not see the ways others are resisting or undermining our own power.

Most of us, to be sure, are not Michael Scott, with an absurdly inflated sense of our own power and importance. Rather, we have a different kind of blindness: an absurdly low estimation of the power we have and how many opportunities we have to use it well. And curiously, this blindness afflicts the visibly powerful as often as the seemingly powerless.

## MAPPING POWER

If you've ever had a job interview in a corporate environment (hopefully a less dysfunctional one than Dunder Mifflin), you've learned something about power. You probably polished your shoes, selected your clothing carefully and tried to remember everything your mother taught you about manners. You arrived at the interview location a few minutes early, perhaps circling the block a few times. As you approached the door of the building, you felt something between mild anticipation and flat-out panic. Like other moments of delight or terror, this is probably one you still remember even years later. In fact, just recalling the experience right now may be enough to elevate your heart rate ever so slightly, whether or not you got the job.

On the other hand, at one time or another you may have been the interviewer, with an interview on your calendar for the day. Chances are, for you this was not an especially notable day. You dressed for work as usual, arrived on time or not according to your custom. You certainly were interested in the outcome of the interview—hiring the right people is one of the most important responsibilities any leader has—but unless this was an unusual situation, you were not especially anxious. Your pulse and breathing were at their resting pace. Years from now you are unlikely to remember this day, even if the candidate got the job.

Both persons in this encounter have power. The interviewer has power, of course—the ability to hire or not, the ability to shape the conversation, to decide when the meeting is over. But why is she interviewing? Precisely because the organization lacks all the power it needs. There is an open position, a deficit of power, that needs to be filled with a person, and that person may just be the one being interviewed. The interviewee may have (and certainly hopes he has) exactly the power that the interviewer lacks.

But one of the deepest resources of power potentially present in every job interview does not belong to either the interviewer or the interviewee. It is the creative power that could be unleashed if it was shared. Even though there is an undeniable asymmetry of power in any interview, interviews at their best are not rituals of dominance and submission, but explorations of collaboration, envisioning the cultural goods that will only come into being if the interviewer and candidate find a way to work together.

There is not one simple kind of power present in a job interview. Power here takes multiple forms, each with their own possibilities and limitations. It is like the terrain of a varied landscape. A dusty path may run alongside a fertile plowed field, which may run down to the edge of a languid river, while further on are mown grass, thickets along windbreaks and perhaps in the distance some rocky hills. Every part of the terrain has its own qualities, its own capacity for giving life, and its own dangers.

Imagine that you asked each person to map the terrain of power—the ability to make something of the world—in that interview and the events surrounding it. Significant parts of the landscape for the hiring manager might include other people: her own boss, other stakeholders in the organization's success, the abilities of other candidates for the position. She might also be able to sketch the hidden land mines and privileged code words that lead to ideas and people being dismissed or applauded in this company's particular culture. (In one company, expressions of macho bravado are essential to winning respect; in another what is rewarded is congenial collaboration.) And she might have some understanding of the opportunities and threats that are before the organization, the larger geography within which her company is trying to carve out a niche. Much of this knowledge of the landscape is unavailable to the candidate for the job, just as a visitor to a farm will never be able to grasp the properties of the soil and the rhythms of life there in the way the farmer does.

But there is one aspect of the map that the hiring manager would have a very hard time drawing accurately, and that is her own power. What she does not see—cannot see—is all the preparation that went into the interviewee's day, the elevated heart rate and last-minute shoe polishing, the extra turns around the block. She cannot see these things because they are intentionally hidden from her, kept from troubling her so that the interviewee can put his best foot forward.

Our own power is almost never represented clearly on our map. A friend of mine retired after twenty years as the executive director of a private foundation and began offering his services as a consultant. For the first time in decades he was the employee rather than the employer. "I was in a meeting with one of my clients, and I thought we had covered everything we needed to do that day. So I stood up. But my client said, 'Have a seat, Rob, we're not quite done.' Not until that moment had I realized that for twenty years, whenever I stood up, the meeting was over."

## TERRA INCOGNITA

My friend Rob had stumbled over a previously unmapped dimension of power—the ability of the person paying the bills to start and stop meetings at will. As far as I know, Rob, a gregarious and generous man, never abused his power to bring conversations to an end. But just because power is not abused does not mean that it is neutral or unimportant. Rob's view of the world was both expanded and constricted by his position of power, expanded because of the people he got to meet, the good work he helped to fund, the warm relationships he formed over years of collaboration with ministries around the world. But also constricted, because for two decades he rarely experienced a very basic human reality: the sense of being dependent on someone who has less at stake in the relationship than you do.

Without knowing it, Rob was navigating blind through the very terrain it was his job to understand. Who knows whether, without any ill intentions, he had stopped a meeting just before his counterpart was about to give voice to a brilliant new idea or an important insight? Unmapped power is a perilous thing.

Unmapped power is also usually wasted power. Rob's power to end a meeting was an inescapable fact of his position. But lacking an awareness that he even had such power, he was unable to make anything of it.

If Rob's power to end a meeting had been on his mental map, he might have worked to minimize the danger that he would cut off another person's creativity and insight by saying something like, "It seems to me that we've covered what we need to in this meeting, but I want to make sure you have had the chance to say everything that is important to you." In some situations he might have wanted to explicitly hand his power over: "I won't get up from this table until you feel we've reached a creative conclusion." (Of course that carries some risks if your conversation partner is there to solicit a financial gift for their organization!) In other situations he might admit, "I should warn you up front that I will have to end our meeting at a certain time."

In all these cases, he would be actively working with the power he had, rather than taking it for granted. But while his power remained unmapped, its potential for good and ill remained unknowable—to Rob. To the people on the other side of the table, it was, of course, as clear as could be.

## MARKING THE MAP

A few paragraphs ago I did something that is quite common these days, but still uncommon enough that it can remind us of the hidden patterns of power most of us take for granted. Required by English grammar to choose a gender for our imaginary hiring manager, I chose to use feminine pronouns for her, and masculine pronouns for the candidate for the job. There is nothing especially unusual about this arrangement, except that even now, with women well represented in the workforce and in leadership, it is still considerably more common for a hiring manager to be a man, especially when those applying for the position are men. (Women still tend to be managers most often in traditionally feminine fields.)

Some readers will have passed over this choice of words without even noticing, but to many—I suspect most—readers there will have been a momentary pause, maybe not even fully recognized at a conscious level. To some the use of the feminine pronoun will have been downright distracting, throwing off your train of thought altogether and prompting either gratitude for my inclusiveness or irritation at my political correctness.

Whatever your response, in that moment a previously invisible pattern of power was brought to light. Until it was interrupted, it could be taken for granted that a typical hiring manager would be male. Indeed, until a generation ago this was the overwhelming likelihood in the business world, and even more so the unquestioned practice in writers' choice of pronouns. Linguists would say that the masculine pronoun was "unmarked"—unremarkable even when used to refer to both men and women. But in a change that both accompanied and accelerated changed patterns of male and female leadership in the public realm, for many readers and writers the word *he* is now "marked" as male, not just generically human. For these readers it would have been equally distracting if I had used the masculine pronoun, especially if I did so consistently throughout the book: it would seem that I was implying that managers (or people in general!) were always male.

When we survey the terrain of power, we tend to map some features and ignore others. Every map marks some aspects of the territory it covers, while leaving others unmarked. Indeed, maps are valuable precisely because they are marked—maps are not just photographs but carefully limited drawings that focus on especially significant features of the terrain.

In 2010, for instance, Google introduced a "bicycle view" for its online maps. With one click in a checkbox, bike trails and bike-friendly streets suddenly appear in dark green, while interstate highways become nearly invisible, grayed-out lines in the background. Highways are the boldest and most colorful features on the basic map, but on the bicycle map, they barely exist. The basic map of my city, Philadelphia, shows you the twists and turns of the Schuylkill River running west of the city, with the Schuylkill Expressway shadowing its curves, but it will never tell you that there is a twenty-two-mile-long trail along that same river for bicyclists, skaters and joggers. The trails were unmarked, even though they were there all along.

Yet whatever features may or may not be marked on any given map, *they are all there at all times*, and all of them may shape the traveler's experience through a given city or countryside. My GPS may tell me nothing about whether there are cows in the fields along my route, but that won't stop my children from celebrating and counting them as we drive by. The cows may be unmarked for drivers, but not for a ten-year-old. The map used by a city planner to survey existing buildings may show nothing about the families who inhabit a given neighborhood slated for redevelopment, but they may assert themselves in surprising ways at a public hearing. I can choose to leave the topographic lines undisplayed on Google Maps, but the hills will still assert themselves when I follow the route laid out for my forty-five-mile bike trip tomorrow.

As with maps of the physical world, so with power. Each of us navigates through our encounters with other people with some features of power strongly marked. A light-skinned American of European descent may hardly notice if she is in a room full of "white" people, whereas another American who is a dark-skinned descendant of Africans will hardly be able to help noticing. For one, light skin color is unmarked; for the other, it is strongly marked, but it is there all the same. The only difference, we might say, is whether it is on the map—whether it is part of our conscious awareness.

Whether a feature of power is mapped or not has its own effects on what we make of the world. (For that reason, in this section I am marking the word *white* with quote marks so that it does not itself pass for unremarkable terrain. The story of what Americans have made of the words *white* and *black* is a complex tale that goes far beyond skin color.) For the "white" person, being in a comfortable cultural environment may make her more free to laugh, to be creative or to object to something she disagrees with. There are no roadblocks marked on her map.

On the other hand, for a black woman who finds herself in a room of white folks, the experience may well seem constraining. At the same time, precisely because her cultural background is "marked" she may be singled out and given particular authority to speak—for example the times when, disconcertingly, she is expected to give a comprehensive representation of the way "black folks" feel about a given issue.

Whether unmarked or marked, then, our maps of power both constrain culture making and make it possible. And whether mapped or unmapped, the reality of power is always there, both limiting and freeing in various combinations. It is the territory we all travel through together, all carrying different maps.

Maps work because they hide some features of the terrain we cross. So it is inevitable, indeed necessary, that real features of power in any setting are hidden to many or all of those who travel together. With the exception of brief illustrations, neither you nor I would benefit from constant interruptions in this book to point out the rules of English grammar that make communication possible; we benefit from the unmarked fact that this book follows those rules. But we also benefit from the cartographers of grammar—the teachers, editors and proofreaders who over time explained this terrain to us, so that we are able to make the most of the world with it. We even benefit from those who explored language's unmapped edges, poets and prophets who stretched the boundaries of speech and diction in order to give expression to the previously inexpressible.

If unmapped power is perilous and wasted, how can we accurately map the reality of power in our midst, not least the power that is hidden from the powerful, and the power that is hidden from the powerless? In one way the answer is disarmingly simple. We need more than one cartographer. None of us can map our power for ourselves. We need one another to fill out our maps, to point out the resources we have of which we are unaware, and to warn us when we are at risk of misusing something we don't even know we have.

Such mapping requires trust, because drawing the map is itself an exercise in power that can be used well or abused. Trust can coexist with confrontation and critique, but only when it is undergirded by a confidence that we are for each other—allies in one another's flourishing, cultivating and creating—rather than using our insights into one another's power to win our own game.

And whether we are for each other depends very much on whether we believe power is a gift, and whether power can multiply when it is shared. If power is essentially a curse, none of us would wish it on a friend, and we would probably prefer not to know how much we have. If power is essentially limited and can only be redistributed, so that when I have more power you have less, all our relationships will be characterized by competition or at best negotiation. Only if power is fundamentally good, and fundamentally fruitful, can we trust one another to accurately and generously map the power that we have and share.

## POWER WITHOUT TRUST

Early in Scripture we encounter a story fraught with lessons about the limits of power without trust. The human story begins in Genesis with a calling to disperse, to "fill the earth" with the fruitfulness of human cultivation and creation. It is, in other words, a call to power: to the creative work of exploration and engagement with the astonishingly diverse world, good though wild, where God has placed his image bearers.

One group of early human beings, though, resists this call to fruitful multiplication. They settle in the plain of Shinar and survey the threats of a world without trust: "Come, let us build ourselves a city, and a tower with its top in the heavens, and let us make a name for ourselves; otherwise we shall be scattered abroad upon the face of the whole earth" (Genesis 11:4). They are the citizens of Babel, heirs to the distorted and disturbed world after the Fall, and their preoccupations betray their conception of power.

On the one hand, they grasp some essential truths. Power is not just about the ability to build artifacts like cities and towers; it is also the ability to "make a name," to identify and interpret the world. And cities and towers, to judge from subsequent history and the new city promised at the end of Scripture, are very much within the original divine mandate to be fruitful and multiply.

But alongside these positive qualities are a darker set of convictions about power that taint the work of Babel. For the citizens of Babel, power is meant to be exercised in the cause of self-interest. It is characterized by scarcity and needs to be hoarded rather than spread. At the same time, the scale of the builders' plans, compared to their technological resources, suggests an unrealistically exaggerated view of what human power can actually achieve—a hubris which is the other side of scarcity and hoarding. Such grandiose plans, driven by a deeper, equally grandiose fear of dissolution, require vigilance if not aggression against both human beings and the gods (the tower will both provide superior visibility over the surrounding plain and invade the sacred upper realm of the heavens). The bravado of Babel conceals an undercurrent of fear; this seemingly ambitious building project is actually the result of diminished human ambition and a growing human sense of vulnerability.

The measure Babel's tower builders use is the measure they get—their jaundiced and fearful view of power leads to God's judgment and intervention. God's own reflection on Babel's ambition invokes the language of power and possibility: "this is only the beginning of what they will do; nothing that they propose to do will now be impossible for them" (Genesis 11:6). Unchecked power, driven by self-interest, scarcity, grandiosity and aggression, is deadly to God's original fruitful purposes. So God intervenes—not with the violence that the tower builders fear but with a burst of creativity, multiplying the languages at the construction site. The sudden introduction of linguistic diversity could be an opportunity for creativity and cooperation, but in a society poisoned by fear of outsiders it simply leads to dissension and dissolution.

Early readers of Genesis would have associated primeval Babel with later Babylon, the great city in the Mesopotamian plain, not far from present-day Baghdad. And in our own time Baghdad has been the scene of terrible lessons in the hiddenness of power. Few men have ever ruled a nation with as self-interested, scarcity-minded, grandiose and aggressive a vision of power as Saddam Hussein. Hussein ruled Iraq, especially its Kurd and Shia communities, with ferocious and capricious terror. His ability to turn his violence on anyone, even members of his own family, sunk him deeper and deeper into the blind madness of power.

One gauge of the depth of Hussein's madness and blindness was his refusal to bend to the international community's demand for clarity about Iraq's capability for nuclear and chemical warfare. We now know that Hussein's relentless quest for weapons of mass destruction had been forced to a halt by international sanctions in the mid-1990s. Yet by continuing to deny U.N. inspectors access to critical facilities, and by ignoring international calls for accountability, Hussein provoked the United States and its allies into a war, with the aim of eradicating weapons that Hussein surely knew did not exist.

Or did he know? We will probably never know for sure, but it is entirely possible that Saddam Hussein *did* believe his country still possessed, or was close to possessing, nuclear weapons. Who around the dictator would have had any incentive to tell him the truth about the country's stalled military programs, when generals were routinely executed for much more minor offenses?

Either way, Hussein's mad quest for power made him blind and led to his destruction. But like the demonic Balrog in *The Lord of the Rings*, Hussein's descent into the abyss managed to snare his most powerful foe as well. The United States was also blind, notwithstanding its massive resources of intelligence gathering and military strength, its spy satellites and night-vision goggles. So its power, when wielded against the dictator, destroyed as much or more than it saved. Future generations will have to judge whether the Iraq War was the mistake most Americans now believe that it was. Those generations will also know, as we cannot yet know, whether it was the decisive swipe of the demon's tail that dragged the American experiment itself into the void, weighed down by economic debt and diminished credibility, but they will have no doubt that it was a searing demonstration of the blindness of power.

From Michael Scott, the cartoon of folly, to Saddam Hussein, the dreadful reality of unchecked and unaccountable power, may seem like a great distance. But it is mostly a matter of opportunity and circumstances. Fortunately most of us blunder through life in settings more like *The Office* than Hussein's palaces or the White House's Situation Room. But all of us have enough power to do great damage, to others and ourselves, if our maps are deficient and our vision blinkered. Unmapped and unknown, power's grip is hard to shake.

# FORCE, COERCION AND VIOLENCE

A**ll politics is a struggle** for power; the ultimate kind of power is violence." This is C. Wright Mills's crisp statement in his influential 1956 book *The Power Elite*. It perfectly sums up a whole way of understanding how power works in society, very likely the most common understanding. The point of this book is that Mills is wrong. No—more strongly than that: the point of this book is that if Christianity is true, Mills is wrong, and if Mills is right, then Christianity is not true and Christian faith is foolish.

Mills chose his words carefully. He did not say, "the ultimate kind of power is force." That would be a statement from physics. Force is what happens when one physical body acts on another. It is a very real kind of power; when I push on something with sufficient energy, it moves, whether I am closing a door or pushing my daughter on a swing. But force is neutral, even beneficial, or so my daughter would say at the height of the swing's glorious arc.

Mills did not even say, "the ultimate kind of power is coercion." This is what many believe. Coercion is the ability to get someone else to act in accordance with your will, in spite of their will. The great German sociologist Max Weber defined power (using the German word *Macht*) as "any probability of imposing one's will within a social relationship even against resistance." That last phrase is crucial. Power for Weber is about overcoming resistance; it is about the ability to coerce. Even Weber's definition of authority, what he called *Herrschaft*, has more than a hint of coercive power: "the probability of securing obedience to definite commands." For Weber and many before or since, power is not real unless it can speak in the imperative mood—"make it so"—and expect a response whether or not those commanded agree with the command.

No, Mills identified power not with force or even coercion, but with violence. And *violence* is not just another word for force. Violence is force that is intended to damage, force that undermines dignity. Violence does not respect its object's limits and intended good. When I close a door violently, I push it beyond its limits, stressing its hinges, slamming it into the frame. I may well leave the door less valuable than it was before my act of violence, perhaps irreparably so.

I can be violent with many things in the world, but it is hard to do anything terribly violent to, say, an outcropping of granite. Granite is so hard and so simple that it is hard to do much to undermine its dignity. In fact, you are more likely to lose some of your own dignity in a violent encounter with granite than the other way around. This suggests that the potential for violence increases not just with our physical ability to exert force but with the dignity of the target of our force. This is the reason we most often use the word *violence* to refer to force used, disproportionately and degradingly, against human beings. Of all the created things in the world, humans are the ones who have the most dignity to lose, so they are the ones most vulnerable to violence. A slap with the hand that would do nothing at all to a slab of granite can be an act of grievous violence against a human being.

And consequently, *violence* is also a word of judgment. "Good violence" is an oxymoron; the closest we can come is "justified violence," which implies, of course, that violence is not just in itself. It must be justified—its justice must be argued for and will always be in doubt. For we sense that there is an irreparable loss whenever violence is done. A door can be replaced. But innocence cannot be replaced, and innocence is always lost, along with many other infinitely precious things, in the wake of violence.

## THE EXCESS OF VIOLENCE

Force operates by mathematical symmetry. I push the door with a certain amount of effort, and it opens to a corresponding degree. But violence tends to have a quality of excess in which both sides end up losing. It is not just the door that loses some of its dignity, its fittingness, when I slam it against the wall; I lose a bit of my dignity as well. This is why even though popular entertainment in our culture often features egregious amounts of violence, it must always be explained by even more egregious villainy or audiences become uncomfortable, if not downright angry. Even our cartoon-violence-saturated culture is uneasy with gratuitous violence. We sense that the stain of perpetrating or even simply witnessing violence can only be washed away with the justification of a greater evil. Otherwise the losses from violence are too great to bear.

So the enemies in violent films are unspeakably and irredeemably evil—only this can assuage our uneasiness with the violence the hero wields. Significantly, in Disney's animated films, which are meant for children with tender consciences, the villain always does himself in at the end, whatever battle has taken place right up to the precipice. Gaston battles with the good-hearted Beast, but falls from the tower as the Beast tries to save him; Syndrome is sucked into his own airplane by his own cape as he utters one final taunt against the Incredibles, sparing us the complexity of witnessing our heroes meting out the ultimate vengeance. Filmmakers like Quentin Tarantino, who flaunt this convention that violence must always be less damning than the evil it resists, make their audiences very uncomfortable indeed—uncomfortable enough that they often explain their enjoyment in lengthy essays lest anyone think they simply were taken in by some dignity-destroying pornography.

So it is a weighty statement indeed to say that "the ultimate kind of power is violence." It would be one thing to say that *one* kind of power is violence. But Mills says it is the *ultimate* kind. The word *ultimate* implies that there is a kind of hierarchy of power, with violence at its root or apex. Mills is saying either that power, in its deepest essence, is violent, or that power, in its fullest expression, is violent, or he may be saying both at once. At one or perhaps both ends of the spectrum of power we find the destruction of dignity and the loss of innocence.

But this means that other uses of power that are not quite so obviously compromised as violence are still part of a system that "ultimately" tilts toward violence. Mills's immediate target is politics. It is one thing to observe that all politics is a struggle for power. (By the way, is this true? As the sociologist Daniel Bell asked in a pointed review of Mills's book, is *all* politics a struggle? Is politics never a matter of discovery of mutually beneficial ways to govern groups of human beings? Is it never a matter of inspiration and hope rather than struggle and conflict? Surely *some* politics, perhaps *most* politics, perhaps *all politics at certain times in certain places,* perhaps even *all politics at one time or another,* is a struggle for power. But all politics, all the time, everywhere?) But what Mills is up to in the second half of his statement is insinuating that forms of power that do not *appear* to be violent—say, a vote on the floor of the House of Representatives—actually partake in a system that is *ultimately* about violence. For if the ultimate kind of power is violence, then it seems hard to avoid the conclusion that any true exercise of power is originally or eventually violent, the more so the more successful the exercise is.

This is, in fact, the worldview of Mills, and it saturates every page of his agenda-setting book. His writing drips with disdain for the "power elite" of business, the military and politics. He alternately belittles and dismisses any suggestion that wealth could result from creativity, for example, pointing out that it is not inventors who get rich but those who finance and popularize inventions, and those who get really rich bypass invention altogether and simply "appropriate" wealth from the right connections with fellow elites in the military and politics. Mills cannot believe that the "power elite" have created anything good or that any genuine wealth, in the sense of common welfare, has resulted from the use of their power.

To be sure, Mills was unusually cynical, though perhaps not so unusual among his fellow sociologists. And there was much to be cynical about in the 1950s, more than most Americans were yet aware, giddy as they were from the postwar economic expansion and superficially satisfied with their place in the world. Even Dwight Eisenhower, who presided over the power elite Mills critiqued, coined the phrase "the military-industrial complex" to warn his fellow Americans of its dangers. In the 1960s and 1970s the broader society caught up with Mills's suspicion, not least because of the disastrous violence of Vietnam, implemented by the very politicians and corporate technocrats that Mills had indicted a decade earlier.

But the alternative to Mills's cynicism does not have to be Polyanna's naiveté. There is another way. Rather than saying that violence is the ultimate kind of power, we should say instead that violence is the ultimate *distortion* of power. Violence is the worst way that power can go wrong, and all the other ways that power can go wrong do indeed lead us down the slippery slope to violence. And violence—uses of force that undermine the dignity of human beings and other created things—is the clearest sign that power has indeed gone astray. Violence is the last refuge of frustrated god players and idols gone bad, lashing out at those that will not bend to their demands and give in to their quest for control.

But there is a crucial difference between saying that violence is the ultimate distortion of power and saying that all power is ultimately rooted in violence. If all power is rooted in violence, then anyone attempting to exercise power—or anyone who finds themselves with power, privilege or status, whether they like it or not—must imagine themselves perched on a steep and slippery slope that leads to violence, and must be constantly trying to avoid slipping down that slope. Even if we manage to avoid slipping all the way down, we will never be able to shake the accusation that ultimately what we are involved in is degrading. And indeed this is how many sensitive people feel about their own power, and others': that it is just a few slippery steps from exploitation and domination. The most reasonable conclusion from such a view would seem to be that the farther we can get from the ultimate power, the better, which suggests that the best amount of power to have is none.

But if violence is a distortion, then in our use of power we will find ourselves not on a slippery slope but at a crossroads. Down one path lies the distortion of power, and at the end of that path is violence. But down another path lies creative power. Take one direction in our use of power and we will indeed contribute to the degradation of dignity—others' and our own. But take another direction and our power can contribute to the expression and even restoration of human flourishing.

One of the most memorable events of my own lifetime perfectly illustrates the possibilities of power to restore and sustain dignity. Indeed, it was a political event at the apex of the very system about which C. Wright Mills was so cynical, and I think it is fair to say that Mills never imagined it would happen. On January 20, 2009, Barack Obama was inaugurated as president of the United States. The election of an African American to the presidency, and the dignified, memorable and moving ceremony that ushered him into office, was a thoroughly political event, and certainly the culmination of a tremendous exercise of many kinds of power, including the "struggle" for power that Mills described. But this political event not only embodied the remarkable heritage of United States politics that every inauguration represents, a nonviolent transition of power from one executive to another, which should only astonish us all the more since it has happened more than forty consecutive times in the history of the nation. It was also a milestone in the use of power to restore dignity after a history of violence. I kept my eleven-year-old son home from school to watch the ceremony because I wanted him to see power at its best. And it is not irrelevant to add that I had made the difficult decision to vote against Barack Obama in the 2008 election. But my political differences with Obama and his party had nothing to do with the import of that day. Like millions of other Americans of every political persuasion, on that frigid Tuesday in January I celebrated and I wept.

Obama's 2008 campaign, it is worth remembering, began with a hard-fought primary in which all the usual mechanisms of political power were arrayed against him. Mills's "power elite," at least the Democratic half, were firmly in the court of Hillary Clinton, Obama's primary opponent. Obama's victory was not the result of cynically wielded camouflaged violence but the result of tremendous creativity—not just his extraordinary gifts at public communication but also his staff's canny use of online networks and grassroots organizing. Barack Obama's rise to power is a tremendous challenge to cynicism about the possibilities inherent even in the manifestly broken and distorted political realities of the United States. What my son and I watched with awe that Tuesday was not simply a well-disguised and precarious intermediate step on the way to ultimate violence. Instead, what we saw, and what the world celebrated, was power rightly used— power that restored dignity not just to the targets of violence and their descendants, but also to the heirs of its perpetrators, and that created the conditions for future flourishing.

This does not mean that President Obama has, in the succeeding years, always taken the right turn at every crossroads in the enormously complex task of using his power well. We cannot afford to be optimists about power any more than we can afford to be cynics. Power, especially concentrated power, always places us at that crossroads where we must choose between creation and destruction, flourishing and violence. It's the very essence of realism to recognize that fallen human beings will often choose the wrong course.

But Mills was wrong—very possibly wrong about politics, and certainly wrong about power. We can make a strong case that he was wrong even from a purely political event like a presidential inauguration, but Christians make an even stronger case from another event in history that was also deeply political and deeply violent. In the light of the crucifixion and resurrection of Jesus of Nazareth, Christians have come to the glad conclusion that violence is not the ultimate kind of power. Far from it. For all its twisted terror it is nonetheless a weak, defeatable and indeed vanquished kind of power. True power is creation, and the truest power is resurrection, the new creation that can restore flourishing even when violence has done its worst.

## WORDS FOR POWER

The words we use for power do not all mean the same thing. *Violence* is physical force that has exceeded legitimate bounds; it does unnecessary harm or does harm for an unjust cause or without just authorization. Violence is wrong by definition. Violence is in fact the word we use to judge force as wrong, just as *murder* is the word we use to name killing that we have judged to be wrong. (To say that someone killed someone else is a statement of fact, whereas to say that someone murdered someone else is to make a moral claim about that killing.) Violence is wrong, at its heart, because it deprives image bearers of dignity, not just liberty. This is why torture, which by definition breaches the integrity of the human body and psyche, is always wrong. This is why we reserve our harshest judgments for the acts that most violate dignity.

*Domination* is pervasive and complete control over a person or a group of people. And for Christians at least, domination is by definition wrong. It is the "absolute power" that "corrupts absolutely," and it violates the

freedom for which human beings are designed—not absolute freedom
from anyone or from any responsibility to others (which is actually its
own sort of slavery), but freedom in relationships of mutual love and submission rather than mere fear and obedience. Domination is the mode of
"the rulers of the Gentiles," who "lord it over" their subjects. "It will not be
so among you" (Matthew 20:25-26). Domination and violence are both
wrong—violence by its very definition, and domination by virtue of its
inevitable effects on both ruler and ruled.

But force and even coercion, in and of themselves, are not so value
laden. *Force* can sometimes be a very good thing. The so-called
Heimlich maneuver popularized by posters in commercial kitchens
and university dining halls involves thrusting a fist backwards into a
choking person's stomach "with a hard, upward movement" (according
to the U.K.'s National Health Service guide to rescuing a choking
victim). Done properly, the Heimlich maneuver can save a life; done
properly, it also is quite likely to break a rib. It is certainly forceful, and
it can be harmful—but it is not violent. Chances are that if you ever are
on the receiving end of a successful application of the Heimlich maneuver, you will be inexpressibly grateful.

*Coercion* is a broader idea than force, because coercion can be exercised
just with the *threat* of force, as when a gun-wielding robber motions with
his gun for everyone to lie down on the floor. Sometimes the threat of
force is very distant. When my boss asks me to complete a task by a
deadline, I'm motivated to work late in the night at least in part by the possibility that failure would lead to my being fired. Firing itself is not an act
of force (at least not at the enlightened offices of Christianity Today), but
should I refuse to clean out my desk and leave the building, eventually
force could be applied by the local police to remove me. To be sure, that
possible use of force is distant when I am racing to meet a deadline, but it
is unmistakably there.

Part of the authority that comes with any supervisory role is coercive.
But any authority that relies too much on coercion soon can rely on
nothing *but* coercion to sustain its power. If the only power my boss has
over me is the threat of force, he has been reduced to just one step above a
gun-wielding robber waving his weapon about wildly to compel some

Thank you for your business!
Have a nice day!

Customer Copy

Revolution Physical

Merchant ID: 5987783                    Term ID: 001

## Sale - Approved

Date: 09/28/16                          Time: 12:51:22
Card Type: Visa
Entry Method: Swiped
Card #: XXXXXXXXXXXX0789

Invoice #:      2445
Approval Code:  06834B
Customer Ref:   NUTR - $25 copay

**Amount**      **$25.00**

I agree to pay the above total amount according to the card

level of cooperation. In fact, since my boss cannot in fact fire a gun at me without being carted off by the police, he is in some ways worse off than the robber. The leader who can only lead through fear is in a very precarious position indeed.

But there are other forms of coercion where even the threat of force may be absent. Catherine and I raised two children without ever spanking them. Certainly we sometimes used force: more than once I recall rather firmly removing a screaming two-year-old from the living room to a place they would have not gone on their own. But thanks partly to the temperaments of our children and partly to a fair amount of on-the-fly creativity, inflicting pain for the sake of punishment simply never became necessary; we found that other sanctions were enough to teach them that our authority had to be respected.

We had no absolute policy against striking our children, though we will always be grateful we never felt it was necessary. But there is one punishment that we never contemplated using: the "silent treatment." The silent treatment involves no force. It is simply the refusal to speak to someone, even if they implore you to speak to them. Unlike "time out," which involves removing the offender to a position of isolation, the silent treatment doesn't even require the offender to leave the room or sit in a corner. It is the removal of the *offended*—the refusal on the part of the offended parent to acknowledge the existence, let alone the entreaties, of their child until the punishment is complete. And as anyone can tell you who was on the receiving end of the silent treatment, there is nothing more devastating. Almost every child would rather be spanked than ignored.

Violence, domination, force and coercion are all forms of power. The question is how they relate to one another, and to power itself. In a great deal of casual conversation inside and outside the Christian community, you might well think that all of these terms are practically synonymous: power *is* coercion, which *is* force, which *is* violence, which leads to domination. So a pastor can summarize the cult of Caesar with the words "power, might and domination," as if they were all the same thing. In fact, coercion, whether direct or indirect, is the *weakest* and ultimately *least consequential* form of power, especially considered from the horizons of the good original creation and the glorious ending to the story of the world. Even within the horizons of our own sinful and fallen history, coercive power divorced from creative power is remarkably unstable and very often much less effective than those who wield it would hope. And it is striking how frequently this insight has been neglected; even a sophisticated ethicist like John Howard Yoder can often use the word *power* as a straight synonym for violence.

The most commonly held Christian position, articulated by Augustine, is that there is such a thing as legitimate force. Even lethal force may not be excessively violent when it is wielded by just authorities in service of a just cause. This is the burden of the "just war" tradition, which—while not pretending that lethal or injurious force is ever a good thing in itself— holds that war is love's response to a neighbor threatened by violence. In the face of violence threatened against the innocent, love requires that human beings and the societies they sustain not stand passively by. The silent treatment is not enough. Nor is vigilantism—unorganized and unauthorized force—acceptable. The only loving response is to invest the responsibility for measured force in accountable governments that act on behalf of the common good.

Anabaptists disagree, and the debate between the Anabaptists and the Augustinians is by far the most important and well-developed conversation about power and its Christian limits. It is such well-traveled territory that I will not retrace it here. But the mistake both Augustinians and Anabaptists often make is Mills's mistake—to think that power is ultimately about force, if not violence, and to concentrate all our Christian attention on the appropriate limits for force.

The hard truth is that no society can survive without coercion. John Howard Yoder himself, for all his important contributions to Christian ethics, was a serial abuser of his power over women. In a painful episode of church discipline he was placed under strict limits by his Anabaptist community. It is exceedingly unlikely that Yoder ever would have undertaken this process of repentance and restoration without the coercive powers available to his church. At the extreme, which thankfully Yoder's own case did not require, those powers would have been exercised in the truly terrible recourse of "shunning," the communal equivalent of the silent treatment, in which the offender is barred from all relationship with those he previously called brothers and sisters.

The powers that came to bear on Yoder were not violent. They were authorized, measured and accountable. But they were still coercive. And if a social ethicist like Yoder required such coercion, how much more inevitable is it that any community will have to coerce from time to time in order to prevent harm?

When I was a chaplain at Harvard University, the chaplains' organization, whose members were mostly pacifists of varying degrees of radical commitment, invited a captain in Harvard's police department to address them. (Like many university security departments, Harvard does indeed employ fully licensed officers of the peace.) The complexity of power was on full display as we gathered in an oak-walled conference room in an elegant church building near campus. On the one hand, the officer was the only person in the room who openly carried a firearm—he had direct access to the instruments of force. But when he began to speak, his South Boston accent immediately signaled that he probably had not had the elite educations that most of us in the room had enjoyed. The first few minutes of his speech were tinged with the brusque bluntness I've often encountered when those from blue-collar backgrounds or professions interact with people they suspect may treat them condescendingly.

But as the presentation continued, this officer turned out to be a committed Christian and a thoughtful one. He quoted Jesus' Sermon on the Mount, "Blessed are the peacemakers," as the foundation of his work. "Our job is to make and keep the peace in this community," he said. He described the ways he and his fellow officers worked to build relationships with faculty, staff and students long before trouble came, so that at times of crisis they could resolve conflict with the minimum of force. He spoke of the role of prayer in a vocation that brought him into regular contact with the drunk, disturbed or dangerous.

By the end of our time with the officer, something had shifted in the room. Not only were we in the presence of a person of great intelligence and insight, we were encountering someone whose vocation had compelled him to learn holiness, someone who was set apart for one of Jesus' highest priorities. We had met someone who used coercive power creatively, and whose stewardship of the community's coercive power made it possible for many others to cultivate and create in peace.

Cynics, their academic cousins the Foucauldians, and anarchists will say that "officer of the peace" is an Orwellian euphemism for an agent of state power. But others will see in that remarkable title an aspiration to legitimate and limited restraining force for the good of a community. Blessed are the peacemakers.

## WHY COERCION IS NEVER ENOUGH

We all recognize the blunt power of a gun pointed at one's chest, or even the less direct but still compelling power of financial reward. Other forms of power, by contrast, seems vaguer and less secure.

Forcible power—whether Weber's *Macht* or *Herrschaft*—can compel obedience of a certain kind. But there are many kinds of human behavior that cannot be compelled by force at all. The command "Be spontaneous!" is impossible to obey. Any response will be anything but spontaneous. All the more so for the command "Be creative!" There is nothing more likely to snuff out creativity than being on the wrong end of the barrel of a gun, and any true creativity in response to compulsion will be subversive, not subservient, to its commanders. The Russian composer Dmitri Shostakovich worked under the thumb of the Stalinist system, producing an extraordinary body of orchestral music that was just patriotic-sounding enough to pass muster with the cultural censors. But the true heartbeat of his terrible and wonderful music is the anguish of a creative soul under compulsion, an eloquent and revolutionary witness to truth, beauty and pain from a world of corrupted power. He was creative in spite of his orders, not because of them.

Similarly, erotic arousal is uncommandable and is never a matter of obedience to compulsion (and often surprises us when we attempt to command even our own bodies). These most fundamental and generative aspects of human life arise not out of obedience but out of our fruitful image bearing. And yet they have undeniable, even unparalleled, ability to make something of the world—the works of artists like Shostakovich are among the most enduring legacies of human culture, and the human race itself is sustained by bodies freely given to one another out of love. Any understanding of power that has no room for uncommanded creativity and fruitfulness seems actually to overlook the mainspring of human life and culture itself. True power would have to include the ability to create the conditions where human beings create in the image of God, not just obey false idols and idolatrous leaders who think that it is better to be feared than loved.

We are also living in an extraordinary time in human history, where most of the traditional paths to coercive power (or even velvet-gloved authority) are proving less sustainable. At this writing the unforgettable dictum from *The Princess Bride* "Never get involved in a land war in Asia!" seems very likely to outlast the effects of the money and military might the United States has poured into Afghanistan. The possession of "hard power" has never been less obviously effective in allowing the powerful to rest soundly in their beds. Instead we find that the most effective commanders of the American military are revising the very calling of the warrior to include endless cups of tea with local officials and construction projects designed to create a cultural environment conducive to peace. Ironically, American might has foundered precisely in countries that might seem to be most firmly rooted in ancient conceptions of power, honor and control. Even premodern societies are postmodern now, in their ability to flexibly resist the application of power and preserve their way of making something of the world.

Closer to home, the erosion of coercive power and obedient submission is even clearer. In an influential 1985 book, *No Sense of Place*, the social critic Joshua Meyrowitz wrote about the way "information control" was slipping out of the hands of Mills's "power elite." For Meyrowitz and most thinkers like him, control was the realest form of power.

More than twenty-five years after Meyrowitz, the deluge of information, pouring through glowing rectangles everywhere we turn, has turned the world of coercive power and compulsive obedience upside down. But it has also revealed something that was true all along: the truest, deepest form of power was never compulsion but creation. Control of information, like other forms of control, is a much more slender and fragile thing than it appears. At one point Meyrowitz uses the example of the 1980s-era car mechanic who has exclusive access to catalogs of parts, repair manuals and directories of

suppliers. The implication is that the mechanic, as long as he retains possession and control of that information, will retain his power and status.

Today, of course, nearly all of that information is only a click away. Yet I
still rely utterly on the authority of my longtime mechanic, Joe Tancredi,
the proprietor of Tancredi's Auto Repair, a reliable, friendly and trustworthy repair shop in our town. In fact, I am much more dependent on
Tancredi's to service my 2010 vehicle than I would have been to service my
much simpler 1982 vehicle. Why? Not because he possesses information I
cannot possess, but because he is *fluent* in the use of that information in a
way I am not and cannot easily become. His fluency goes far beyond the
simple ability to look up information in a book; it is a hard-won competence and intuition with complex systems that is much less like a possession and much more like, well, creative power. His power is, in short,
not something Joe Tancredi *possesses* but something that he has *become*—
a function of his image-bearing identity and character.

So we find ourselves in a world where the coercive model of power is
no longer the only game in town. Instead, coercive power is seen as the
thin and limited thing it has always truly been. The most authoritative car
mechanics in America, until their retirement in 2012, were Tom and Ray
Magliozzi, the constantly chortling hosts of a call-in program on public
radio called *Car Talk*. Tom and Ray's authority came not by virtue of their
command of repair manuals or even their arcane technical knowledge
(most of which would now be available via Google), but their instincts,
their humor, their generosity, and fraternal rivalry and fiercely loyal collaboration. They were genuine authorities of a media age—authoritative
not for what they knew but who they were, and respected not for their
ability to command but for their ability to dignify and ennoble (and get a
good laugh out of) Americans' love-hate affairs with their automobiles.
And they did so not as authority figures pronouncing from a great height
and distance, but as neighbors (proprietors of a neighborhood shop
called the Good News Garage). They had the true authority besides which
coercive power seems transient and thin: the authority of relational, generous, disciplined image bearers who have made something delightful and
true of the world.

## THE PLACE FOR COERCION

So coercion is not the deepest and best form of power. But is there any place for coercion, any role it may legitimately play? Yes. Coercion is needed to protect the possibility of creation. At the very beginning of the Genesis story we find God separating the waters above from the waters below, pushing the sea aside to make room for dry land—all in the interest of multiplying opportunities for diverse and teeming creation. All the more so after the Fall, when the ever more violent demands of idols and the perpetrators of injustice threaten the vulnerable. The legitimate role of coercion is to make room for flourishing, especially by restraining whatever fundamentally threatens the integrity of God's creative image bearers.

And coercion is needed at the end of the whole story as well. The good news of Revelation 21–22 comes after the judgment of Revelation 20—indeed, the whole preceding book—in which the good Creator God pronounces a final and compelling judgment on all that will not bow the knee to true power. Ultimately God will judge the world and banish the agents of idolatrous violence, both heavenly and earthly. We do not want to live in a world without judgment, a world where idols would never be cast down, where injustice would never be recognized, let alone condemned. A God who always deferred such a judgment, with the coercive finality that judgment of evil requires, would not be a God worth worshiping.

But coercion is always penultimate. It is of limited use. Oddly enough, it is too strong to be truly useful as a form of power.

Creative power allows creatures to become themselves, flourishing in their own distinctive ways with their own proper being. To interfere coercively with creatures would be to compromise the very thing God wills them to be: beings of their own, with their own history, agency and destiny. Only a Nietzschean god would want to coerce its creatures. But this means that creative power involves risk—the possibility, indeed the likelihood, of loss. Creative power bears this risk gladly, because true flourishing is only found on the far side of risk.

To be sure, in any given situation the quickest way to the results we seek is generally command and control. But over the long run, the *only* way to the results we seek is creativity and true freedom. Coercive power is instant but short-lived; creative power is patient and enduring.

Force, coercion and violence are all very real forms of power. Indeed, because violence is so real, careful and restrained use of coercion can be a legitimate use of power, here in the middle of the story. But true power always moves beyond "make it so" to "let us make" to "let there be"—and the last word of the world's story is not coercion, but creation.

# 8

# THE LURE OF PRIVILEGE

In January 1999 I was flying on Saudi Arabian Airlines from Mumbai, India, to Riyadh, Saudi Arabia, and then onward to London. I arrived at the Mumbai airport to find a long line. Perhaps seventy-five people were waiting to check in, and nearly every one was an Indian man with a very small suitcase. Saudi Arabia imports the great majority of its manual laborers from places like India, and this 747 flew across the Arabian Sea largely to ferry guest workers back and forth. I had arrived at the end of a long line of Indian men who were, essentially, commuting to work.

Like all lines in India, this one was packed closely together, and we were all sweating in the mid-day heat. But I was fairly sure the plane would not take off without us, so I was in no great hurry. As the single ticket agent checked in each traveler at the far-off counter, I prepared myself for a long wait.

I had been in line for under five minutes when the agent came out from behind the counter, walked down the line until he came to my spot, and said, "Come with me."

When you're several thousand miles from home and an airline agent says that, you obey—an example of Weber's *Herrschaft* in action. So I followed him, up to the front of the line, past all seventy-five Indian men with their suitcases, to the counter. Without another word he took my passport, examined it, printed out a boarding pass, and said, "You may go."

It may say something about how much was missing from my own map of power that literally until those final words, I did not understand what was happening. When I realized that I had just been singled out and effectively ordered to cut in line, I was shocked, not to mention embarrassed. I felt a momentary urge to make a small speech to the men who had been in line before me: "I didn't ask for this! I didn't even want to be taken to the front of the line. We don't do this in America!"

But as I walked off toward the boarding gate, flushed with surprise and embarrassment, I could not detect the slightest surprise or discomfort in that line of men. It gradually dawned on me that not only were they not surprised that I had been ushered to the front of the line—they had expected it the moment I arrived. They had understood what was happening long before I did. They knew about something I was only beginning to understand: the power of privilege.

## THE POWER OF PRIVILEGE

Privilege is a special kind of power. It is a form of power that requires no effort. Indeed, only in unusual circumstances do we become conscious of it at all. Most of the time, privilege just works on behalf of those who have it, never making the slightest demands of them.

The best way I know to define privilege is *the ongoing benefits of past successful exercises of power*. Privilege is the name for all the good things we do not need to try to acquire, because they simply flow to us as a result of past exercises of power.

A simple example is the royalties that are paid to authors of books like this one. As publishers collect revenue from book sales, they pay a certain percentage to the author as payment for their work. Sometimes a publisher will give an author an "advance" on royalties (the upfront payments that show up in the news when they are especially eye-catching in size), but the goal is to sell enough books that the advance is repaid. In practice, this happens all too seldom, but if both author and publisher are fortunate, the book sells better than expected, the advance is repaid, and ongoing sales produce a stream of income that arrives in the form of royalty checks.

Writing and publishing a book is an act, or series of acts, of creative power, full of the "let there be" and "let us make" moments that are the glad heritage of image bearers. But the interesting thing about royalties is that they arrive *after* most or all of the creative work has been done. If an advance was paid, it may take two or three years before the royalty checks begin to arrive. Yet if the book has a long life, those checks may continue to arrive for years. It is a remarkably delicious experience to get checks year after year for work you did long ago. The book is long since finished and requires nothing more of you; it simply goes on serving new readers and producing new revenue, and you enjoy the stream of income.

Writing the book was an act of power and, at least in this highly fiction-alized example which almost never actually comes true for starry-eyed writers, a successful one.

Cashing the royalty checks—the ongoing benefits that keep arriving long after the exercise of power is over—is an experience of privilege.

## ROYALTIES AND RENTS

Royalties are delightful enough. But there are other forms of privilege that require even less of us. To earn royalties, after all, you have to actually write a book. What if you could have all the benefits of writing a book without the inconvenience and difficulty of doing the actual work? Well, one way is to be the child of a successful author. Thanks to the laws of copyright, the royalty checks can continue to arrive even after the author has died. The children of the author, who did nothing at all except be for-tunate enough to choose the right parents, now receive benefits, not from their *own* past successful exercises of power but from another's—an even more pure form of privilege. All inheritances, indeed, are instances of privilege. Someone's image-bearing work is sufficiently successful that it produces abundance beyond what they needed in their own lifetime: the heirs receive the ongoing benefits of that abundance without needing to work for it.

It is no accident, indeed, that we use the word *royalty* for the payments that accrue after an act of creative power has been successful. For the original recipients of royalties were literally the royalty—the members of royal families that passed on the privilege of taxing the land and work of their subjects from generation to generation.

And there are other equally delicious forms of privilege. One form is what the financial world calls "economic rents." These are not the same thing as the rent you pay your landlord. Instead, when economists use the word *rent* they are measuring what they call "market power": the ability of some people, in certain circumstances, to command much higher pay for their work than they would actually require to do the job.

To illustrate rents, we need to move from publishing to professional sports, which offers some of the most fantastic examples of economic rents in our world. The very best professional athletes are paid extraordinary sums to use their talents on the field, court or pitch. When David Beckham, the British soccer star, signed a contract with the Los Angeles Galaxy in 2007, he was promised $50 million per year, for thirty-five games a year—$1.4 million per game, or approximately $15,555 per minute of each match. Beckham and a handful of other human beings are paid these fantastic sums because the market values their skills so highly.

Imagine you could find fourteen-year-old David Beckham, undoubtedly already an accomplished soccer player, and ask him how much he would charge per game to pay soccer when he grows up. Two thousand dollars per game? Twenty thousand per game? Perhaps Beckham was ambitious and self-confident. Maybe he would have asked for $100,000 a game. But it is inconceivable that he would have insisted on $1.4 million per game. David Beckham, we may suppose, loves soccer—at least the fourteen-year-old version did. To get paid to do something you love is one of life's rare gifts. He would surely play for less than $1.4 million. The difference between what he would insist on being paid and his actual ability to command payment in the international soccer market is what economists call rent.

Rents are interesting to economists because *no extra work is done to earn them*. There is no additional exercise of creative power involved when David Beckham takes the soccer field and is paid twice or ten times the amount he would require to play the game. Rents are a kind of unnatural abundance of reward for exercising one's power, which is why economists observe that many people even engage in "rent-seeking behavior," finding positions in the economy that will pay without requiring work. Indeed, collecting rent is a godlike experience. Without needing to do any work, take any risk or contribute in any way, you receive an excess of reward.

Royalties and rents often go together. The additional royalties that arrive when a book does well do not add anything to the creative power exercised by the author. They are a pleasant surprise, an unexpected bonus. So royalties are their own form of rent—more money that arrives, unbidden, without requiring anything of us.

When rents are paid to stars like Beckham or authors who write unexpectedly successful books, most of us may feel a twinge of jealousy and move along. But rent seeking is not always so benign. Corporations that pull strings to get favorable regulations or prevent competitors from entering their market are often seeking rent—compensation they would not need to do the work they do, pure and unproductive excess that can flow straight to profit rather than being invested in real, difficult work. Corrupt officials in governments demand bribes for services, skimming rent off the top, often while neglecting their duties and not even performing the work for which they are paid. Rents can sometimes be a sign of genuine image bearing, but just as often they are a signal of god playing. And whether their sources are benign or malign, as rents accumulate they become privilege.

## THE NEUTRALITY OF PRIVILEGE

Privilege—the accumulated benefits from past successful exercises of power—is perfectly indifferent to whether those exercises of power were creative or oppressive, rooted in image bearing or in idolatry and injustice. Indeed, sometimes you cannot tell whether privilege's sources are good or bad. As a native English speaker, I benefit tremendously from things I did nothing to earn, which is the very definition of privilege. I benefit from a rich tradition of literature, generations of gifted teachers, and the whole history, often glorious, of the Angles and Saxons. I also benefit from the sorry history of British and American imperial adventures, the dominance of Western mass media that pander to human beings' basest instincts, trade agreements that favor incumbent American firms, and millions of fanny-pack toting American tourists. There is no way to separate the benefits that come from good exercises of power from those that were regrettable or worse. They are all benefits; they are all privilege.

Privilege is not bad. To the contrary, it comes in the forms of *benefits*. And privilege is not necessarily exclusive—it can be widely shared. We all benefit from countless past exercises of cultural power, from the invention of indoor plumbing to the translating of the King James Version of the Bible to the first person who dared to eat the allegedly poisonous tomato and found that it was very good. All of the human cultural inheritance is privilege, in this sense, and every person, not just those from dominant cultures, benefits from past exercises of power by their parents and more distant ancestors. "If I have seen further," Isaac Newton said, "it is only by standing on the shoulders of giants." Many exercises of true power begin by cashing in our privilege, using it to launch us further than we could go on our own.

But if privilege is not bad, it is still dangerous. For one thing, we can cash in the benefits of privilege for many purposes other than the exercise of true power. The exercise of true power always involves us in risk, and requires creaturely dependence on God and other people. But we can use our privilege to insulate us from risk, and often from God and other people as well. Relying on my fluent English, I can travel widely and never attempt to understand or make myself understood in another language. The author who collects enough rents in the form of royalties never has to write again, but that is not a good thing for an author who has an image-bearing calling to creativity. A life too devoted to privilege becomes a life swathed in more and more layers of protective bubble wrap, constantly seeking more protection and becoming less and less able to move freely in the world.

And privilege is dangerous because of how easily it becomes invisible. The incident in the Mumbai airport has haunted me ever since. There was nothing I had ever done to deserve to be put in line in front of these hard-working men. If anything, quite the reverse. I was simply the beneficiary of privilege, of rent—a free pass in excess of anything I deserved or even wanted.

But what really has haunted me is this question: How many times have I been put at the front of the line without even knowing there was a line? How many times have I walked through a door that opened, invisibly and silently, for me, but slammed shut for others? How many lines have I cut in a life of privilege?

It is almost impossible to know how much privilege you have. As someone privileged by my skin color, I have literally never spoken a single word to a security guard at a shopping mall or store. But most of my friends of African descent, including those with Ivy League degrees and occupations of higher status than my own, have been followed or indeed confronted by retail security personnel. If they had not told me of these experiences, I never would have believed that such things happened to them. At its worst, privilege is blindness, allowing us to blithely go on in our god playing, not even aware of the insults to image bearers that happen under our noses every day.

## PRIVILEGED PANIC

For many Americans, September 11, 2001, was a sudden plunge into the icy sea of risk and the terror of threats that had seemed safely remote. But my own life-changing encounter with urban terror came in New York's Penn Station a decade earlier, in an episode just as sinister, in its own way, as the attacks of September 11. On May 1, 1992, I arrived in midtown Manhattan on a train from Boston, on my way to a citywide prayer meeting in the Bronx. And I stepped off my inbound train into a sea of chaos.

Two days before, the acquittal of four police officers in the beating of an African American man named Rodney King had set off riots across Los Angeles. With helicopter footage from LA of burning neighborhoods and angry crowds airing constantly on live television, cities across the United States were tinderboxes of hostility and fear.

In New York, it turned out, rumors of riots had spread across Manhattan at mid-day. Businesses were abruptly shutting down, sending their employees home and boarding up their street-level windows. At two o'clock in the afternoon, Penn Station was more crowded than it would normally be at the height of rush hour. As I walked down the train platform, I watched in amazement as terrified white-collar workers tried to squeeze themselves onto overloaded commuter trains, shoving and elbowing one another in barely restrained panic. As they ran toward a boarding train, I heard one say to another, "The blacks are coming over the bridges to burn Manhattan."

Need I mention that nearly everyone getting on the trains was white?

The rumors of riots were entirely false, which is why few readers of this book have the faintest memory that anything unusual happened in Penn Station that long-ago Friday afternoon. The rumors were also absurd—in LA

that weekend and in nearly every other riot in American history, the neighborhoods most affected by racial anger were the neighborhoods of the aggrieved
rioters themselves, not privileged places that enjoy reliable policing. The idea
that "the blacks" (an incredibly offensive generalization) might somehow
mount an assault on the shops and office towers of Midtown was risible to say
the least. And yet millions of commuters found it believable enough to flee the
city as fast as the Long Island Rail Road could carry them.

That afternoon it occurred to me that the placid calm of my own suburban upbringing had been as thin as the walnut veneer on a cheap TV
stand. Just under the surface was a throbbing fear of vulnerability and risk,
so raw and fierce that it could be stirred into panicked flight by the merest
suggestion of a real threat. As unfounded and unprovoked as it was, the
terror I witnessed in Penn Station was as real, and as powerfully shaping a
force, as the daily boredom of the 4:19 train to Montauk, and as real as the
terror that gripped the nation a decade later on a brilliant fall morning.
The idolatry of privilege lay quietly under the surface, unmapped, waiting
for the slightest provocation to stir it into raging action.

## OUR PLACE IN THE LINE

There is another, even more dubious form of privilege. Many kinds of
privilege, like the power that produces them, are not fixed in quantity and
can be widely shared. I can enjoy the benefits of the English language
without taking away from your enjoyment of them in any way. But there is
another kind of privilege that cannot be shared without loss. It is intrinsi-
cally scarce, and its pursuit leads to some of the most egregious acts of god
playing. The name for it is status.

Status—at root, "where you stand"—is about your place in line. It is
about the human drive to be ranked above another, to be counted more
worthy than another. It is the rush of third graders to line up at the
classroom door, each pushing and shoving to avoid being last. It is the
subtle calculations we often make when we enter a room, sizing up who is
most popular, who is most pretty, who is most powerful. Status is about
counting, numbering, ranking and ultimately about excluding.

We begin life as image bearers, each one with infinite dignity and worth.
But from the day we are born we inherit a certain status. Status is pure

privilege; it is never based on what we are currently aspiring to or achieving, but on what has been done before, often long before. We are born into families with greater or lesser economic means. We inherit features that are strikingly attractive or painfully plain. We live in districts with "good schools" or "bad schools." And every one of these inherited qualities is ranked, sometimes vividly and directly, sometimes implicitly and obliquely. We rarely have any control over where we land in these rankings; they are assigned based on realities that long preceded us. But our status follows us, or maybe more accurately hovers over us, opening certain doors and closing others. Wherever there are limited resources that are distributed on the basis of privilege, status is at work.

Status itself is by definition a scarce resource. There can only be one person who is first in line. The scene in Penn Station that May day was so chaotic because space was limited. The thronging commuters' race for the trains was a race for position, a race to occupy a relatively few slots. My experience in the Mumbai airport was likewise an experience not just of privilege in general but status in particular. Indeed it was the dissonance between my social status—a tall, white, obviously middle-class man with a blue U.S. passport—and my place in the check-in line that created such a sense of discomfort for the airline agent. Though my status was invisible to me, it was inescapably important to him, so much so that he stopped what he was doing to correct the imbalance. Once my visible place in line matched my invisible status, the stress was relieved for the agent and very possibly for many of the other men in line as well.

If privilege is neutral and sometimes beneficial, I have come to believe that status is rarely anything but dangerous. Of course there is a place for recognizing and even ranking achievement. It would be foolish to pretend that just because I am an image bearer of infinite worth, that I am worth as much on the soccer field as David Beckham. In limited domains like a given sport, profession or business, we rely on rankings and scarcity to determine and celebrate what is most productive and fruitful.

But the quest for status rarely stays within the bounds of a limited domain. Instead, we begin to chase status itself. And because there will never be enough status, because every move up in the line requires that someone else move back in the line, the quest for status pitches us against our fellow image bearers. The near violence of the train platforms in Penn Station was a terrifying reminder of how fiercely human beings can defend their status, but of course the wider situation was far worse. An entire population was attempting to protect its status, its one-up advantage over the less privileged. Status is an implacable idol; it can never deliver enough, and the more you pursue it, the more it will demand.

James and John have already been chosen. They are among the Twelve. Of course we know that the Twelve are not chosen for any special merit or privilege they possess—a motley crew of fishermen and tax collectors with strong local accents. But James and John have tasted the satisfactions of the inside track, the charms of the inner circle, the self-importance of those granted admittance while others are left outside. So they approach Jesus at an opportune time to ask for status. In Matthew's telling, their mother is the one who makes the request, not the last time a parent would seek to advance the status of their children. "Declare that these two sons of mine will sit, one at your right hand and one at your left, in your kingdom" (Matthew 20:21). Jesus' response is dismissive if not indifferent:

> "You do not know what you are asking. Are you able to drink the cup that I am about to drink?" They said to him, "We are able." He said to them, "You will indeed drink my cup, but to sit at my right hand and at my left, this is not mine to grant, but it is for those for whom it has been prepared by my Father." (Matthew 20:22-23)

James and John ask for status—but Jesus responds with a question about power. Are they able to actually risk everything in the way he will shortly risk everything, drinking the cup of wrath to its dregs? When this goes straight over the disciples' heads, Jesus makes an extraordinary prediction. They will in fact identify this deeply with their Lord. One day James and John will taste the same cup as Jesus. They will be closer to him in glory than they can ever imagine, after paying the highest possible cost.

But as for status, Jesus turns them away. It is not something he is even concerned with; it is the business of his Father. Who will be first in the kingdom of heaven? Who knows? Not Jesus. It will be someone no one expected, someone for whom it was prepared without them asking. When the disciples become angry at the brothers' line-jumping, Jesus makes this clear.

You know that the rulers of the Gentiles lord it over them, and their great ones are tyrants over them. It will not be so among you; but whoever wishes to be great among you must be your servant, and whoever wishes to be first among you must be your slave; just as the Son of Man came not to be served but to serve, and to give his life a ransom for many. (Matthew 20:25-28)

Ultimately the best reason to be wary of status and privilege is how little they mattered to Jesus. "It will not be so among you"—the priorities of Jesus are to spend his privilege, not to conserve it. As Paul would put it, quoting one of the first Christian hymns, the one who was in the very form of God, the one who could have claimed ultimate status, the one who deserved all privilege, did not consider it something to be grasped, and emptied himself, taking the form of a servant. Did that mean he was not the Son of Man and Son of God? No. It was precisely because he was the true Son of Man, the true Image Bearer and the Icon of the true God that he had not the slightest interest in gripping tightly to status and privilege. Because he did not grasp them, they had no grip on him, and because he became last and servant of all, he is now highly exalted, Lord of all—the only one in heaven, on earth or under the earth who deserves his place in line.

## THE PEACE OF THE CITY

On that Friday in May 1992, I was on my way to a prayer meeting in the Bronx, the first of a whole weekend of gatherings for prayer around the city that had been planned long before the riots in Los Angeles. I got on the 7 train with my friend and host Mac Pier, a longtime servant of the church in New York City. In those days when gentrification barely reached the Upper West Side, on that afternoon when the whole city retreated behind boarded-up windows and closed gates, we were surely the only two white guys voluntarily taking a train to the Bronx. We arrived at a small Spanish-speaking Pentecostal church where the prayer meeting was to be held and found it packed with representatives of every one of the Bronx's nations and tongues.

What happened that night was one of the most extraordinary experiences of worship I ever expect to encounter this side of the new Jerusalem.

An outpouring of intercession, grief, hope and joy shook the rafters of the building—hour after hour of praise and prayer, song and shouting, dancing and weeping. In that building, apart from a few privileged guests, were the least, those without status, those who could not call 911 and expect the police to come, those with no enclaves of privilege to retreat to in the time of trouble. But they were not intending to retreat. They called out to God for the protection of their homes and neighborhoods and for the peace of their city. They praised the One who had made himself the friend of sinners and the servant of all. After the service was over they poured out into the empty streets, bearers of hope and joy in a frightened city.

That night on the eleven o'clock news, befuddled anchors talked to puzzled reporters on location in places like the Bronx, searching over their satellite uplinks for something newsworthy. The streets were quiet; there were no riots, there was no looting. "Well," one reporter said to her news desk that night, "all we can say tonight in New York is that people are praying."

There is a power loose in the world that those who grip their privilege and status will never know.

# EXPLORATION

## JOHN 13—JESUS, POWER AND PRIVILEGE

I t is not uncommon to hear preachers say that Jesus of Nazareth "gave up power," pointing out the ways that his life and death challenged the existing powers of his day. It is indeed true that Jesus taught and lived a life of complete nonviolence (toward his fellow human beings—he seems not to have objected to catching fish). When the forces of institutionalized violence concentrated all their fury on him at his trial and crucifixion,

> like a lamb that is led to the slaughter,
>> and like a sheep that before its shearers is silent,
> so he did not open his mouth. . . .
> although he had done no violence. (Isaiah 53:7, 9)

Jesus' silence before, and submission to, the unjust violence visited upon him is one of the most stunning parts of his whole story.

And yet the idea that Jesus "gave up power" would have been inconceivable to his first biographers and the early Christians who reflected on his life, death and resurrection. Precisely because they were witnesses to his resurrection after a violent death, the New Testament writers could no longer acquiesce to the idolatrous fiction that violence is the truest form of power. Instead, they had seen with their own eyes, and touched with their hands, the evidence that a much greater power was at work in the world than Rome could ever muster. And when they reflected back on the life of Jesus, from his extraordinary birth to his last night as a mortal man, what they remembered was his extraordinary power—his unpredictable, creative, compelling presence that both fulfilled the ancient prophecies of the anointed One and also defied and redefined all expectations of how that One would exercise his power.

Of all the Gospel writers, John is the one who most directly addresses the power that was at work in Jesus at every moment of his ministry. With exquisite precision and complexity John crafts a story of successively more and more powerful signs. Jesus son of Joseph from Nazareth is indeed, as Philip tells his brother Nathanael in the opening lines of the Gospel, "the one Moses wrote about in the Law, and about whom the prophets also wrote" (John 1:45 NIV), the one Nathanael identifies (after personally encountering Jesus' clairvoyant power) as "the Son of God" and "the King of Israel."

As John's story of this unlikely Son and King comes to its climax, the storyteller slows down time like a careful filmmaker, devoting more and more attention to the scenes in the days before Jesus' death. On the night before Jesus' arrest the pace slows even more as Jesus, gathered with his disciples around a table, brings his closest followers more deeply than before into the heart of his mission, with an action, a teaching and a prayer.

> During supper Jesus, knowing that the Father had given all things into his hands, and that he had come from God and was going to God, got up from the table, took off his outer robe, and tied a towel around himself. Then he poured water into a basin and began to wash the disciples' feet and to wipe them with the towel that was tied around him. (John 13:2-5)

As if to ward off any suggestion that Jesus is somehow losing his wits under the pressure of the moment, John places this unexpected deed in the broadest possible context. Jesus knows that, far from being powerless, he holds "all things" in his hands. He knows where (and Whom) he has come from. He knows where (and to Whom) he is going. In short, the action and passion that is about to follow is not the sign of someone who has lost power, but someone who has been given all power.

And what an action it is that John records. With a few quick motions, Jesus leaves his expected place at the center of attention and honor, disrobes and picks up the last item in the room that any of his disciples would have expected him to touch: the towel for washing guests' feet. Even today many cultures preserve the sense of shame that accompanied the feet in Jesus' day—the lowest part of the body, the one most covered in the grime of the world (far more grimy, in Jesus' day, than our modern sidewalks) and the most likely to smell of creaturely sweat and toil. To touch another person's feet was an act of profound subjugation, fit only for a slave or a supplicant. The feet were the antipodes of power, kept away from the table toward which all guests leaned, accorded the least attention and attended to by the least dignified. At a normal feast, some household slave would have performed the footwashing. That matter of personal hygiene would have been taken care of with as little ceremony and comment as happens in a modern household at dinner when someone leaves to use the toilet. Suddenly here was Jesus, disrobed, drawing everyone's attention to their feet.

It is no surprise that Peter interrupts Jesus' shameful and shocking progression around the table with an incredulous question: "Lord, are you going to wash my feet?" and then a furious protest: "You will never wash my feet!" (John 13:6, 8). Now we are witnessing a much more mundane form of power. Peter has set up an inevitable contest of wills, a zero-sum game. Either Jesus will win or Peter. Here are Weber's definitions of *Herrschaft* and *Macht* perfectly embodied. Which of Jesus or Peter has the ability to "secure obedience to definite commands"? Who has the ability to "overcome resistance"? This is power in the most ordinary sense of the word—the capacity to coerce another to obey.

And Jesus wins. Jesus is Peter's Teacher and Lord. Peter, for all his blustering, would lay down his life for him. So when Jesus replies, "Unless I wash you, you have no share with me," Peter changes his tune: "Lord, not my feet only but also my hands and my head!" (vv. 8-9). Jesus has won. He has overcome resistance and secured obedience. And Peter, in losing the argument, has won too—won a place at Jesus' table in his perplexing new kingdom.

As Jesus sits down, John gives one more reminder of his power. "Do you know what I have done to you?" Jesus asks. "You call me Teacher and Lord—and you are right, for that is what I am" (vv. 12-13). There is not an ounce here of false humility. There are no more powerful roles in these disciples' world than rabbi and *kyrios*—the titles given to Jewish leaders and the lordship ascribed to Caesar himself. Jesus claims them both. He wins direct contests of wills. He has come from God and is going to God. He is, John wants us to see, completely at home with power.

And we, reading this story millennia later, recognize the creative cultural power at work in it as well. Every Maundy Thursday, the night before Good Friday in the Western liturgical calendar, Christians around the world gather to wash one another's feet. Two thousand years after the Teacher and Lord knelt with a towel around his waist, his followers, servants and messengers continue to imitate his example. There is no act of culture-making power more extraordinary than creating a ritual, an act that continues to bear witness to truth from generation to generation, long after the first persons who experienced it lay in the dust of death. The persistence down to this day of the act Jesus performed at that table, and the acts from that night that the other Gospels report—taking, blessing, breaking and giving the bread and wine—is the ultimate test and sign of his power. In this moment, Jesus creates culture, forever transforming the meaning of towel, loaf and cup, forever altering the way teachers and masters will see their roles, and the way their students and servants will see them.

## THE END OF PRIVILEGE

There is no point in this story where Jesus gives up power—instead, it is the culmination and demonstration of his power. What Jesus gives up in this story is not power but privilege and status.

It was the privilege of the most powerful person in the room, after all, to never have to worry about feet being washed. When you were a respected rabbi, such things simply happened without your needing to lower yourself to the indignity of requesting them. Should the ritual of footwashing somehow be neglected by the servants attending the feast, it would have been the job of the least powerful guest present, making a quick and entirely subconscious calculation of status, to quickly take up the towel and perform the duty. (Anyone who has been in homes in any number of traditional cultures, or for that matter for a modern Super Bowl Sunday where the men sit watching the game while the women bring the food and clear the dishes, will know how taken for granted this calculation would have been. Most of those serving, let alone those served, would not even be aware that they had made it.) But it is precisely these calculations of status and these indicators of privilege that Jesus shows himself completely unconcerned with.

And when we begin to reflect on the life and ministry of Jesus, we find that this is a consistent pattern. Jesus is rarely if ever diffident about using his power, the power that allowed him to forgive and heal, proclaim and teach, feed thousands and calm storms. What he is not only diffident about, but positively averse to, is reaping the privilege that would so naturally be offered in the wake of these acts of power. After Jesus heals Peter's mother-in-law in Mark 1 and the entire village is gathering around her door, he goes off to a lonely place, prays and leaves town. After he has fed the thousands and the crowds are clamoring to make him king, he gets in a boat and goes to the Gentile country on the other side. After the crowds have acclaimed him with palm branches and shouts of "Hosanna to the Son of David," with more truth in their words than even they know, Jesus, "having looked around at everything," simply leaves the city for a night in a suburban home. He simply never accumulates privilege.

And Jesus consistently shows absolute indifference to status. This is not because he doubts or does not know his place as the Beloved Son of the Father—it is, in fact, because he *does* know his place. But Jesus "did not count equality with God something to be grasped." Even this ultimate status—the status which the serpent and every future idol dangles beguilingly in front of bewitched humanity—is not something the true Son of God needs to grip. Those who are preoccupied with status must constantly expend their energy on sorting out the status of those around them. But Jesus, completely unconcerned with his own rank or place in the pecking order, shows a corresponding lack of interest in associating with the "right sort" of people. He meets procurators and prostitutes, tax collectors and zealots, synagogue leaders and women with twelve years of disabling medical troubles, with precisely the same care and truthful attention. He never fails to honor the image of God in each of these daughters and sons; he never pays the slightest compliment to the exaggerated images and roles they play.

For those of us preoccupied with protecting our privilege and raising our status, this indifference of Jesus is terrifying. It prompts the kind of outburst that came from Peter. It is holy power, utterly purified, without an ounce of self-protection or self-regard. Jesus' only use of power was to create, never to protect himself or to exalt himself. Perhaps this is the deepest explanation of his nonviolence. Violence, even when used in justifiable self-defense, does nothing to restore, redeem or create. It only damages in return. And Jesus simply never had a thought except to restore, redeem and create a new community among whom power would be used always and only for flourishing. In such a community, privilege and status can only be disdained and discarded. They are distractions from the real calling of image bearers: to be fruitful and multiply, far as the curse is found.

As John prepares to tell this story, he tells us that Jesus, "having loved his own who were in the world, . . . loved them to the end" (John 13:1). The Messiah wrapped in a servant's grimy towel is not giving up power. He is restoring it to its original purpose, cleansed of its distortions—the power to love a lovely and loveless world to the uttermost. None of his power is reserved for carefully guarding privilege or meticulously accounting for status; every bit of it is poured into this one end.

**PART THREE**

# INSTITUTIONS AND
# CREATIVE POWER
### FROM GENERATION TO GENERATION

# THE GIFT OF INSTITUTIONS

There aren't many words less popular in our world than *institution*. We remember with horror when persons with mental illnesses or cognitive disabilities were "institutionalized," cut off from families and communities in a life that was less than life. Many people declare their appreciation for spirituality, but their distance from "institutional religion." Many of my own generational cohort, so-called Generation X, have avoided positions of institutional responsibility long after previous generations had settled into them, and until very recently I was one of them. The well-known Christian speaker and performance artist Rob Bell spoke for many of us when he rhetorically asked a group of pastors in October 2010, "Do you ever feel like you signed up for a revolution and ended up running a corporation?" Implicit in Bell's question was a deep suspicion of institutions—both in the ideal of being a radical revolutionary and in the horror of being a mere bureaucratic functionary. Perhaps it is not surprising that a year later, Bell left the church he founded for a less institutionally constrained life in the City of Angels.

But institutions are the only way that the gift of power can be fully expressed, because institutions are essential for flourishing.

*Institution* is the name that sociologists have given to any deeply and persistently organized pattern of human behavior. "A football" is a cultural artifact, but "football" is a cultural institution: a rich and complex system of behaviors, beliefs, patterns and possibilities that can be handed on from one generation to the next. And it is within institutions, in this broad sense of the word, that our most significant human experiences take place. Institutions are at the heart of culture making, which means they are at the heart of human flourishing and the comprehensive flourishing of creation that we call *shalom*. Without institutions, in fact, human beings would be as feeble and futile as a flat football.

Institutions create and distribute power, the ability to make something of the world. The game of football—the institution—is an opportunity for kinds of image bearing that would be impossible in a world without it. When a quarterback spots an open wide receiver far down the field and throws a perfectly targeted pass, we jump out of our seats and cheer (or, if we're rooting for the other team, shake our heads in resigned admiration) because we have just witnessed a particular kind of flourishing: human beings performing astonishing feats of strength, agility, discernment and foresight under tremendous pressure.

Yet this moment of flourishing would mean little without the institution that surrounds it—the defensive and offensive lines contesting to block or advance the pass, the officials to certify fair play, the coaches who helped design and perfect the play, and the crowd to witness it, cheer, invest it with significance and cherish it in memory. Without all these other players that remarkable pass would be much less remarkable, and it would not be remarked. It would not be noted and rehearsed and replayed so that all its significance can be celebrated. And so it is not just the quarterback nor just the receiver who is invested with power in a given play—all the other "players," whether they are on the field or on the couch, are engaged in particular kinds of making something of the world. They are able to exercise their own particular culture-making power only because there are others, past and present, who have made the game what it is.

So on a given midwinter Sunday afternoon in America, millions of people take up various image-bearing roles through the institution of football. If the institution disappeared, even if it left behind all of its artifacts, the distinctive kinds of power that the institution makes possible would also disappear, and Sunday afternoons would be a lot more boring. *Boredom*, after all, is simply a word for frustrated image bearing. We are made to exercise our power creating and cultivating in the world, and when we find ourselves with nothing to create or cultivate we are bored, dissatisfied for very good reason. Ironically, *institution* is a word that itself sounds boring, suggesting a place where little creativity or cultivation can be found, but in the fullest sense of the word, institutions are the environments where image bearers flourish in all their astonishing variety. Healthy institutions are the ultimate antidote to boredom; they are the context within which our lives become vivid, meaningful and alive.

This does not mean that institutions are always beneficial—quite the contrary. Just as institutions make image bearing possible, so they also make possible, and perpetuate in the deepest and most lasting ways, the twin distortions of idolatry and injustice. Nor are all institutions equally beneficial or harmful. Football is a game of strength and aggression, a kind of stylized warfare, but in some societies at some times, equally elaborate institutions including officials, stadia and cheering crowds gathered around combat that was literally mortal. Surely football is an improvement over the gladiatorial games. But by occupying so many millions on a given Sunday afternoon, football may also crowd out other institutions that might be far more suited to comprehensive flourishing.

If we want to make creative and conscious choices about the institutions we invest our lives in—and that we allow to invest our lives with meaning and power—we will have to decide whether we believe they produce image bearing or merely idolatry and injustice. But whatever we decide, we will have to choose some institution. We may leave the institution of the church for the institution of Hollywood, or go in the exact opposite direction, but we are very unlikely to flourish, or create opportunities for others to flourish, if we try to avoid institutions altogether.

So if we want our power to be used for the comprehensive flourishing of the world, we will have to understand institutions: how they function, how they fail, and how we can be agents of their health and renewal.

## THE FOOTBALL, THE STADIUM, THE PLAYERS AND THE GAME

Institutions have four essential elements. Take the game of (American) football. It depends on particular *artifacts*—the football itself, helmets and pads, and upright goalposts, just to name some of the most distinctive ones. Nearly every fully developed institution, in fact, has an artifact or two that are so closely associated with it that they can serve as symbols for the entire game. A football, a football helmet or a set of goalposts are all that Americans need to invoke the whole complex institution called football. These artifacts are produced in profusion for all the different places the game is played, from Pee Wee football and backyard pickup games to the Super Bowl.

A second kind of cultural good, though, is also part of the institution of football, and it is found in smaller numbers while possessing greater significance: the stadiums where major football games are played. Like the smaller-scale artifacts, these are tangible results of human culture making, but they are distinctive in their scale—larger by orders of magnitude— and in their role, which is providing the *arena* within which the game is played with the greatest intensity and significance. An arena provides the context where all the participants in a football game, not just players but coaches, crew, referees, broadcasters and fans, can participate most fully and wholeheartedly, and where the artifacts associated with the game are used most skillfully and meaningfully.

The institution of football requires a third kind of cultural good, this one entirely intangible: the *rules of the game*. These may be written down in tangible form in a rulebook, but they exist primarily in the minds and expertise of the participants in the institution (not just the players, coaches and referees, but the crowd as well). They describe what is allowed and what is forbidden, what is rewarded and what is punished.

Finally, the *rules* prescribe *roles*, the different parts played by different people within the institution. Each role has its own freedom and responsibility; each role makes something distinctive of the world. And the rules describe or at least suggest what it means to be a flourishing participant, one who is fulfilling the expectations of their role—for example, the unwritten but ironclad rule that at the end of the game, one player will be selected as Most Valuable.

*Artifacts, arenas, rules* and *roles*—these are the essential ingredients that make an institution. In games like football, all of these are vividly defined. In fact, *game* is the name for a kind of institution where all four ingredients can be specified very precisely. We can know exactly when a player is in and out of bounds; we know exactly what constitutes winning; most of the roles (including the fans!) can be identified by distinctive clothing or labels. Other human institutions are much less well defined. But these four ingredients are present even when they are not laid out so clearly as in football. In fact, once you start to think of institutions as persistent collections of artifacts, arenas, rules and roles, you start to see them everywhere and realize that almost all human life takes place within the elaborate "games" that institutions make possible.

So, the care of human health is an institution, the institution of medicine. Its artifacts, in modern Western culture, include thermometers and surgical instruments, blood pressure cuffs and white coats. In other cultures the artifacts may include acupuncture needles or rare and magical talismans. Its arenas, in the Western context, are the buildings that house the practice of medicine, especially doctor's offices, pharmacies and hospitals. And medicine has rules, lots of rules. Some are written down, like the instructions that accompany a medication. Some are clearly communicated in the course of training, like the proper procedure for diagnosing a complaint of chest pain. Some are largely implicit but just as powerful, like the expectation that patients will undress for a physical exam. Finally, medicine has roles. The doctor has one set of responsibilities and freedoms, the nurse has another, the pharmacist has still another, and patients have their own role to play. It is the convergence of these artifacts, arenas, rules and roles that make the institution of medicine what it is, for better and worse.

Interestingly, often these ingredients can be separated from one another and the institution will still function, at least to some extent. You can take away the football arena and play the game of football in a back yard, and it is still truly a game of football. You could even take away as central an artifact as the football itself: if a group arranged themselves in two facing lines on an unmarked field and one player in the center hiked a ball made of old rags to someone standing behind them, who then handed it off or passed it to one of their teammates, anyone familiar with the game would recognize it as football. Just the constellation of rules and roles would be enough to make it such a game.

But not all human institutions can be so easily separated from their distinctive artifacts and arenas. The practice of Western medicine requires an array of instruments—artifacts—that make it effective. Even highly trained doctors who have been inducted into the rules and roles of medicine find that their power is limited without access to drugs or diagnostic and therapeutic instruments. They may find themselves nearly as helpless as anyone else if a medical emergency occurs during an airplane flight or on a trip to a distant country where the artifacts of Western medicine are not available. Likewise, artifacts can be all but useless without the proper arena: the surgical sterility of a hospital or well-managed office is the only thing that makes it safe to perform any number of otherwise routine medical procedures. And without the training in rules and roles that medical professionals receive, even a hospital well stocked with medical equipment would be of very little use in caring for the sick.

It is only when artifacts, arena, rules and roles come together that we have a truly viable institution. For only the distinctive combination of artifacts, arena, rules and roles can sustain an institution on the large scale of shared culture. A pickup game in the backyard is football, but if that were all there was to football it would not be the force in American life that it is today. That requires equipment and stadiums, much more highly defined rules, and more differentiated roles. Indeed, the way that cultural change becomes widely available and influential is through a process of *institutionalization*, in which cultural innovation becomes available to society through the creation of artifacts, arenas, rules and roles.

Institutionalization can happen very slowly. The creation of modern medicine took generations and traces its roots back over two thousand years (as the ancient artifact of the Hippocratic caduceus, the symbol of medicine, reminds us). Or, especially in an age of media, it can happen with astonishing speed. Think about the institutionalization of what was initially called "The Facebook," a site for students at Harvard College to share photos, short updates and the all-important "relationship status" with their classmates. In 2004 Facebook was little more than a cultural artifact, albeit one generating intense interest at Harvard and the handful of other campuses where it was available. But when it opened in 2006 to anyone over thirteen with an email address, it rapidly became an arena as well—a context within which countless games of "social networking" were played.

Along the way both written and unwritten rules developed for the players in the game, some of which were hammered out through controversy and conflict between the Facebook programmers and their users, others of which simply emerged as millions of people sorted out their relationships with their newly connected "friends." Other media and institutional authorities helped in the negotiation of these rules, initially so unclear, by exploring the difficult edge cases. Should high school teachers "friend" their students? How about the other way around? What kinds of pictures should a fourteen-year-old, or twenty-four-year-old, make visible to their parents, future employers or the public?

And then another phase in Facebook's institutionalization began, as it launched its "initial public offering" on the stock market, joining an arena (in this case, a market) with its own artifacts, rules and roles that helps establish businesses as institutions in a global economy.

At each step in Facebook's institutionalization, power was created and redistributed—"redistributed" because there have always been social networks, which Facebook visualized and profited from, but also "created" because Facebook gave its users, and its owners, new artifacts, arenas, rules and roles within which to create and cultivate, as well as perpetuate various idolatries and injustices. The institutionalization of Facebook did more than simply rearrange existing forms of power. It created new power, including the financial form of power that we call wealth. There is more power for image bearing in the world, as well as more power for idolatry and injustice, because a cultural artifact called "The Facebook" became the institution called "Facebook."

## ABRAHAM, ISAAC AND JACOB

Institutions allow culture to spread across the world. The other football, the one Americans insist on calling soccer, is one of the most visible global institutions, played on every continent with roughly the same rules and roles, its arenas producing some of the planet's most visible heroes. If part of the divine commission to image bearers is to "be fruitful and multiply," institutions allow the fruits of their image bearing to multiply and reach far more people than a single individual or even single community ever could.

But institutions do something even more remarkable. They make it possible for culture to spread across time, over generations of human history. When a set of artifacts, arenas, rules and roles can be passed from

one generation to another, and then to another, the process of institutionalization is truly complete. The most powerful institutions can last for
dozens of generations relatively unchanged, fading into the background
and sinking deep into the collective cultural subconsciousness. They
simply are taken for granted as the way the world works. Language is one
of the most persistent human institutions, with its collection of artifacts
(words, books, idioms, clichés), arenas (schools, theaters), rules
(grammar), and roles (in many languages, there are different word endings
for different genders, or different forms of address for close friends and
distant acquaintances). No human being invents language—instead, it
simply is the part of the world we inherit, a rich and inexhaustible world
built on the past.

How long does it take before we can consider a cultural pattern an institution? I would suggest that the minimum number of generations is three.
For it is the third generation of any cultural pattern who truly grow up in a
world where the artifacts, arenas, rules and roles of that institution can be
taken for granted. Take the institution of telephone communication.
There were no telephones in the rural communities of my grandparents'
childhoods, and my parents remember the early, awkward days of hand-
cranked phones and party lines. But I have never lived in a house without
a telephone. It is simply part of my world, along with all the patterns of life
it sustains. Meanwhile, I have lived through the introduction of the mobile
phone (I vividly remember my first experience placing a call from a "car
phone"), but even my own children cannot conceive of a world without
them. My grandchildren are likely never to hear a "dial tone." They will be
the third generation of mobile telephony, and, never having known any
other kind, they will be the first for whom the mobile telephone is a cultural institution rather than a novel cultural artifact.

Could this be the reason the Hebrew Bible so often describes the
people of Israel as the family of "Abraham, Isaac, and Jacob"? Why are the
people of Israel so often named by three generations, not just one? Because it took no less than three generations for the promises of God to
Abraham to sink deeply enough into the memory and imagination of his
descendants to be transmittable across future generations—deeply
enough, indeed, that that original promise survives even to our own day,

countless generations later. Of course, the story of Israel played itself out over several dozen generations in the span of the Old Testament. But it is telling that Genesis, the book of "beginnings," ends with the death of Jacob, the third generation.

In the span of time recorded from Genesis 12 to Genesis 50, Abraham and his descendants acquire crucial *artifacts* that will anchor their identity as the people of "the Most High God"—perhaps most notably, the practice of circumcision that marks the males of each generation, setting this distinctive nation apart from the pagan nations that will always surround them. We may also suppose that even in this early period the stories we now have recorded in Genesis 1–11—the primordial narrative of the Most High God's dealing with his creation—began to be formalized and passed on. They also acquired distinctive names, Abram renamed as Abraham, Jacob renamed as Israel, and the decisive encounters with God that gave rise to those names.

In this same time, Abraham's family goes from being one of many small bands of nomads in the ancient Near East to a "nation." Indeed, a pagan empire, in this case Egypt, becomes the *arena* within which God's people acquire a clear identity as a people. (Not for the last time: exile in Babylon would be the crucible of a new stage of Israel's identity, and both Jesus of Nazareth and his apostles would come face to face with the imperial functionaries of Rome.) The rise of Joseph to power in Egypt allows his extended family (seventy direct descendants of Jacob, according to Exodus 1:5) not only to survive a famine but to establish themselves as a "nation," enough so that generations later, when Joseph's warm relations with Pharaoh are forgotten and his descendants have been reduced to slavery, they have not assimilated but instead retain their distinctive patterns of language and worship.

Over the three Genesis generations, rules and roles begin to emerge—most of all concerning how this nation would relate to their God. The ancient Near East was full of rules and roles for the worship of tribal deities, but already in Genesis the Most High God is rewriting the rules and upending the roles that the peoples around Abraham's tribe took for granted. The first generations also see intense conflict to define the rules and roles of how Abraham's children will relate to one another and the sometimes hostile people around them, from Abraham's tendency to lie to powerful protectors at crucial moments, to the simmering conflict between Jacob and Esau, to Sarah's cruelty to Hagar, to the final act, Joseph's betrayal by his brothers, which brings all the scheming dysfunction of Abraham's family to the boiling point. All of these conflicts embody a contest for the rules and roles that will define the people of Israel, and they are brought to a cathartic climax when the unrecognizable Joseph confronts and then embraces his brothers, implicitly naming all of this multigenerational family's mistrust and deceit and yet also forgiving it with the redemptive words, "You meant it for evil, but God meant it for good." The final chapters of Genesis establish the deepest rule of all: in spite of their brokenness and betrayal of one another and God himself, the Most High God will never fail to bless them and rescue them, even from themselves.

## FOUR INGREDIENTS PLUS THREE GENERATIONS

The recipe for an institution, then, is four ingredients plus three generations: artifacts, arenas, rules and roles that are passed on to the founding generation's children's children. Fail to follow this recipe by neglecting the transmission over generations and you are likely to leave little of cultural significance behind—at best, a few mysterious artifacts and hazy, nostalgic memories. Likewise, fail to follow this recipe by neglecting one of the four essential ingredients, and enduring impact is equally unlikely, because only the fourfold combination of artifacts, arenas, rules and roles is strong enough to sustain a cultural innovation through time. Sustainable institutions are built on highly distinctive, meaningful and valuable artifacts that make something worthwhile of the world; they find a home in uniquely suitable arenas; they transmit a clear set of "rules" about what counts as a faithful performance of the institution's story; and they provide a range of roles for different people to play. Institutions that fail in one of these dimensions tend to diminish in significance and often fade from influence altogether.

The most durable institution in culture is the one that gives us generations in the first place: the family. The biological process of the generation of children is natural (we share it with all creatures that reproduce sexually), but the family is a cultural institution of great depth and staying power. As far back as we can see in the human story, human beings have cherished a cultural institution that makes meaning out of the biological reality of parents and children. Of course, the family has taken on myriad forms in the great variety of human cultures. But in every culture it is a central institution—because without this institution, no culture survives very long.

So every culture has essential family *artifacts*, cultural goods unique to the institution that come to stand for its meaning. Not all of them are homebound: adorning countless cubicles and taxicabs across the world are family pictures, portraits of workers' parents, children and relatives that remind us that there is someone with a deeper claim on their life than their customers or employers. In some places, pictures of parents and ancestors will be adorned with garlands of flowers or set in a niche with a stick of incense. Family celebrations like Mother's Day, Father's Day and birthdays have rituals and artifacts of their own.

The family also has its distinctive *arena*—the home. The home is the environment where the unique intimacy, dependence, cooperation and conflict of family takes place. Father, mother, child and sibling can all be strictly natural roles; everyone has a biological father or mother whether or not they ever lived with them in a home. But to move from the strictly biological to the richly cultural, these roles almost always have to be played out in an arena, and no arena is quite like the home for its intensity of interaction, where human beings share bed and board day after day and night after night, making a life together over years or decades even as work, school, hobbies and friendships shift and change. It is in the home that we most often learn the fundamental *rules* of being a family member and for that matter a human being—what we eat and how we cook, how we address our elders and how we play with children, what counts as success at work and what we do with our leisure, what topics we talk about openly and what topics are never to be discussed. Most of these rules are learned far before we know we are learning them, and so homes embed us in culture before we know it, shaping us at the most formative time of our lives, and involving us in the shaping of others at the most formative and dependent seasons of their lives.

The family creates an environment for human beings to play multiple roles. Father, mother, child; brother or sister (including the roles assigned to the eldest, older, younger and youngest); grandparents; parents-in-law and children-in-law; uncles, aunts and cousins—any given member of the family may play several of these roles at once, and may play most of them over the course of a lifetime. Associated with each are explicit and unwritten rules and expectations, and even specific artifacts (such as wedding rings for the father and mother).

Obviously, for all sorts of reasons nearly every family departs from the standard type in some way. In many families the rules or roles are scrambled by events like divorce or separation, premature death, as well as the slower but steadier dislocations caused by children growing up and parents growing old. This does not necessarily mean that the institution is redefined by these events; everyone involved in the institution may still ascribe to the same ideal artifacts, arenas, rules and roles. A "homeless" family may still hope to move into a home one day. Children who lose their fathers or mothers to death, divorce or even the parents' own neglect can still hunger for a person to fill that role.

Cohabiting couples in the United States may seem to be rewriting the rules, but usually at least one member cherishes the hope that the relationship will eventually turn into a marriage and family. At the turn of the twenty-first century many young adults in the West, especially in economically marginal communities and occupations, were delaying marriage, replacing it with cohabitation or single parenting, until they could afford all the artifacts associated with the institution—so that the institution was reinforced almost as much in the breach as in the observance. The movement for gay rights, one of the most consequential cultural innovations in Western culture, only truly gained widespread momentum in America when it became identified with the cause of gay marriage; that is, when it was presented as a progressive but also deeply conservative way of fulfilling the human calling to family. Indeed, what makes institutions so powerful in human cultures is the way they shape our aspirations and hopes even when our performance of them departs dramatically from the traditional ideal. The backyard quarterback might not be able to last for two minutes on an NFL field, but that doesn't mean that he doesn't have the Super Bowl in mind as he throws a pass. In the same way, many of us are shaped as much by the family we were taught to long for, but never had, as by the actual flawed and fragile homes we know. Such is the power of institutions to define what human beings are for and how they flourish.

## SEX AND INSTITUTIONS

Institutions are essential for flourishing. Flourishing is not just a matter of multiplication; it also requires differentiation. The lilies of the field are clothed in the glory not of uniformity, even glorious uniformity, but glorious variation within their common form. Lilies on a summer hillside in Palestine do not just multiply in an orderly grid, they *teem*. Indeed, one of the remarkable consequences of sexual reproduction, which mixes genes from two parents in unpredictable and unrepeatable combinations, is that it guarantees teeming rather than just multiplication. No child is exactly like its parents, and the more we learn about the influence of the environment on genetic expression, the more we understand why even twins whose DNA is identical can turn out to be subtly but truly different in personality, gifts and calling. Those who bear the image of the Creator God are meant to teem. When the Creator commands his image bearers to "be fruitful and multiply," this is not a command to fill the world with clones or mechanical replicas, but to fill the world with marvelously different refractions of the image.

Sexual reproduction guarantees biological teeming, and therefore flourishing; and institutions make possible cultural teeming and therefore flourishing. They create and preserve the conditions for abundant differentiation, not just in our physical or natural form but the roles we play in the world culture has made. In an institution of any complexity the roles of the various participants are differentiated, or to put it another way, different persons in different roles have different kinds of power. In the game of soccer only the goalies have the "power" to use their hands. Only the referee can call a foul. Only the players and referees can be on the field while the game is being played. Only the coach can decide which players are sent into the game or taken out of it. Only the crowd can chant insulting slogans without running the risk of a technical foul. (That may not seem to all of us like an essential part of the flourishing of soccer, but if nothing else, the chants of British soccer fans are a reminder of the way that creativity bursts forth in the most unlikely places.)

This differentiation is essential to the existence and flourishing of the institution itself. Soccer would be impossible if twenty thousand people in a stadium all tried to play on the field, all had the authority to start and stop play, and so forth. But differentiation is also essential to human flourishing—because institutions at their best create a host of roles suited to the different abilities, interests and stages of human life.

So the institution of the family, by making room for various roles, gives us opportunities to explore an abundant range of possibilities that would be unavailable if we all, say, grew hydroponically, isolated monads with no essential roles and responsibilities. Even a single role—say, my role as a son—has required me to develop different capacities at different times. In childhood I learned and practiced dependence and obedience; in adolescence I learned how to balance bonds with friends and loyalty to family; in young adulthood I learned to include my parents in crucial moments of pain and joy, along with decisions about where to live and whom to marry; later in my adulthood I will, if my own parents' experiences with my grandparents are any guide, have to learn to bear with new infirmities and limitations, and help them navigate through choices about health in the last season of life. And one day I will learn to say goodbye, mourn and keep alive memories of two image bearers that would otherwise be lost to the world.

Son or daughter is the one role that every human being plays in one way or another. Each stage of this role, if entered into wholeheartedly and boldly, requires and forms new capacities in us. But most of us play other roles in our family that also stretch and shape us. As an uncle I play with my nieces and nephews in a different way than I do with my own children, and in a different way again than I do with the children of close friends. In this abundance of roles is the opportunity to explore the astonishing complexity and diversity inherent in becoming an image bearer. And the institution of family also makes room for even more complexity and diversity by yoking together men and women, different both biologically and in the way we play our roles, so that I get to witness and support fellow image bearers as they play roles—wife, mother, daughter—that I will never be able to play. Only as we take our place within a highly differentiated institution like the family do we see all the range of possibilities that must be explored and expressed for image bearing to flourish.

To be sure, not all institutions lend themselves to the image of wild-flowers teeming on a hillside. The opening ceremonies of the 2008 Summer Olympics in Beijing, planned with extraordinary precision, often seemed like a study in uniformity, featuring a cast of thousands who had been drilled to eliminate any expression of individual difference, a vision of the "harmonious society" to which China's leaders aspire. To some observers this uniformity was thrilling; to others, perhaps especially in the West, it was chilling. We Westerners are uneasy with a society that so relentlessly polishes away the differences between individuals, subordinating them to the interests of the state.

Yet a knee-jerk rejection of official China's vision of "harmony" should be tempered by two further thoughts. First, the very differences in culture that made the Beijing opening ceremonies in 2008 look so different from the London opening ceremonies in 2012 are themselves part of the "teeming" of image bearing. Certain kinds of human flourishing require a high degree of coordination and conformity, and the cultures that especially value that level of uniformity have kept alive an aspect of image-bearing diversity that would otherwise be lost.

There are kinds of flourishing that actually require practiced uniformity. A solo violinist can and must explore the individual capacities of her instrument and her own interpretation of a given piece, eliciting surprise and discovery in even the most familiar musical score, but the violinists in a symphony orchestra must play with strictly unified intonation, articulation and bowing to achieve the pinnacle of orchestral sound. One of the most essential institutions for cultural flourishing in the European Middle Ages was the monastic movement, whose members dressed alike and took vows of obedience—and yet out of these highly uniform communities came the cultural conservation and creativity that Thomas Cahill could say (with a little hyperbole) "saved civilization." To a Westerner, the harmony prized by official China may look more like monotony, but it may also be that China is keeping alive human possibilities that can easily be lost in the chaos of individualism.

Indeed, while all flourishing requires teeming, it also requires certain kinds of consistency and order reflected in Genesis's celebratory words, "God created the great creatures of the sea and every living thing with which the water teems, ... *according to their kinds*" (Genesis 1:21 NIV, italics added). The teeming of the world takes place within forms, "according to their kinds," that give structure, rhythm and patterns to the world's creatures. True shalom, comprehensive flourishing, mirrors the pattern of the Trinity itself, in which there is both unity and diversity. The choice between teeming and order, diversity and unity, is a false choice. True abundant life is found where "the one" and "the many" meet in "the three." Healthy institutions provide the ordered context in which surprise and diversity can flourish, but they also provide the diverse and varied environment that makes order healthy rather than repressive.

## THE GIFT OF UNEQUAL POWER

The different roles and rules found in any institution distribute power, the ability to make something of the world, but they almost never distribute power equally, in either quantity or quality. The soloist in a concerto or the striker on the soccer field has a unique kind of power, based on a mysterious combination of innate talent, ferocious personal discipline, and the decisions of others—including those of us in the crowd—to grant them the opportunity to use their abilities in such a singular way. Toward the end of the first movement of many classical concertos, the entire orchestra stops playing, the conductor puts down the wand, and the soloist is given the freedom to play an extended, virtuosic "cadenza" unlike anything played by any other instrumentalist that evening.

Almost by definition, institutions can grant certain individuals an unequal quantity of power. The striker receives more passes while in scoring position than anyone else on the team—that is what being the striker means. In many churches the pastor, often equipped with a special device I have come to call the Wireless Headset of Authority, will talk, uninterrupted, for thirty minutes or more, while it is entirely possible that the average person in the congregation will not say a single word. It's not hard to figure out who has the power in any large gathering in our mediated culture: they are the ones with a microphone, their image projected larger than life above the crowd.

There are at least two ways of looking at this inequality. We are right to wonder whether granting so few people so much power is good for them, let alone the rest of us—whether it contributes to comprehensive flourishing. The best test of any institution, and especially of any institution's roles and rules for using power, is *whether everyone flourishes* when everyone indwells their roles and plays by the rules, or whether only a few of the participants experience abundance and growth.

Clearly, in many institutions the unequal distribution of power is not gift but theft—stealing from image bearers their capacity to bear the image in fruitful, multiplying, teeming ways and granting a small minority the pleasure of exercising their talents or merely strutting their stuff. The granting of the power of amplification to "worship teams" in American Christianity has done more than anything since the Protestant Reformation to undermine congregational song. Once Protestants were known for their lively and joyful corporate singing, but today in many of our largest and most imitated churches the only music worth admiring comes from multithousand-watt sound systems while the vast majority of image bearers in the room sing weakly or not at all. Who can doubt that when power is concentrated in the hands (or voices) of a few, the total amount of image bearing in the institution often diminishes rather than flourishes?

And yet not all unequal power prevents flourishing. In fact, sometimes unequal distribution is *essential* to flourishing. This is the essential insight in Paul's language of "spiritual gifts"—particular kinds of power that when properly used "build up the body." While there is a kind of amplified worship leadership that is merely self-serving and sucks the life out of corporate worship, there are individuals and worship teams that have the genuine gift of turning amplified music into an occasion for total praise shared by the whole community. And equally to the point, many or most of us in the congregation would *not* flourish if a microphone were placed a centimeter from our mouths or a guitar were put in our hands, nor would our fellow church members. As a worship musician I have worked hard to cultivate the power to play the piano, and my experience is that when I do so prayerfully and excellently, the music of the people flourishes, but the same would certainly not be true if you put me behind a drum set.

The truth is that no matter how distorted it can become, the unequal distribution of power in institutions is essential to the gift that institutions bring. Certain kinds of flourishing are only possible if we grant individuals outsized proportions of certain kinds of power. And when that power is handled in image-bearing ways, it can lead to comprehensive flourishing of a kind that would be unreachable otherwise. *Some* of the American enthusiasm for spectator sports may be the result of failed image bearing—fathers who should be playing touch football with their children in the back yard instead of eating pretzels and gaining weight while they yell at a screen. Some, but not all. There is a kind of flourishing that is only available in a stadium with thousands of others, watching people at the brief height of their abilities take tremendous risks and occasionally triumph. We leave these experiences hopeful, astonished and ideally more empowered for our own lives.

We should be neither incurable romantics nor incurable cynics about our institutions, but at their best they make possible experiences that give human beings the closest taste we ever get to the glory that waits to be revealed fully in God's very good creation. The healthiest institutions, indeed, make it possible to exercise even terrifying amounts of power without becoming captive to idolatry and injustice, because they surround those unique power bearers with artifacts, arenas, rules and image bearers in other roles who hold them accountable to their responsibility for comprehensive flourishing, not private thriving.

And it is also true that *every* role in human institutions comes with certain kinds of power that others do not possess. The crowd at a soccer game is free *not* to play soccer—something that is not true of the players, not if they want to stay in the game. Members of the crowd may watch intently or stand and cheer, but they are also perfectly free to check their email on their smartphone or leave the stadium altogether. I can flourish in certain ways at a game precisely because I do *not* have to be on the field. As someone who frequently wears the Wireless Headset of Authority, I also know just how great a gift it is to sit attentively and listen to someone who has put in hours or years of preparation to communicate something that I need to hear in order to flourish.

And we should never forget that the most basic power in any institution is the power to distribute power. This power is *always* shared. The crowd makes the game, and the stars of the game, just as much as do the referees or the coaches. No crowd, no stars. And this too is a function of image bearing. Even in the most oppressive environments, the relentless human impulse toward image bearing can assert itself, even in the face of deadly force, as happened in 2011's "Arab Spring," 1989's protests in Tiananmen Square, the marches in the American South of the 1960s, and back through every era of history. Ultimately, every member of any human institution bears some power and some responsibility for its flourishing. Our best leaders and our most admired celebrities, along with our most feared tyrants and despots, only have their unequal power as long as the image bearers in their institutions grant it to them. All of us have a stake, and a choice, in whether the artifacts, arenas, rules and roles of our institutions bring bane or blessing to their inhabitants and to the world we are meant to tend and keep.

## THE POSTERITY GOSPEL

Even an institution as central as the family can be lost if its essential artifacts, arenas, rules and roles are disrupted over several generations. In our own time the most dramatic example may be China, where the state-sponsored One Child policy, even though it has been unevenly enforced and recently relaxed, has disrupted centuries-old rules and roles, and where sex-selective abortion has produced a generation with tens of millions more men than women. Institutions, like cultures, are amazingly fragile things. In a few short decades, everything Chinese families once thought they knew about what it meant to be a parent or child has been turned upside down, leaving a new generation to scramble to construct new environments that might preserve the possibility of flourishing. Similar developments, less dramatically coercive but no less far-reaching in their effects, have overtaken the advanced industrial economies of Japan and Western Europe, which face an unprecedented, upside-down demographic pyramid with far more elders than children.

When the institution of the family breaks down in this way, there are two options. Either people will find a way to refound the institution from scratch, creating novel artifacts, arenas, rules and roles, or, given how difficult it is to reinvent such a deeply rooted institution as the family, other institutions will take its place, however inadequately. The corporation, the state or the army acquire new power to provide the shelter and direction for human flourishing that the family once provided, or that task can be turned over to the mass-mediated consumer society itself, as seen in the astonishing phenomenon of Japan's *hikikomori*, the hundreds of thousands of young men who close themselves into their bedrooms and live virtually their whole lives through video games, comic books and the Internet.

The greatest risk to human flourishing, then, is not institutionalization but the loss of institutions. In our time we have seen the rise of the "prosperity gospel," which in its crassest forms promises quick wealth in mechanical proportion to faith. But the prosperity gospel has not only a thin and unbiblical understanding of wealth (which in Scripture is never a private matter but an occasion for blessing for whole communities, not to mention the fruit and source of justice)—it has a thin and unbiblical understanding of *time*. In the biblical mindset, prosperity that does not last is not true prosperity at all. The only biblical prosperity gospel is a *posterity* gospel—the promise that generation after generation will know the goodness of God through the properly stewarded abundance of God's world.

Institutions are the way the teeming abundance of human creativity and culture are handed on to future generations. So posterity, not just prosperity, is the promise of God to Abraham: countless descendants and blessing poured out on entire nations not yet born. Posterity, not just prosperity, is God's promise to David, a succession of sons in his line on the throne. And posterity was what the average Israelite prayed for as well—"may you see your children's children!"—a wish that before death one would see the evidence that shalom and abundance would continue in one's own line after death. There is nothing quick about shalom. True shalom endures.

One of the great tragedies of the church in America is how many of our most creative leaders poured their energies into creating forms of church life that served just a single generation. Even when these efforts were built around something larger than a single personality, they were doomed to seem dated and "irrelevant" even to the children of their founders. Perhaps a new generation of leaders will arise who want to build for posterity, to plant seeds that will take generations to bear fruit, to nurture forms of culture that will be seen as blessings by our children's children. If we are serious about flourishing, across space and through time, we will be serious about institutions.

# 10

## PRINCIPALITIES, POWERS AND BROKEN INSTITUTIONS

I am writing these words while a recording of J. S. Bach's cantata "O heilges Geist und Wasserbad" plays in the background. This particular recording is quite a complex cultural artifact, the product of three centuries simultaneously: the cantata was written in 1715, recorded in 1976, and played on my computer using the music-streaming service Spotify, which was invented in 2008. And I have chosen it, strangely enough, because as a cultural artifact it is half, or maybe three-quarters, dead.

Bach's cantata is partly dead—to me—because it is sung in German, a language I do not speak or understand. This turns out to be a useful quality for background music. Like many writers, I cannot concentrate on crafting my own words when someone is singing English lyrics, so someone singing in an unintelligible language—a "game" I have never learned—is just the ticket. But of course this means that much of the original significance of this cantata is lost to me as I listen. All that remains is the music itself, a glorious remainder to be sure, but nothing like the original composition in a setting where both music and meaning flourished together.

And for many modern Americans, not just the lyrics but the music as well is practically dead. For the music is its own kind of game with rules and roles, and in the case of Bach's baroque music some of the rules are especially complex. When a bass sings the syllables "vo-hihn" over and over, the game being played is not just the German word *wohin?* but a musical game of repetition that would have been full of meaning to its original listeners. I have been inducted into this musical game, so I can appreciate it, but many of my neighbors would find it merely puzzling. They know the rules of the game of modern pop or hip-hop, but the rules and roles of Bach's musical world are lost to them. Cut off from the structures that gave it musical and lyrical meaning, Bach's carefully crafted cantata is doubly lost.

This cantata is near death in yet another way, for what I am hearing is very far from the way it was written to be heard. The cantata I hear is presented as a single, continuous work of six movements—a strictly musical performance. But its original context was neither a concert hall nor a recording studio, but a church at a particular place and time. Bach wrote it for a service held on Trinity Sunday, 1715, in the German city of Weimar, probably in the court chapel where he was the "Konzertmeister." Within the halls of that chapel the cantata of the day would have been combined with Scripture readings, a sermon and the celebration of the Eucharist. Those present for that original "performance" would have included not just instrumentalists and singers but clergy and a congregation, rustling and probably coughing in the pews. When I listen to the beautiful but disembodied music that comes from a pair of speakers in my basement office, flanking a glowing rectangle that holds these very words, I can easily forget the context of worship that would have made Bach's choice of tunes and text so alive to his original hearers—nor, for that matter, do I have any hint of the institutional context of power and privilege, status and prestige, that suffused a court chapel full of men and women dressed in the robes of the local nobility.

When artifacts are shorn from their original context of institutions and structures—whether a cantata used as background music or a football included in some futuristic archaeological exhibit—something essential is lost. (One Amazon reviewer of a recording of the *St. Matthew Passion*, a work of fierce tension and emotion that is perhaps the greatest of all Bach's choral works, wrote innocently that it was wonderfully "relaxing" to listen to. Relaxing!) Of course something may also be gained: the purity and precision of a modern recording may allow me to hear things in Bach's exquisite music that escaped the original congregation, just as a painting that might have once hung far above an inaccessible altar in a church can be examined more closely when it is mounted at eye level on the wall of a museum. But artifacts that become truly homeless, with no one to tend the structures that gave them life and no institutions to provide a hospitable home for their performance, soon cross over from the land of the living to the land of archaeology, or perhaps worse, background music. They can gesture mutely across time, but future generations may be able to make out little of what they are saying about what it once meant to be human at that particular place and time—to be a worshiper in Weimar on Trinity Sunday, 1715, in the halls of the prince's chapel. Only artifacts that remain connected to flourishing institutions truly live. And only cultures that can sustain those institutions have any hope of flourishing life.

## INSTITUTIONS IN CRISIS

Every institution, like every human being, is haunted by the fear of death. And for good reason—institutions decline and die. The flourishing musical world that Johann Sebastian Bach knew is now a shadow of its former self, the province of a relative handful of specialists who perform his music in secular concert halls to aging audiences rather than as innovative, improvisational offerings of devotion in churches filled with worshipers.

Institutions, like people, can die of multiple causes, and most often do. They can die of *broken artifacts*, when the artifacts at the heart of an institution's life are no longer available, attractive or plausible focuses of human attention and effort. This happens perhaps most often when artifacts are superseded by more compelling competitors. When wooden wheels were replaced by steel wheels with rubber tires, the beautifully handcrafted wooden wheel became a nostalgic lawn ornament rather than a useful part of every buggy and wagon. As we live through the most rapid extinction of human languages in history, countless people are deciding that their own mother tongue is not viable in a world dominated by a handful of global languages.

Institutions can also die of *disappearing arenas*. The decline of Bach's sacred music as a living tradition can be traced in part to the decline first of the public liturgical worship it was meant to serve, and then to the collapse of audiences for "classical" music in the twentieth and twenty-first centuries. Indeed, as Spotify's perfectly comprehensive catalog of Bach recordings attests, Bach's musical artifacts are still very much with us, and in one sense more accessible than ever. There are still organs, musical scores, recordings and the other traces of Bach's prodigious creativity; what is missing are not so much the artifacts as the settings where those artifacts might be put to regular use. There are even plenty of classical musicians today (too many for the job market), those who have learned to inhabit the rules and roles of baroque musical performance, but there are not enough *arenas* for them to perform in. At least at our fleeting moment in cultural history, the biggest arena for the performance of music is television shows like *American Idol*, which attracted over 21 million viewers for its final episode in 2012 (and reached as many as 30 million listeners each week over the previous decade). By contrast, in the middle of that same decade only about 21 million adults attended a classical music performance any given *year*. So while Bach's cantatas still exist as artifacts, cantata performance, let alone cantata-as-worship, is floundering as an institution—above all, for a lack of an arena.

The health of arenas is especially important for the survival of institutions because, in many cases, arenas provide a large number of people with paradigms of flourishing, the exemplary individuals and communities who model what we can become at our human best. When I play the Bach cello suites or the fugues from the Well-Tempered Clavier in my living room, I am participating in the cultural heritage of Bach and Western music, but I do so largely for my own enjoyment and the pleasure (hopefully) of my family and a few friends. But when I sit in a concert hall or, better yet, a German cathedral and hear Bach performed by people who have honed their skills and practiced together over weeks, months and years, and when that experience is shared with hundreds or thousands of other audience members or, better yet, worshipers, I encounter this cultural tradition in its richest and most powerful form—an experience that can shape my poor but real imitation in the privacy of my home.

Very few institutions thrive when they are left solely to "professionals," people who have made it their life's work to master a given domain of culture. Football is a powerful institution in American life because of pickup football

games in backyards, not just the Super Bowl, and because of all the grada-
tions of skill and performance and participation in between, from games
under the Friday night lights in small Texas towns to a Pac-12 game in front
of 130,000 fans, from Tom Brady arcing a pass downfield to a dad tossing the
ball to his daughter. A similar line can be traced from Mariah Carey to the
latest *American Idol* winner to Americans warbling melismas in the shower.
Even today in parts of Europe, you might walk down a quiet street in the
evening and hear families playing classical music together, as Dietrich Bonhoeffer's family did a century ago. Both ends of the spectrum, amateur and
professional, contribute to an institution's thriving.

But when an institution's arenas disappear or lose their hold on our
shared imagination, it is beginning to decline. The daily newspaper was a
central institution of American life in the twentieth century, providing the
arena in which politics and journalism were practiced at a professional
level, where the roles and rules of journalism were set and modeled, and
in turn setting the agenda for much of America's political and cultural life.
But these arenas are swiftly disappearing or giving way to the very different arena of the Web, and as the arena disappears, the particular forms
of flourishing that newspaper journalism made possible, for individuals
and communities, also begins to disappear. Perhaps what will replace it
will be even more conducive to civic and personal flourishing, as professional journalists with access to the printing press are replaced by a billion
tweeting amateurs, or perhaps, as we lose access to models of professional
journalistic truth telling and evidence gathering, the standards for public
discourse will decline. It is surely too soon to tell what institutions will
emerge from the ferment of the Internet, but it is clear that some institutions from a previous media era will die.

As artifacts are lost and arenas disappear, the rules that once provided
structure and direction for flourishing begin to fade from memory or
from plausibility. Journalists, for example, prided themselves for a time on
a set of rules that were summed up in the (somewhat unrealistic) word
*objectivity*. No human being can achieve a truly "objective" view of any
situation, especially highly contested matters of politics or culture—but
journalists followed well-defined rules about the obligation to include opposing points of view, the number and nature of sources that were needed

to establish the truthfulness of a story, and the delicate balance between guaranteeing confidentiality and not being used as a mouthpiece for hints and allegations that those sources would not publish under their own names. But as the arenas for this kind of journalism shrank in number and cultural significance, the rules that several generations of journalists lived by began to fade in relevance, often placing the journalistic institutions that still followed those rules in the awkward situation of reporting on items of innuendo and rumor that had appeared, and were dominating the news cycle, in less rule-bound outlets.

Finally, as institutions die *roles* disappear, which is another way of saying that particular kinds of power disappear. Unique constellations of human capacities no longer find expression because there is no institutional context in which those gifts and skills might be discovered or developed. This loss is easiest to see in the form of particular occupations and activities which once provided rich contexts for image bearing but now have all but vanished. The rise of the automobile ended the era of the horse as a workaday companion of human beings, and with the passing of the horse ended not just the dirty and dreary tasks of cleaning stables but the unique image bearing embodied in the millennia-old relationship between human beings and horses. (My family happens to live only an hour's drive from Lancaster County, Pennsylvania, where the Amish keep alive the institutions of horse-drawn wagons and farm equipment, and on our frequent bicycle trips through Amish country we see the rich skills and interactions between young and old and the horses that power many aspects of Amish life, something our own culture has almost entirely forgotten.) But of course it was not just the automobile as an artifact that ended the era of the horse. What eventually crowded out the horse was the automobile's institutional arenas (interstate highways), rules (including the prohibition of work animals on many roads), and new roles (which included many new opportunities for human image bearing and god playing, from mechanics to race car drivers).

What are we to make of the life and death of institutions? Institutions are in the process of being created, thriving, dying and disappearing all around us. Not all institutional decline is bad by any means. But we should not be quick to celebrate the passing of cultural patterns that have endured for generations, because for every institutionalized pattern of idolatry and injustice that is replaced with a far healthier set of artifacts, arenas, rules and roles, there are others that kept thriving possibilities for human beings alive (and for nonhuman creatures like horses, and for the rest of the created world) that are put in peril with the institution's disappearance.

What is lost when institutions die is, in a word, power—the potential for image bearing. When oppressive institutions decline, especially when they are replaced with institutions better suited to comprehensive flourishing, we rightly celebrate, but we should never wish for the decline of institutions in general, because to wish for that is to wish for a world emptied of the artifacts, arenas, patterns of life and richly differentiated roles that fulfill God's original intention for his image bearers to be fruitful and multiply.

## ALL INSTITUTIONS FAIL

If three generations is the minimum life span for a cultural pattern to be called an institution, the maximum life span can be measured in centuries or even millennia. On most mornings I pray the Morning Prayer service from the Book of Common Prayer, using a form that is different only in minor respects from the one set down by Thomas Cranmer in the sixteenth century. On most Sunday mornings I sit in an arena whose architecture and purpose would be immediately recognizable to Cranmer, playing a role according to certain rules (the "liturgy") using artifacts that are hundreds or thousands of years old. Indeed, the pattern of worship in "liturgical" churches like mine is not that different from the worship of Christians in the first centuries of the church, which in turn was not that different from the pattern of worship in synagogues for several hundred years after the Jewish return from exile. The church is a living institution, meaning that it is constantly changing and responding to its environment just like living creatures do, but for all the change there is an essential continuity between the arena, artifacts, rules and roles my church community experiences every Sunday morning and more than a thousand years of history.

But just because an institution has lasted for many generations does not mean it will never decline or die. In fact, the liturgical denomination that my own congregation is a part of has declined dramatically in the past hundred years, and drastically in the last ten years, by almost any measure—finances, converts, adherents or cultural influence. (By the grace of God, our particular congregation continues to thrive, but it is the exception.) Its arenas are disappearing—on the way to our church we pass another building that once belonged to our denomination but now is host to a thriving nondenominational church. My denomination's artifacts are less and less familiar to our culture, and less and less appealing to most of its children, partly because it has done such a poor job of inducting them into the rules and roles that would make them stewards of its particular forms of flourishing.

Indeed, for all its connections to a historically rich tradition of flourishing, our denomination also was enmeshed from its very beginning in much less salutary traditions and institutions: founded by a willful king who would not discipline his lust either for sex or power, treated as a sanctuary for privileged and risk-averse elites, and ultimately susceptible to the totalizing, secularizing stories told by the modern era. These compromises with other forms of power and god playing left it weakened and disoriented when the idols of a previous generation ceased to deliver on their promises and came to collect ever more outrageous sacrifices.

All the same, our denomination is not dying simply because it has failed. *All* institutions fail. This is one of the central lessons of the very first book of the Bible, with its host of less than edifying stories about the founding three generations of the people of Israel. The founding of God's chosen people is shot through with human compromise and failure—idolatry of a very literal sort (Abraham's family apparently continues to travel with household gods [Genesis 31:34]) and equally literal god playing, as when Abraham takes the generative power promised by God into his own hands by sleeping with Sarah's maid Hagar.

Just as Genesis shows us how frail and fragile even God-breathed institutions can be, so do the first pages of the New Testament. The disciples in the Gospels can be confused and bumbling when they are not blustering and self-seeking, and even after the world-upending events of Resurrection, Ascension and Pentecost, we see Paul and Barnabas abruptly parting ways over a personnel decision, Peter and Paul in a very public argument about whom they will eat with, and nearly every epistle author, whether Paul, Peter, John, James or Jude, beside themselves with concern for the heresies, divisions and follies creeping into the communities they founded. Even Luke's glowing description of the earliest days of the Jerusalem church may be a not-so-subtle reminder to Theophilus and his community of how quickly that first love could be lost—not to mention that even the Acts of the Apostles' earliest chapters feature a dispute over equal treatment for ethnic minorities and a case of financial deception.

So it is with every institution that lasts long enough for its founding generation's unique image bearing and equally unique patterns of idolatry and injustice to be imprinted on their successors: *By the third generation, every institution has failed.* This is true not just in biblical history but elsewhere as well: the third generation of the United States of America had to fight a terrible Civil War to address the idolatry and injustice that had been written into the founding documents.

Some institutions, by the common or special grace of God, plant themselves deeply enough in the soil of image bearing that they sustain creativity and flourishing in spite of their failures. But others not only fail but die—or worse.

## ZOMBIE INSTITUTIONS

In the imagination of American popular culture, there is a fate worse than death. The undead lurch through the world, hungry for human flesh, unthinking, unfeeling, remorseless and relentless. Less than alive, they cannot be placated or persuaded; beyond death, they cannot easily be killed. Zombies are a parable of deadly power—power that brings no flourishing, is mute and inert, yet threatens to consume all life and love.

People who watch zombie movies do not generally believe that there are former human beings, now the living dead, stalking the earth. Unfortunately, their institutional equivalents are all too real. They are institutions that refuse to die and indeed often seem impossible to kill: complexes of arenas, artifacts, rules and roles that do not contribute anything to comprehensive flourishing but continue to exist, rather than passing unlamented into the dim memory of history. If Bach's music or newspaper journalism are formerly thriving institutions, now near death, these institutions are stubbornly vital, yet without being truly alive.

As odd as it seems, the most common place to find zombies outside of
the movie theater is in the financial pages (if you can still find a newspaper
with pages). In Japan and Europe in the early twenty-first century a substantial number of banks were stuffed with nonperforming loans. They
were kept alive only by the indulgence of government agencies that pre-
ferred the appearance of a functioning banking sector to the reality of
having to declare billions of dollars' worth of actual losses. Unlike fictional
zombies, "zombie banks" do depend on an outside source of support—
usually a nation's central banks—but like the fictional creatures, they are
hard to kill. The benefits of keeping a zombie bank lurching forward, as
opposed to exposing its rotten balance sheet for the world to see, can
seem overwhelming.

Zombie banks contribute nothing to the flourishing, economic or otherwise,
of their host nations. In fact, they absorb substantial amounts of government
revenues since they cannot support themselves. They are deceptively
healthy from the outside: zombie banks frequently have an impressive *arena*
in the form of headquarters in prestigious locations and plenty of branch
offices (even if you rarely see anyone enter or leave). They preserve the *artifacts* of banking; you can open an account at a zombie bank, perhaps even
obtain a loan from one, and you will encounter nattily dressed executives
and tellers during the usual banking hours. But what has really corroded in
zombie banks is the *rules* and *roles* of banking. The rules of banking say that
bad loans need to be "written down" on the bank's balance sheet—when
there is no chance that a loan will be repaid, the fact needs to be acknowl-
edged by reducing or eliminating its value as an asset. But in zombie banks
these rules are ignored, and new, unwritten rules emerge: the truth will have
to be artfully concealed for the institution to go on, because to register the
real losses would reveal that these institutions are unsustainable. As the
rules are changed, the roles of everyone from the teller to the CEO become
distorted. Employees may continue to go through the motions of banking,
but in fact they are contributing in one way or another to a lie. What once
was about banking becomes about the appearance of banking. The result, of
course, is diminishing, not flourishing. Human beings who were made to
cultivate and create real prosperity and power in the world are reduced to
*simulating* prosperity and power.

For make no mistake: while in one sense zombie banks are powerful institutions (powerful enough to convince government officials to tolerate their half-truths and outright misrepresentations of their strength), they do not create power. Instead they slowly but surely leach power from an economic system. More and more resources of time and money go into the appearance of power, while less and less go into its actual exercise in ways that would create opportunity and true wealth. Like the fictional monsters they are named after, zombie banks can only use their power in their own interests, and in doing so they consume and undermine the power of others, not least by employing countless people in living-dead-end jobs rather than in occupations that would reward honesty, hard work and creativity. Perhaps the worst cost of zombie banks is the way they absorb the energy and creativity of thousands of image bearers, giving them something to do but not bearing any fruit from their work.

If only banks were the only zombie institutions. But in fact zombie institutions can be found in every part of culture. Zombie institutions are institutions that have not faced the truth about their own failure. And because of their access to privilege—their ability to continue collecting rent—they continue to exist, crowding out institutions that might create true shalom. Zombie institutions are dedicated first and only to their own preservation, not to anyone's flourishing.

So there are zombie businesses, like *The Office*'s companies Dunder Mifflin and Wernham Hogg Paper, where no apparent fruitful work ever happens. Because they are insulated from market forces and prone to "rent-seeking," government agencies seem to be a particular danger zone for zombification. In my youth, sad to say, my closest encounter with a zombie institution seemed to be the Department of Motor Vehicles, where employees dulled by low expectations slowly and sullenly served frustrated citizens under pallid fluorescent lights. (Astonishingly enough, years later an energetic political appointee actually instilled in that same government department a sense of mission and customer service, and my most recent visit to the DMV in the state where I grew up was a positively surreal experience of hospitality, efficiency and pride in one's work.)

Worst of all is when one encounters zombie churches. Because every church is built and sustained by volunteers, almost every church was at some point a thriving institution that contributed to real flourishing. But over time the imperatives of self-preservation can create a risk-averse culture that prevents continued learning and growth. Zombie churches exist to keep the lights on rather than to be the light in dark places; they turn inward rather than outward; they serve insiders and ignore outsiders.

The paradox of institutional life is very much like the paradox of individual life: only those who are willing to die can truly live. Only institutions that squarely face their own decay and decline can avoid the fate of the zombies.

## INSTITUTIONS OF IDOLATRY, INSTITUTIONS OF INJUSTICE

Institutions at their best make room for image bearing at its best, in all the abundance which God originally intended. But nothing in this world east of Eden has escaped the corruption of the divine image, certainly not institutions. For the patterns that institutions sustain with their artifacts, arenas, rules and roles are not just the patterns of image bearing but the patterns of god playing and god making played out over space and time until they become woven into the very fabric of culture. These institutions consistently fail to provide for the comprehensive flourishing that is the test of shalom—instead, within their matrix some enjoy absurd levels of godlike autonomy and affluence, while others are robbed of even the most basic dignity image bearers should enjoy.

Consider again the moneylender in Gudiyatham, extracting rent from his position of privilege from the poor families who depend on him for loans. This picture of injustice is incomplete if we look only at the single moneylender and a few exploited families. For in fact there are thousands of such moneylenders in thousands of villages, each pursuing their own prosperity by exploiting others. The system of "bonded labor" is an institution, with well-established artifacts, arenas, rules and roles, that has persisted for generations. Changing that system is not a matter of removing a single wicked actor from the stage; there are countless more waiting to play their part in a well-established pattern of exploitation. This is why World Vision's intervention in Gudiyatham had to be so wide-ranging and so patient.

In their important book about race and religion in America, *Divided by Faith*, sociologists Michael O. Emerson and Christian Smith observe that what most distinguishes white evangelical Protestants from black Protestants is not their theology or even their desire for racial reconciliation, but evangelicals' lack of institutional thinking. When evangelicals think about solving social problems like the legacy of slavery and racism in the United States, they think almost exclusively in terms of personal, one-on-one relationships—which is why so many white evangelicals can imagine the problem of racism is solved if they simply have a handful of friends of other races. To think of race this way is to miss the fact that race and racism are *institutional* realities built on a complex set of artifacts, arenas, rules and roles. A few friendships that happen outside of those arenas and temporarily suspend a few of those rules and roles do little to change the multigenerational patterns of distorted image bearing and god playing based on skin color. Black Christians instinctively know that for the gospel to keep transforming America's sorry racial story, it will have to keep challenging these deeply ingrained patterns and the structures that even now perpetuate them—while white evangelicals, who identify racism with a handful of dismantled artifacts like twentieth-century Jim Crow laws and legally segregated schools, cannot imagine that racism has a continuing institutional reality.

The artifacts of racism may be largely gone—there are no longer signs over water fountains that say "Whites Only." But racism was never a matter just of artifacts. Nor do the privileges racism gave to the god players in its system disappear just because the outward exercise of domination has ceased. The basic law of cultural change—the only way to change culture is to make more of it—applies to institutions as well. Until new institutions are created, the power of the old institutions can persist for generations. These new institutions will take at least three generations to be truly rooted in a society. It is surely no accident that Barack Obama, whose election was a milestone in America's emergence from its racist history, was elected in 2008 on a surge of support from emerging adults, the third generation after the civil rights movement, the children's children of those tumultuous years. It takes three generations, at the very least, for the worst institutions of injustice to begin to lose their grip. Lincoln's terrifying words did not apply to the Civil War itself, by the grace of God:

If God wills that it continue until all the wealth piled by the bondsman's two hundred and fifty years of unrequited toil shall be sunk, and until every drop of blood drawn with the lash shall be paid by another drawn with the sword, as was said three thousand years ago, so still it must be said "the judgments of the Lord are true and righteous altogether."

But 150 years after the Civil War, 250 years sounds none too pessimistic for the task of creating cultural institutions in the United States that allow image bearers to flourish no matter the color of their skin. On many days, it seems we are much further away indeed.

As with injustice, so with idolatry. Human institutions are the carriers not just of god playing but of god making. This, indeed, is the biblical view of all human religions, emphatically including the distortions of the biblical faith itself. The human drive to make images of god is both part of our created dignity and part of our fallen idolatry, the mark of our quest for reconciliation and reunion with our Creator. So all human religions contain some elements of image bearing, as their extraordinary art, music, architecture and literature attest; all human religions sustain institutions that create some measure of flourishing. But the biblical view is that to the extent human religions are constructed by human effort rather than by God's gracious self-giving and revelation, they inevitably participate in the deceptions of idolatry as well. Jesus' central charge against the Pharisees was not their adherence to God's revealed Torah, a gift from God designed to make Israel a distinctive, image-bearing people—it was all the layers of human addition to Torah that created distinctions of privilege, status and exclusion. These additions laid burdens on God's "little ones"—the most vulnerable image bearers—"too heavy for them to bear," allowing the Pharisees to exult in their righteousness while relegating others to the demeaning category of "sinner."

As idolatry and injustice always go together—injustice requiring idolatry to justify exploitation, idolatry leading to injustice as the idols fail to deliver and demand ever greater sacrifices—so with the entrenched cultural patterns we call institutions. There is always a false god lurking behind every system of injustice, the god of nationalism or racism or misogyny, wealth or lust or power itself, which promises godlike abilities to some at the expense of others. And every institution that sustains the worship of a false god ends up neglecting the most vulnerable. The little ones are sacrificed on the altar of the idols' demands, not once but generation after generation, until we forget that there ever could have been a way for every person and every created thing to flourish. This, in a word, is sin, not a few isolated acts but a pattern embedded into every human act, even and maybe especially our well-intentioned acts. Only by seeing sin as an institutional reality—embedded in concrete artifacts, played out in terrifying large and visible arenas, dictating rules that enslave rather than set free, and turning naturally differentiated roles into oppressively rigid structures of status and privilege—can we understand the damage idolatry and injustice have done.

## PRINCIPALITIES AND POWERS

The first-century Mediterranean world did not know about zombies, but it did know about shadowy powers that lurked behind human institutions and indeed the whole natural world. The Greeks called them the *stoicheia,* a word that in our English Bibles is translated "elements" or "elementary principles." A handful of times in Paul's letters we find references to them, as when Paul refers to "the *stoicheia* of the *kosmos*" (Colossians 2:8) that once kept his Colossian readers bound in ignorance. The *stoicheia* are closely linked to two other words that show up together in Paul's later letters: the *archai* and the *exousiai,* often translated "the principalities and the powers" or "the rulers and authorities."

Though there is a lively debate about the exact meaning of these terms, several things seem clear from these passing yet pointed references to the elements, rulers and authorities. First, in their present form they are opposed to God. These powers, whatever exactly they are, challenge the true Source of power. And in a decisive confrontation at the cross, these powers have been exposed for what they are: deceptive, "weak and beggarly" (Galatians 4:9), and ultimately powerless against God's creating and redeeming power.

Second, these powers are more than just "flesh and blood"—they have an existence in "the heavenly places," that is, in N. T. Wright's useful modern metaphor, the "control room," the realm where the ultimate battle for sovereignty over the world takes place. But the "spiritual" or "heavenly"

nature of these powers does not mean they have no effect on earth. Quite
the opposite: it is by these powers that human beings are "enslaved."

Third and perhaps most suggestive, Paul in both Colossians and Galatians seems to consider the *stoicheia* to be connected with the pagan observance of "special days, and months, and seasons, and years" (Galatians
4:10) and "matters of food and drink" (Colossians 2:16). That is, they are at
the root of pagan cultural patterns—the deep structures of time and ritual,
passed on from generation to generation, that order the pagan world.

In the early Christians' view, then, there are powerful patterns of life,
with more than a merely earthly reality, that have enslaved God's image
bearers, cutting them off from sight and life. It may well be that Paul envi-
sions these "rulers and authorities" as having a personal quality much like
the messengers or angels who come from God—demonic beings beyond
ordinary human experience—but their rule is embodied in human existence in the form of elemental patterns that shape and constrain human
life. They are, in a word, institutional. They prescribe certain rules and
roles; they are made known in specific artifacts and associated with specific arenas of activity. But unlike image-bearing institutions that lead to
flourishing, these rulers and authorities have taken power over people, degrading and diminishing the image of God.

Paul says something telling about Christ's victory over the rulers and
authorities in Colossians 2:15: "He disarmed the rulers and authorities
and made a public example of them, triumphing over them in [the cross]."
It is remarkable that Christ's victory comes not through the resurrection—
the vindicating event that Paul referred to just a few sentences earlier—
but through the cross. Why was the cross the site of Christ's victory over
these demonic, pervasive, invisible but powerful forces?

The answer may lie in something we do not always fully appreciate
about the crucifixion of Jesus: just how institutional it was. The central
institutions of Jesus' world—the Roman occupying army and its procurator, the Romans' client king Herod, and the religious establishment led
by the Jerusalem Sanhedrin and its high priest—all play pivotal roles in
the trials that lead to Jesus' condemnation. And in doing so all of them are
revealed to be deeply corrupt. The witnesses for the prosecution cannot
agree. The overnight trial is a travesty of both Roman and Jewish legal

procedure. It becomes clear that these institutions, far from safeguarding flourishing and protecting the innocent, exist only for their own self-preservation and the protection of the powerful. Perhaps it is not surprising that those whose offices require them to take responsibility for judgment attempt to shirk it and hand the case on to others: the Sanhedrin to Pilate, Pilate to Herod, Herod back to Pilate, and finally Pilate to the crowd. Even the most powerful actors in these institutions have lost their ability to say yes to truth and no to lies. They are, to use Jesus' words, "whitewashed tombs" that deal death rather than bringing life. They are zombies.

This, I believe, is the reason that Paul saw the cross as the place of real victory over the rulers and authorities of his age—and every age. The cross "disarms" the reigning institutions of first-century Judea by revealing them for what they are. They are instruments of injustice, and they are implements of idolatry. Like all idols, at the cross they exact the ultimate price, demanding the sacrifice of the Father's Son in order to preserve their privilege. But in doing so they reveal their true character—and God reveals his true character. In public (making "a public example of them," as Paul says), for all to see, we are given the choice between the power of false gods and the power of the true God. Malcolm Muggeridge grasped what was happening:

> The climax of Jesus's earthly ministry, His Crucifixion, amounted to a re-ductio ad absurdum of what the Devil has on offer—which is power. Likewise, Pilate's ironical billing of Jesus on the Cross as "King of the Jews" misfires in the light of Jesus's true destiny as "God's Almighty Word leaping down from Heaven out of His Royal Throne." Again, the mockery of the Roman soldiers misfires when they dress Jesus up in a scarlet robe, put a crown of thorns on His head, give Him a reed to hold in His hand as a sceptre, and then kneel down before Him in obeisance, chanting: "Hail, King of the Jews!" The soldiers are not, as they suppose, just ridiculing a poor, distrought [*sic*] and deluded man about to be crucified, but holding up to ridicule all who exercise power, thereby making power itself derisory, so that thenceforth thorns will be woven into every crown, and under every scarlet robe there will be stricken flesh.

Of course we will want to amend Muggeridge's observation: what is being ridiculed at the cross is not "power" in general—not creative, image-bearing power—but idolatrous power, the power which the rulers and authorities have claimed for their own. And what is revealed at the cross is true power, the power that willingly bears the pain of wounds and thorns, the power that gives up even an only Son in order to bring life.

To live after the cross, and after the resurrection that vindicated the cross's suffering and sacrifice, is to live in a world where the fundamental elements of the world, the patterns of life that bring fear and death, have been disarmed. No matter how deeply embedded these institutions have become, no matter how taken for granted they have been in their exaggerated promises and their rapacious demands, the cross has excavated them and ruined them. The zombies have lost their power to control and terrify; the living dead have been overcome by one who went to the grave and returned, and now lives to breathe life into the image bearers he came to rescue.

All that remains is for us, made and restored in his image, to rise to our calling—to exercise true power—even in the very institutions that now bear the marks of failure. Is it possible to exercise leadership in the institutions of the world without becoming captive to the principalities and powers that exploit them, to dispatch and even resurrect zombie institutions without becoming zombies ourselves, to bring back to life institutions that are failing and gasping for air? There is only one reason to hope that it can be done: if it already has.

# BECOMING TRUSTEES

The single culture-making endeavor I am most astonished by and grateful for in my lifetime is the Christian human rights organization International Justice Mission (IJM). The story of IJM has been told elsewhere (including briefly in my previous book) so I will not rehearse it here, but IJM's mission and methods shed unique lights on power at its worst and best, and the crucial gifts that only institutions can bring to those who would be image bearers rather than god players.

IJM combats idolatry and injustice in some of their most rancid manifestations. There is no more reprehensible god playing than the use of children for sexual gratification, the exploitation of widows and their children by distant relatives after the death of a father, the misuse of police powers to extort false confessions and protect the perpetrators of sexual violence, or the serial enslavement of generation after generation to extract payments on unpayable debts. All of these and more are abuses of power that IJM targets in countries around the world where the public justice system does not work on behalf of the poor and powerless.

These abuses of power are deeply institutionalized, which is why they persist. Prostitution, police corruption and bonded labor are institutions just as much as the symphony orchestra or football. Each has all the ingredients of a stable institution. Prostitution, for example, has its distinctive artifacts (which is why you are likely to know immediately, wherever you are in the world, when you have arrived in a neighborhood where women are prostituted), arenas (the "red light districts" created by official decree or neglect), rules (informal but coercively maintained patterns of behavior by pimps, those they exploit, and the johns who purchase their service), and roles. And while many of these abuses of power have been exacerbated by modernity and globalization, they are rooted in patterns that go back for generations if not centuries or millennia, and that function at the deepest level of shared assumptions about the way the world works, so much so that it can be difficult for anyone to imagine an alternative. Rather than creating an environment of comprehensive flourishing, these institutions foster comprehensive devastation of the image-bearing capacity of human beings and, almost always, the degradation of the cultural and natural environment as well.

Yet what is striking about IJM's response to these institutionalized patterns of injustice is how institutional it is in turn. The core of IJM's strategy in every country where it works is *to strengthen the institutions that have the legitimate authority to restrain evil*—the police, judiciary and prisons— and *to strengthen institutions that can restore image bearing among the victims of evil*—social work, counseling and economic development organizations that help those whose image has been marred by abuse recover their dignity and capacity. I remember the jubilation among IJM's staff and supporters in April 2011 when a local official near Chennai, India, identified as S. Kandaswamy in news reports, took the initiative to raid a brick kiln where 143 families, a total of 522 people, had been enslaved. Police under his direction freed the laborers, commandeered the use of a local high school to provide them with health care, and arrested the owner of the brick kiln. Our joy was not just for the hundreds of men, women and children who no longer would be robbed of the dignity of hard work freely done and properly paid, but for the image bearing of this public servant. By properly playing the role that he had been given in the institution of the local government, rather than using his power for self-interest or simply neglecting his power altogether, he not only was able to do concrete good for those directly affected but begin to change an institutional pattern that had persisted for generations.

Just a few weeks before this raid and the bold actions of this local official, one thousand staff and friends of IJM had gathered in a Washington,

DC, hotel ballroom for a weekend of prayer for IJM's most urgent needs. We spent an agonizing, energizing night praying specifically for the end of bonded labor in the countries where it persists. It seemed like an audacious and impossible thing to pray for—and it was, because to pray for the end of bonded labor is to pray for nothing less than an institutional revolution. And yet I believe that nearly everyone in the room that night would affirm that as we tried to muster up enough faith even to dare to ask that bonded labor might be eradicated in our lifetime, the Spirit came with extraordinary power, pouring out on us the willingness to ask something none of us could possibly bring about with our own resources or power.

Is it only a coincidence that four weeks later, this local official took up the image-bearing power granted to him by his position? Is it inconceivable that in his nation of a billion image bearers, we will in our own lifetime see the renewal of institutions that are intended for flourishing, and the withering of institutions that have stolen the true freedom of slaves and slave owners alike? If and when that happens, it will be an *institutional* change, not just a single news story, momentary revival or pyrrhic victory, but a change in artifacts, arenas, rules and roles that will be handed down from generation to generation until it is inconceivable to some future generation that people were ever enslaved. Only this will fully answer our prayers that weekend in Washington.

## AN INSTITUTIONAL JUSTICE MISSION

There are many ingredients in the success of IJM, probably the most influential new Christian nonprofit of the last twenty-five years—its crystal clear mission, its dynamic founder, its supremely talented staff, and their profound cultivation of prayer and dependence on the power of God. But there are two more that are surprising and quite exceptional. The first is IJM's unapologetically institutional character. Even when IJM was a handful of twenty- and thirty-somethings working out of a rented house in the suburbs of Washington, DC, its logo included a formal round seal. The seal came complete with an ornate map of the world, the Latin motto QUAERITE IUDICIUM SUBVENITE OPPRESSO (from Isaiah 1:17, "seek justice, rescue the oppressed"), and engraved flourishes that could easily belong to a government agency. In its fifteen years of existence, as the professional work world slipped comfortably down the slope from business casual to untucked shirts to hoodies, IJM retained a crisp, strict business-formal dress code. In many law firms, associates and partners only wear ties and suits when they are going to court; IJM's staff, from interns to the president, look ready to litigate every hour of the day.

All this is more surprising when you consider that some of IJM's key leaders, like founder Gary Haugen and senior vice president Sharon Cohn Wu, are members of two of the most institutionally antipathetic groups in American history: Generation X and evangelical Christians. Their demographic cohort is, as we already noted, nearly allergic to institutional leadership, and their fellow Christians are often institutionally naive, yet IJM's leaders have created a most unlikely creature: a startup institution.

To be sure, IJM has yet to face the most basic test of institutionalization: it is still in its first generation of leadership, and there are no guarantees of how it will manage its transition to the second and third generations and beyond. But in hundreds of hours spent as a volunteer and friend of IJM I have noted both the high regard IJM's staff have for their founder and a distinct sense of lack of dependence on him. No one at IJM would want to do their job without Gary, but there is no doubt they could and would. IJM itself has become an arena in which a distinctive set of artifacts, rules and roles can be sustained in the world, not just the temporary extension of a charismatic and compelling personality.

Often when evangelicals have ventured abroad in mission, they have carried their institutional blindness with them, relieving immediate needs without asking what institutional conditions created the need in the first place, and preaching a gospel that has the power to transform hearts but not social structures (partly, to be sure, in reaction to a version of the Christian faith that offered no hope *beyond* changing social structures). But from the beginning IJM took a very different approach. Built into its DNA was its founder's experience investigating police corruption for the Civil Rights Division of the United States Department of Justice, which involved daily reminders of how broken America's own public justice institutions could become. So rather than setting out to "free slaves" with minimal recourse to local institutions of law enforcement, IJM sought to partner with institutions at the local, national and international level. It was a thoroughly *institutional* justice mission—signaled by the artifacts of its formal seal and dress code, and operating in the arenas of government and diplomacy rather than the more typical charitable realm of individual need and relief.

In recent years, as IJM has grown, it has focused more of its resources on what its documents call "structural transformation," which is to say, changing and strengthening the institutions of justice. Yet part of the genius of IJM's approach is that it is not *merely* institutional in its approach to structural change. Excess institutionalism led an earlier generation of culturally engaged Protestants astray. As they became identified with and eventually submerged into culturally dominant institutions, they lost touch with personal commitment and transformation—the dramatic, miraculous, irreplaceable restoration of image bearing that accompanies conversion and faith in Christ. The individual matters because the individual is an image bearer even in the midst of the most suffocating structures. And IJM's litigation-ready dress code is an artifact that reinforces a basic commitment to take on individual cases at the grass roots rather than simply try to work the levers of power at a distance. IJM's lawyers dress for court because they go to court on behalf of specific poor, exploited, destitute and desperate clients, not just on behalf of "systemic change." But the long-range success of IJM hinges less on individual dramatic victories than on the way those victories will reshape the artifacts, arenas, rules and roles of justice for clients whom IJM will never represent—and for image bearers who will never become clients in the first place, because they will live in societies freed of the tyranny of injustice at its worst.

And this leads to the second truly distinctive feature of IJM: it advocates on behalf of the powerless without becoming cynical about power. Close encounters with the worst that idolatry and injustice can do often lead to a profound disillusionment with power itself. To some extent this is inevitable. If the police in your neighborhood do little but harass, extort and intimidate, it is very unlikely that you will be able to envision police work as an image-bearing act of peacemaking through the wise and limited use of power. You will naturally be inclined to conclude that the problem is power itself.

This is just the posture of many activists who live in the midst of broken institutions that have robbed citizens of their image-bearing dignity and elevated a handful of individuals to idolatrous levels of exploitation and self-enrichment. The community organizing movement that emerged from the work of Saul Alinsky was based on just such an adversarial relationship to existing power. Alinsky's work is relentlessly zero-sum, simply seeking to marshal sufficient power among the currently disenfranchised to compel the powerful to act against their own interests.

Yet though IJM's staff are exposed daily to powerful persons who are indifferent to the poor and oppressed, they retain a faith in the potential for restoring image bearing not just in spite of institutions and their appointed representatives, but through them. Indeed, this faith is an essential component of the structural transformation that IJM seeks. For at the very heart of corruption and injustice is the very misconception of power that attracts so many radicals: the Nietzschean suspicion that deep down, society is nothing more than a continual clash of competing interest groups who can only advance at others' expense. In such an environment all victories are temporary, all power must be jealously hoarded, and positions of power are to be used as ruthlessly as possible for the benefit of one's own kind. Even revolution in such a society—overthrow of the existing representatives of power—would simply replace one kind of corruption and one set of corrupt actors with another.

IJM's vision is far more hopeful. This does not mean that IJM is anything but realistic about how much pressure is necessary to persuade the official representatives of power to do what is right. But by relentlessly pressing the claims of the oppressed for justice with those very officials, calling on them to take up their own image-bearing role in the institutions they represent, IJM holds out a vision of comprehensive flourishing for everyone, including those who hold official positions. The vision of IJM is not an India without powerful institutions—it is in fact an India with *more* truly powerful institutions, institutions that liberate every citizen to play his or her role in freedom with dignity. IJM is working toward an India full of S. Kandaswamys and full of families who reap the fruit of their labor in justice. Such an India will not be empty of power; it will be full of power at its best, the power that brings shalom.

## OVERLORDS AND UNDERLORDS

When institutions are broken, three characteristic patterns of failed image bearing almost always occur together. The first is the *broken image of the poor*. The "poor" in a broken institution are those whose roles are so constricted by the institution's rules that they are unable to exercise their creative and cultivating power. This loss of power is always multidimensional and, in the worst situations, total—not just the loss of the ability to choose and leave a job, but parents' loss of ability to provide security and nurture for their children, children's loss of ability to play and learn rather than merely labor, and the excruciating physical disempowerment of malnutrition and beatings.

The second failure of image bearing is the *exaggerated image* of those we might call the "overlords," a name that captures both what they do—"lord it over" others, exploiting the poor in the quest for idolatrous godlikeness—and what they are. Overlords are overly lordly, distorted by their hoarding and misuse of power into an inflated caricature of the true lordship originally granted to image bearers and exemplified by history's one true Image Bearer. And their power is overly dedicated to their own lordship, not to comprehensive flourishing but private benefit that comes at the expense of the image-bearing capacity of the poor.

But wherever overlords reign, you will almost always find another failure of image bearing, characteristic of neither overlords nor the poor: the *neglected image* of the powerful but passive. We might coin a name for these neglectful image bearers and call them the "underlords." They do not lack power—sometimes they may have a great deal—and they do not use it conspicuously in the service of their own self-aggrandizement. Rather, they simply, passively fail to play the role that they are meant to play; they are unfaithful not by abusing their power but by not using it at all. They are like a slothful referee in soccer, who can spoil a game by neglecting his duties to rein in the unfair power-grabbing of "overlords" on the field who seek to win by mere strength or stealth. It is not the referee's calls that matter, and it is not that the referee seeks excessive glory or victories for himself. It is the calls he *does not make* that make all the difference.

Most failures of image bearing have vastly greater consequences than a game won or lost. The scandalous truths about the Roman Catholic

Church that burst into the open in the 2000s were not just about "overlord" priests idolatrously abusing young people, robbing them of their image-bearing dignity while playing a hideously exploitative parody of the God they were sworn to serve. There was also the role of "underlords" in the church hierarchy who passively enabled the abuse by inaction or inadequate action. Many of these institutional actors were nominally more powerful than those they malignly neglected to discipline—up to and including bishops, archbishops and cardinals—and they were certainly greater in number than the abusers. But they failed to use their power to curb idolatry and to protect the vulnerable. The outrage was not just what some did, but what many others did not do.

So we find that in any failing institution, as common as the abuse of power is the neglect of power. In fact, the abuse of power may be quite concentrated among relatively few actors. What is widely spread whenever institutions fail is the failure to exercise power. The neglect of power, not the willful abuse of power, is what makes the difference between flourishing and failure in almost every institution. The sign of flourishing is when countless people exercise their power within the rules and roles of an institution; the sign of failure is when most people within the institution simply cease to act.

Gary Haugen of IJM observes informally that most public justice systems around the world follow a 15-70-15 principle. Consider a typical police force in a city somewhere in the developing world. More often than not you will find that 15 percent of the force's officers are incorruptible—they simply cannot be bribed or bought, no matter how meager their own pay or the cost to advancement in their career. And 15 percent, the "overlords," are pervasively and incorrigibly corrupt, bent on extracting rents and using their power for their own gain, no matter how wealthy and powerful they may already be. But the middle 70 percent, the great majority of those with some power in the system, are neither incorruptible nor corrupt. They are ordinary people trying to eke out a living in a messy world, beset by external and internal pressures, who can be swayed in either direction. Surround them with incorruptible peers and superiors, and they will probably carry out the duties of their office honestly. But surround them with pervasively corrupt overlords, and they will follow suit, perpetrating their own forms of petty corruption and never challenging the corruption they see around them.

The society is shaped not so much by the choices of the incorruptible 15 percent, nor by the corrupt 15 percent, but the wavering 70 percent—the "underlords" who forfeit much of their image-bearing and image-restoring power to others. The good news is that if you can find a way to shift the balance ever so slightly between the fortunes of those who uphold the law and those who undermine it, loading the teeter-totter of corruption just a little bit more at the end of the incorruptible 15 percent, the 70 percent will shift as well. And in a relatively short time you can shift from an 85 percent corrupt force to one that is 85 percent clean. The bad news is that it is also possible to shift the teeter-totter just slightly toward corruption and end up with a system that is 85 percent corrupt. The sober truth is that the neglected power of the underlords is what often makes the difference. The underlords are not the poor, those who are at the mercy of the system and who may have learned the hard way that any move toward honesty and flourishing is likely to be undermined and punished by those with extra power. The underlords have real power in the system—if they will use it.

The dynamics that affect a citywide police force or indeed an entire nation also apply to institutions as small as an individual family. Like all institutions, the family distributes power unevenly. And very often our deepest failures as parents are not so much the abuse of power, the work of overlords, but the neglect of our power, the slothfulness of underlords. In my own extended family, and in my own home, the deepest violations of shalom have not taken the form of abuse. Instead they have taken the form of absence: the unwillingness to bear the pain of conflict or the vulnerability of intimacy, the flight into solitary life in a distant corner of the house or into travel far from home. And the losers from our rent-preserving, privilege-guarding, self-protective withholding of true power are the "poor"—our children and indeed each of us at our moments of greatest physical and emotional vulnerability, facing the world without the loving community and trust that are the bedrock of true shalom. We have not had many overlords in the Crouch and Bennett clans in the past few generations, but we have had underlords. If only I were not among them.

The role of the underlords, those who neglect their power, is a central concern of one of the great works of American and Christian history, Dr. Martin Luther King Jr.'s 1963 "Letter from Birmingham Jail." King addressed his letter to his "Dear Fellow Clergymen," white pastors who had questioned the "untimely" and technically illegal protests that had landed King and many of his fellow leaders in jail. King's scathingly restrained response to these "white moderates" is an indictment of the passivity of underlords:

> I have almost reached the regrettable conclusion that the Negro's great stumbling block in his stride toward freedom is not the White Citizen's Counciler or the Ku Klux Klanner, but the white moderate, who is more devoted to "order" than to justice; who prefers a negative peace which is the absence of tension to a positive peace which is the presence of justice; who constantly says: "I agree with you in the goal you seek, but I cannot agree with your methods of direct action." . . . Shallow understanding from people of good will is more frustrating than absolute misunderstanding from people of ill will. Lukewarm acceptance is much more bewildering than outright rejection.

Here are all the elements of the passive 70 percent, "more cautious than courageous" in King's phrase: those who will not act to bring justice and shalom, people of basically good will and substantial privilege who will not put their power behind their "lukewarm acceptance" of the relatively powerless who are claiming their image-bearing calling at great risk and cost. "We will have to repent in this generation not merely for the hateful words and actions of the bad people but for the appalling silence of the good people," King wrote. Silence is the underlords' failure.

## THE ROBE AND THE RING

I once spoke with the chief executive of a nonprofit organization that was in the throes of a third-generation transition. At the end of a long and difficult day, he reflected on a few conversations that had offered hope for the future. He summarized them this way: "The trustees of an institution are those who have forgiven it."

I don't think he was referring to a board of trustees in the formal or legal sense, but to those who could truly be trusted to lead at all levels in the organization. In his simple statement are several essential truths about institutions. First, institutions are fallen—they embody and perpetuate our human contradictions at their worst. For this reason they need "trustees": those who can be trusted to preserve and provide for what is best, most suited to image bearing, and to weed out what is worst, most implicated in idolatry and injustice.

Yet these trustees will only be able to be truly trusted with this responsibility if they have both named the failings of the institution and forgiven it for failing others and for failing themselves. They are not trustees who pretend that their institutions somehow escape the idolatry and injustice that shadow even the noblest human efforts, but neither are they trustees who have seen the dark truth about their own institutions and cynically refused to extend mercy and hope. Trustees have seen, and borne, the worst that institutions can do—and yet they have somehow escaped the abyss of cynicism. Instead they enter into the life of their institutions, embodying a better way, bearing the institution's pain and offering hope.

So perhaps it is not surprising that the book of Genesis, the story of how the people of God came over three generations to be the bearers of God's own redemptive power within the world that had forgotten him, culminates with the story of the training of a trustee.

Joseph, the fourth generation of the family of Abraham and Sarah, comes of age amidst that fractious family's simmering pot of jealousies, rivalries and ambition. And the pot boils over when Jacob's extravagant favor for Joseph—symbolized in the "robe of many colors" he commissions for Joseph to wear—is compounded by Joseph's imprudently reported dreams of his family bowing down before him like the sun, moon and stars before a cosmic god. His brothers angrily mock Joseph's visions of power: "Are you indeed to reign over us? Are you indeed to have dominion over us?" (Genesis 37:8). The brothers believe they know full well what Joseph's dream means: like a Nietzschean god, he aims to expand his dominion until there is no room for them. So they resort to a perfectly Nietzschean solution, conspiring to destroy him altogether, a plan only averted at the last minute by the scruples of Judah, who suggests (very slightly to his credit) that they sell their brother into slavery instead. So Joseph is trafficked to the land of Egypt, his robe returned to his grieving father torn and covered in blood. Now even the chosen redemptive family has descended to the infighting of Cain and Abel, and the young Joseph is cast off in a far country, all his dreams of power seemingly at an end.

In the house of his first master, the captain of the guard, Joseph proves so trustworthy that he is eventually left alone in the house day after day. But here, as with the dreams of his youth, Joseph's foolish confidence in his own power leaves him vulnerable, this time to the desire and then fury of his master's wife. Thrown into prison, Joseph is once more rendered powerless. He witnesses the arbitrary injustice of Pharaoh's household when one cellmate is restored to his post while another is summarily executed. Joseph has now seen the dark underside of two systems: his family of origin and the country of his enslavement. And each time he has been humiliated, scorned and shamed, figuratively buried and forgotten.

Yet God is with this image bearer. He is part of a larger story he cannot yet imagine. Once more Joseph rises to power, this time at the very right hand of Pharaoh, and this time he is not only trustworthy but, we can well suppose, chastened enough to use his power carefully. Carefully, but boldly. When God uses Joseph to interpret Pharaoh's dream about seven fat cows and seven lean cows, Joseph is not slow to counsel Pharaoh about how to use his power for the flourishing of the whole land. And in response, Joseph becomes Pharaoh's vice regent (and son-in-law): "Removing his signet ring from his hand, Pharaoh put it on Joseph's hand; he arrayed him in garments of fine linen, and put a gold chain around his neck" (Genesis 41:42). Over the next seven years, Joseph presides over carefully stewarded abundance (grain "in such abundance—like the sand of the sea—that he stopped measuring it"). Then comes the famine that is the real test of leadership, and here too Joseph stewards the wealth and power of Egypt in such a way that not only Egypt but the neighboring countries, and Joseph's own family, are rescued from famine.

The sequence of scenes where Joseph comes to recognize his brothers, then tests them to their breaking point, then finally reveals himself to them with weeping so loud that it is heard throughout Pharaoh's house, are among the most moving in all literature. Like the rest of the story of Abraham's children, like any family's story, there is nothing neat or simple about these scenes, but they end with an astonishing reconciliation, as the son who had been given up for dead saves the lives of his whole family, embracing them and forgiving them everything.

And then there is one final scene, on the very last page of Genesis. After Jacob's death, Joseph's brothers come nervously to supplicate him and ask for forgiveness.

> Then his brothers also wept, fell down before him, and said, "We are here as your slaves." But Joseph said to them, "Do not be afraid! Am I in the place of God? Even though you intended to do harm to me, God intended it for good, in order to preserve a numerous people, as he is doing today. So have no fear; I myself will provide for you and your little ones." In this way he reassured them, speaking kindly to them. (Genesis 50:18-21)

Everything Joseph's brothers had feared comes true—and nothing they had feared comes true. Here they are bowing down before their inconceivably powerful brother. But his only thought is for reconciliation and the restoration of abundance. The humbling extremities of his story have made Joseph an image bearer, not a god player—"Am I in the place of God?" he asks. Whatever dreams of god playing Joseph might once have cherished have come to an end, because Joseph has forgiven. His power now is used to bless and to create institutions that will provide for future generations. He has become a trustee: entrusted, trusting and trustworthy. The institution that is Israel will fall again into injustice and idolatry. It will need future trustees, the judges, kings and prophets who will sometimes succeed and sometimes fail to forgive and lead their people. But Israel will always carry in its story of institutional beginnings a memory of the meaning of true power.

## BECOMING TRUSTEES

It is amazing how consistently the stories of even the most complex institutions come down to their trustees, the ones who, at their best, bear the institution's pain and brokenness, forgive it and serve it. It is amazing how consistently the fate of institutions hinges on a few people, and their own personal character, how much even one person can tip the balance toward devastating injustice or toward redeeming abundance. And it is amazing how often the most trustworthy trustees are those who have personally experienced the worst that idolatry and injustice can do. There is good news for all those who have been thrown into the pit by the Nietzschean power plays of every human structure and system—God does not forget his image bearers even in the deepest and darkest prison. And there is hard news for those who seem like the children of privilege, the ones who are handed the robe and ring even before they deserve it; they too will be broken by the very institutions they thought they would rule, and will have to choose whether to forgive and serve them nonetheless, to seek destructive dominance, or to descend into a hell of their own disappointment.

It might seem like it should not be this way. Surely institutional problems require institutional solutions. But this is not the witness of Scripture. Instead, over and over, both the most likely suspects and the most unlikely ones are called by God to become trustees. God works through the favorite son Joseph, and God works through the Canaanite prostitute Rahab. God calls Saul, the tall and dominant warrior, and God calls David, the youngest son keeping the sheep. Esther and Ruth, Nehemiah and Ezekiel, Hezekiah and Jeremiah—the story of the institutions of the world hinges not on institutions but on persons. It hinges on image bearers, and on their very personal responses to the injustice and idolatry that surround them, whether they become caught up in god playing or humbled in worship, corroded by cynicism or sustained by hope, bitter or forgiving.

So the institutions of our time will be changed not by impersonal institutional forces; they will be changed by trustees, the image bearers who face their institutions' failings, forgive them and lead toward a better way. One of them is named S. Kandaswamy. One of them could be you.

# EXPLORATION

## PHILEMON—THE PECULIAR INSTITUTION

I f there is one abuse of power that sets the pattern for all other abuses, one
institution that reminds us how pervasively corrupt institutions can
become, one zombie that has been harder than all the rest to kill—it is slavery.

In Galatians 3:28, Paul famously proclaims that three divisions of identity
have been set aside in Christ: male and female, Jew and "Greek" (meaning
Gentile), slave and free. But one of these is not like the others. Our identity
as male and female is rooted in the creation of humankind in God's image,
male and female. Our cultural identity is rooted in the divine command to
be fruitful and multiply, filling the earth, with all the cultural diversity that
would naturally ensue; the Jewish nation arose in response to the redemptive call of God to Abram the Aramean. But the status of "slave" and
"free" has no such root in the original goodness of creation or the creative
goodness of redemption. It is a distortion of the Fall, an echo of the violence that began with Cain and Abel and has haunted the human story ever
since. From the wars that furnished the Roman imperium with slaves from
among its subjugated peoples to the coercion and deceit that sustains
modern-day trafficking, slavery has always required violence to survive, because it is the ultimate expression of god playing and image breaking.

Faced with the distortions of power between husbands and wives that
led to divorce, Jesus could say, "In the beginning it was not so," and go on
to reaffirm the given goodness of gender and marriage (Matthew 19:3-12;

Mark 10:2-11). Faced with alienation between God's chosen people and their ethnically distinct neighbors, he could look forward to the promised future, telling the Samaritan woman at the well that an hour was coming when the special access of the Jews to the true God would give way to universal worship "in spirit and truth" from every nation, just as the prophets foretold (John 4:21-26).

But there is no corresponding good beginning to which slavery could be restored, nor any ultimate future to which it looks forward. It is, to borrow the famous phrase of the Southern senator John Calhoun, a "peculiar institution." In Calhoun's day the word *peculiar* meant belonging to a particular place or people—Calhoun's way of acknowledging and defending the role slavery played in the culture of the American South. Today the word means odd or unusual. But slavery is less odd or unusual than any of us would like to admit. It recurs over and over in human history, whether in the first century or the twenty-first, its endurance a sobering reminder of how far our institutions fall short of creating the conditions for flourishing.

Slavery was anything but peculiar, in either sense, to Paul's contemporaries in the Greco-Roman world. Slavery was so ubiquitous and essential to Roman society that it faded into the background. Like all truly enduring institutions, it became part of the landscape of human expectation, existing naturally and seemingly eternally within the horizons of the possible. There simply *were* some people who were free and some who were slaves, some who were owners and some who were owned.

Yet there was something about slavery that made this most enduring of institutions unstable at the same time. Slaves could and did run away. This was yet another reminder that unlike gender and "nation" or ethnic heritage, the status of slave was a fundamentally arbitrary and potentially temporary state of affairs. And the threat of runaway slaves (who might cart off some of their master's wealth with them) introduced regular tremors into the bedrock of the institution, disrupting its ability to be taken for granted. Every Roman master understood perfectly well that a slave who could gain his freedom would do so, and that some slaves would seize their freedom if they had a chance. And one slave who did so was named Onesimus.

Many aspects of the story of Onesimus are unknown to us, including the details of his encounter with the apostle Paul (probably while Paul was under house arrest in Rome, the city where runaway slaves often fled). Nor do we know what exactly happened after his return to his master Philemon bearing a letter from Paul, Philemon's dear friend, brother and elder in the faith. All we have is a strikingly intimate letter of a few hundred words. Yet we can be sure that the first time it was read it caused astonishment, for it profoundly challenged its first readers' assumptions about the way the world worked. It can still do so today. From the first words to the last, Paul's letter to Philemon is a power letter—a letter about power, to power, with power, against power and for power.

## REORIENTING POWER

Paul begins rearranging his readers' assumptions about power in the very first words. "Paul, a prisoner" invokes the coercive power of Rome to detain anyone who posed a threat to the imperial peace, yet these words are followed immediately by a qualification that changes everything: a prisoner "of Christ Jesus" (Philemon 1). Some English translations give the plausible alternative, "in Christ Jesus," but Paul's words in Greek are in the straightforward genitive case that shows whose prisoner Paul thinks he really is— not Caesar's but Christ's. Before he has even finished his first sentence, Paul has signaled that he lives in a universe of power very different from what his Roman captors, and perhaps his fellow Christians, think it is.

Then, as almost always in his letters, Paul adds the name of his coauthor, "Timothy our brother." Here he takes another word and remakes it, referring to this much younger nonrelative with the equalizing term *brother*, borrowing the intimacy, loyalty and authority of family to signal the ways relationships have been reoriented by the sacrifice of Christ.

The reorientation continues in the next part of the greeting, which is addressed not just "to Philemon our dear friend and co-worker," but also "to Apphia our sister, to Archippus our fellow soldier, and to the church in your house" (vv. 1-2), a greeting that places men and women side by side and places these Roman elites in the context of a whole church. (And here, again, Paul uses the language of family, bridging across the division of Jew and Greek.) This is no private message from one leader to another; it is a communication meant to place Philemon in the awkward position of hearing Paul's request while seated among the community he was privileged to host in his home. Yet while this message is not private, it is personal—after his initial greetings to the whole church, Paul switches to the second person singular ("you" rather than "y'all") and continues addressing Philemon directly and individually up until the final words of the letter.

Through an extraordinary coincidence—or providence—Paul has met Onesimus, the runaway slave of his dear friend Philemon, in the teeming tenements of Rome. And Onesimus has become a Christian, a "brother" in God's new family. It is a sign of how seriously Paul takes the reconciling, world-remaking power of the gospel that he believes this conversion requires healing the breach between master and slave. Paul cannot in good conscience let Onesimus remain in Rome, perpetually in flight from his master who is now his brother. But the gospel compels Paul to go farther, for it is clear that he does not simply intend that Onesimus return, apologize and take up his old subservient place in the household, showing up for church on Sundays in the very house where he is enslaved.

Instead Paul, without ever directly insisting that Philemon take the unprecedented step of granting freedom to a runaway slave, makes it as clear as can be that he expects Philemon will "do even more than I say" (v. 21). To persuade Philemon to be not just clement but generous, Paul pulls out every possible source of authority he can find—every one, that is, except the power to "command you to do your duty." The one role Paul will not step into is that of a master ordering a subordinate. He will not use the coercive power that distorts and diminishes human image bearing. But he will use everything else, from memories of their warm friendship to his role in Philemon's coming to faith, to his status as an "old man," to persuade Philemon to do "your good deed [as] voluntary and not something forced" (v. 14). And at the very end, like Steve Jobs in his famous product announcements, Paul throws in (literally) "one more thing": "prepare a guest room for me, for I am hoping through your prayers to be restored to you" (v. 22). Never have affection and accountability, constraint and hospitality, been combined so perfectly.

What did Philemon do? We do not know. We do know that fifty years later, the Antiochian bishop Ignatius addressed a letter to the church of Ephesus, just down the road from Philemon's home town of Colosse. The name of the bishop of Ephesus was none other than Onesimus. And, of course, we know that this strikingly personal letter was kept, passed on and eventually included in the canon of Scripture, something that hardly would have happened if the influential church elder had done much less than Paul expected.

We also know that the institution of slavery did not end, certainly not in the Roman Empire and probably not even in the church. For the same Paul who wrote so stirringly to Philemon also wrote to the churches of Philemon's region the "household codes" of Ephesians 5–6 and Colossians 3–4, addressing the very same categories that he had declared reconciled in Christ—men and women, free and slave, as well as parents and children—and giving instructions for how to maintain these institutions through mutual submission "in Christ." Many leaders in the first centuries of the church frowned on slave owning, to say the least: Augustine wrote, "By nature, then, in the condition in which God first created man, no man is the slave either of another man or of sin." But at other times, all the way down to John Calhoun's South, Bible-reading Christians found in the household codes—and in Paul's affectionate ambiguity in his letter to Philemon—plenty of precedent to maintain the institution of slavery.

The church did, at long last, fulfill Paul's hopes that Philemon would "do even more than I say." After nineteen centuries, the institution of slavery was overthrown not just on tablets of stone but on tablets of flesh as well. Not a single reader of this book will believe with John Calhoun that slavery should be a cherished institution. Culture has truly changed when what seemed possible to our forebears seems utterly impossible, indeed unthinkable, to us. Though its effects are still with us, the "peculiar institution" is well and truly gone, its image-breaking artifacts, arenas, rules and roles confined to museums and history books, incapable of being recaptured in our imaginations. It took a terribly long time for Christendom to be ready for Paul's visit to our guest room, but eventually the room was prepared.

## OUR PECULIAR INSTITUTIONS

But there are two sobering ironies that should cut short any self-congratulation. The first, as we have already noted, is that there are more human beings in bondage today than were trafficked in the whole history of the Atlantic slave trade. The tablets of stone have been erased and rewritten, but in many societies today slavery is just as possible as

ever. It takes place under cover of deceit and ignorance even in neighborhoods and cities near us.

To be sure, in most of the Western world, slavery is rarely institutionalized
and there are vigorous law enforcement efforts to stamp it out wherever it is
uncovered. But in other parts of the world the use of children's forced labor
to pay parents' debts, the enslavement of girls and women from immigrant
and ethnic minority groups for the commercial sex industry, and the exploitation of children from poor rural families to serve as unpaid servants to
urban ones is as taken for granted, as readily visible yet practically invisible, as
seemingly unstoppable, as slavery was to Philemon, Apphia, Archippus and
Onesimus. That is to say, it is an institution—a complex and deeply rooted
set of practices and beliefs that will require the same patience, courage and
creativity that Paul's letter to Philemon displays if it is ever to be uprooted
altogether. Already both "insiders" and "outsiders" are applying their power,
like Jayakumar and his coworkers in the district of Gudiyatham, to disen-
tangle and defang these peculiar institutions. There are few more compelling
uses for our power than finding ways to join them.

But the second sobering irony is that while we may no longer live in a
world where the institution of slavery is taken for granted, there are other
"peculiar institutions" that grant godlike power to a few and rob others of
their image-bearing dignity. These institutions are completely visible,
tightly woven into history and law, evident for those who have eyes to see
in signs on buildings in many cities and towns, yet also all but invisible,
rarely discussed and easily ignored. Consider just two.

The first is the institution of abortion. At most times and places in
history, of course, women and those with power over them have found
ways to end pregnancies. But in our time like few others in history,
abortion has become an institution—a set of artifacts, arenas, rules and
roles that, like all real institutions, gradually fade into the background and
simply become the taken-for-granted reality of "the world."

The second is incarceration in the United States. Every society has to find
ways to restrain those who do violence and threaten others' lives and liberty.
But today the United States imprisons twice as many people per capita as it
did just thirty years ago, and (at nearly one person out of every hundred)
more any other country in the world: 2.3 million Americans are "institution-

alized" in this manner today, and the effects of their incarceration are both invisible and pervasive. Because of its disparate impact on ethnic minority communities in particular, the institution of incarceration has been called "the new Jim Crow"—seen most of all in the absence of young black men from the home as fathers and from the labor force as productive workers.

Institutions take root when they become routine. Nothing reveals the institutional character of abortion in our time more clearly than the fact that when parents discover that their unborn child carries the genetic markers for Trisomy 21, better known as Down syndrome, at least two-thirds of them choose abortion. This is not abortion as a last-chance, desperate attempt to cope with the harsh realities of unplanned pregnancy; it is abortion as a straightforward solution to a common problem that poses certain challenges, but hardly insurmountable or unspeakably tragic ones, to parents and children. Likewise, in the 1990s, incarceration, previously imposed only at judges' discretion in the case of relatively minor crimes, became mandated as the usual way to deal with repeat offenses, leading to a dramatic increase in the number of people sent to prison. Like slavery in the Roman era and every era, abortion and incarceration have come to be seen less as a harsh necessity or even a necessary evil than a convenient arrangement that makes life considerably easier for those in power. All they require is that we look aside from the damage done to the image-bearing dignity of those who cannot resist or refuse.

If image-bearing institutions consistently lead to flourishing, image-breaking institutions consistently lead to violence. Abortion is a violent act, breaking the intimate physical and spiritual bond of mother and child, destroying one and wounding the other. Incarceration too is associated with extraordinary levels of violence *inside* prisons, however much it has reduced violence outside prisons (though half of prisoners in the United States are serving sentences for nonviolent crimes). Assault and rape are horrifyingly regular features of prison life.

And yet the very nature of "peculiar institutions" is that the violence they involve, which would be horrifying in any other context, becomes the subject of much more ambivalence when it is linked to the ends that the institution seeks to serve. The institutional character of abortion in our time is confirmed by the fact that while I can be confident no reader of this book supports the legalization of slavery, I can be equally confident that many readers of this book will be ambivalent about, or indeed passionately opposed to, the criminalization of abortion. Similarly, the suggestion that the disproportionate incarceration of minorities amounts to a "new Jim Crow" provokes fierce resistance from some quarters, including some Christians who believe they are sincerely pursuing the common good. Like Calhoun on the floor of the Senate, these readers see that abortion or incarceration cannot simply be excised from our society without a host of unintended consequences, and indeed without depriving some people of certain good things, just as Calhoun saw that abolition in the South would (and ultimately did) deprive some people of certain good things. These readers will strenuously resist the idea that the exercise of coercive power in these institutions is a denial of image bearing. In all these ways they are very much in Calhoun's position as he defended the "peculiar institution." Only through a failure of sympathetic imagination can we think that the case for deinstitutionalizing abortion or dramatically changing criminal justice in the United States should be any clearer or simpler to these thoughtful, faithful people than the case for abolishing slavery was to Calhoun—or to Philemon.

And this is not just a matter of theoretical positions on legal and ethical questions. It hits closer to home than that. I can be sure that many readers of this book will have made difficult decisions themselves to terminate pregnancies. Some of my friends have used the technique called "selective reduction" to conceive children through in vitro fertilization, allowing some embryos to come to term while eliminating others in the womb. In practically every church on every Sunday there are women who have undergone abortion and men who fathered the unborn children whose lives were ended. This is not something "out there" in a hostile, secular culture, but "in here" in the life of the Christian community. Likewise, the 2.3 million people incarcerated in this country may be only a distant reality in my suburban, dominant-culture church, but in many American churches the command from Hebrews 13:3 to "remember those who are in prison" brings to mind specific faces of fathers, husbands and brothers (as well as mothers, wives and sisters). And because abortion and incarceration are both subtractive, not creative, institutions, they are manifest most of all in the gaps, the lack and absence we will never truly comprehend—the children who could have been in our Sunday school and our schools, the men who could have been in the pews and in our homes, all the culture that will never be created by those whose freedom to create has been removed. All of this is present, and absent, when we gather for worship, sing and pray, and listen to the Scriptures, including Paul's letter to Philemon.

What could we learn from the way Paul addressed his own peculiar institution? Every broken institution has its abolitionists, those who cry for the immediate destruction of the artifacts and arenas that perpetuate a cultural pattern. Paul's letter certainly does not forbid that kind of activism, which takes place today through organizations like Operation Rescue and the Sentencing Project. Indeed, Paul himself could be every bit as fiercely radical an activist for cultural change as nineteenth-century abolitionists or twentieth-century pro-life demonstrators—just read his letter to the Galatians.

But the letter to Philemon, and the household codes with which it stands in such interesting contrast and tension, suggests that sometimes there is another way. Abolition and criminalization are coercive measures even when they are morally justified. They restrain action, which is to say, they constrain power and cut off the supply of oxygen for image bearing. Paul chooses something different. Though he is "able to command," he does not. Instead, he wants Philemon's good deed to be "voluntary and not something forced." For all the direct and indirect pressure Paul is placing on Philemon, he is concerned above all to preserve Philemon's capacity to act in his own right as an image bearer, not to grudgingly acquiesce to Paul's authority. Nor will Paul let Onesimus off the hook of his own image-bearing responsibility. He is called to stay in relationship with his master, now also his brother in Christ, rather than remaining, like the young prodigal, in the far country. What Paul seeks above all is to restore true power to everyone in Philemon's social world—to Philemon and Onesimus, Apphia and Archippus—the power that comes from love, faith, family, partnership, generosity, hospitality and ultimately grace.

What would a letter like this look like today addressing our own peculiar institutions? Rather than simply calling for the eradication of the institutions of abortion or the immediate repeal of mandatory sentencing, perhaps it would begin where Paul begins, with a wide community, much wider than the single mother or the couple who have received a troubling prenatal diagnosis, much wider than the criminal offender or even that offender's victim. Perhaps it would begin with thanksgiving for these image bearers at their best; perhaps it would be soaked in the language of family, prayer and celebration even as it called them to a more excellent and more difficult way than our current institutions offer. Perhaps it would, like Paul, boldly offer to share freely in paying all the costs—financial and emotional—of bringing children, even those with grave disabilities, to term and placing them in families, or training prisoners to use their energies in service to the community.

Perhaps it would creatively reinterpret the challenge of unexpected or disabled children in just as surprising and hopeful ways as Paul's redefinition of Onesimus, "no longer as a slave but more than a slave, a beloved brother," even as endeavors like the Prison Entrepreneurship Project have reframed urban drug dealers as people with the capacity to be successful entrepreneurs and business builders. Perhaps it would open up avenues of cultural creativity, recognizing that the very image bearers placed in these difficult situations are the ones most likely to "do even more than I say" and create new institutions that welcome those who once would have been excluded.

Paul's letter to Philemon has never been fully satisfying to activists and abolitionists, nor to those who bear the burden of injustice. It seems too incremental, too slow to right systemic wrongs. But it is less slow than it is patient. Paul's expectations of Philemon are indeed radical, but they are couched in the radical patience of love. Institutions, even image-breaking ones, are so deeply woven into our culture that they cannot be ripped out of the cultural fabric without doing serious damage. Only when broken, image-breaking institutions are carefully unwoven and replaced with the power of new imagination and new image-bearing relationships can they be fruitfully discarded. Perhaps this is why Paul's letter, so radical in its expectations, ends with hospitality, friendship and grace. Only as guests and friends of the true Host, the one who is himself preparing a guest room for us, can we unmake our institutions at their worst and be ready to greet him joyfully and wholeheartedly at his own return.

## PART FOUR

# THE END OF POWER

**WE HAD TO CELEBRATE**

12

# DISCIPLINED POWER

I admit that when I think about power, my mind returns again and again to Steve Jobs, one of the most visible, creative and tragic image bearers and god players of our generation. Walter Isaacson's biography of the man is simply stuffed with examples of power gone wrong, and they go far beyond Jobs's profanity-laced temper tantrums and brazen truth bending in the service of creative excellence. The most revealing anecdotes in Isaacson's biography are not the shouting matches but the moments when Jobs himself, and those around him, simply and quietly took his power for granted.

Isaacson recounts the story of how Jobs met Laurene Powell, the woman he ultimately married and spent the rest of his life with, seated in the first row for his lecture in a series called "View from the Top" at Stanford Business School. "'There was a beautiful girl there, so we started chatting while I was waiting to be introduced,' Jobs recalled. They bantered a bit, and Laurene joked that she was sitting there because she had won a raffle, and the prize was that he got to take her to dinner." (By the way, one minor detail ought not to pass without comment: even though Jobs signed emails to perfect strangers with just the name "Steve," Isaacson unfailingly refers to his subject by his last name. One of power's invisible perquisites is that others grant you deference without your having to ask for it. Meanwhile, here and elsewhere in the book Isaacson breaks journalistic convention by referring to figures like Powell by their first names—a none too subtle reinforcing of the asymmetry of power.)

Sure enough, after the lecture Jobs did ask her to dinner.

"How about Saturday?" he asked. She agreed and wrote down her number. Jobs headed to his car to drive up to the Thomas Fogarty winery in the Santa Cruz mountains above Woodside, where the NeXT education sales group was holding a dinner. But he suddenly stopped and turned around. "I thought, wow, I'd rather have dinner with her than the education group, so I ran back to her car and said 'How about dinner *tonight*?'" She said yes.

To most of Isaacson's readers, this probably seems like a perfectly romantic story—the ultimate "meet cute" scene for an attractive couple who talk into the wee hours at a "funky vegetarian restaurant." But the next paragraph reminds us of the currents of power surging through this simple how-they-met anecdote: "Avie Tevanian was sitting at the winery restaurant waiting with the rest of the NeXT education group. 'Steve was sometimes unreliable, but when I talked to him I realized that something special had come up,' he said."

*Steve was sometimes unreliable.* Jobs's biography gives us ample reason to judge that a drastic understatement. Isaacson does not clarify for us when exactly Tevanian and his colleagues found out that the CEO would not be joining them for dinner after all—perhaps a quick cell phone call as Jobs turned the car around, perhaps not until later that evening, perhaps not until the next day. In any event, what every participant in the story seems to take for granted, along with its storyteller, is that Jobs had made the right decision, following his heart to pursue the woman with whom he was about to fall in love.

But in fact, what Jobs had done was play god, a god whose promises do not matter and, indeed, are ostentatiously broken in order to supercharge a new opportunity with the tantalizing taste of forbidden fruit. It is the stuff romantic dreams are made of: throwing caution to the wind, dropping everything for another glimpse of one's crush. It is perfectly understandable. And it is saturated with god playing.

There are two key elements to this superficially charming story. The first is Jobs's willingness to abandon people whose welfare and flourishing he was responsible for as their CEO in exchange for dinner with a "beautiful girl" on the spur of the moment. The second is the distinctive quality of the crisis that prompted breaking that promise, and that is that *there was no crisis*. Powell had already said she would have dinner with Jobs on Saturday night. He was not driving off to the Santa Cruz mountains never to see her again. He had her phone number and, reading between the lines, every reason to believe she would meet him any time, anywhere. Jobs could have invited her to breakfast at 5 a.m. the next morning and she probably would have said yes.

Jobs could have had it all. He could have had a dinner with Laurene Powell on Saturday night—made romantically thrilling, as any lover could testify, by virtue of delay and anticipation—and also kept his promise to his team. Instead he discarded his promise in order to seize something that was already in his grasp. It was not just Jobs's employees who came to know that "Steve was not always reliable," but, as Isaacson's biography makes painfully clear, the family he would eventually form with the beautiful girl he met that night.

## VIEW FROM THE TOP

Yet this is exactly the sort of story we tell all too often about our heroes—or, better put, our idols—stories of breaking the rules in order to get the girl, bending the truth to serve some great cause, committing crimes in order to achieve justice. False god players believe that to have what we really need and want, we have to break our promises. We believe this, as Jobs's choices that night show, even when it is patently not true. The lie that pulses at the heart of every act of idolatry and injustice is that we are unfairly constrained by our promises, duties and obligations—all of which are marks of our creatureliness, our dependence and contingency on others—rather than graciously freed by them. God playing demands not just the chance to make our dreams come true but the freedom to discard our obligations to people who no longer seem to serve our immediate interests.

This is one reason that so many people who achieve exceptional fame and power also exhibit a pattern of serial divorce and remarriage. To be sure, by all accounts, Steve Jobs ended up being a faithful and devoted husband to Laurene Powell (though the same cannot be said of his relationship with Chrisann Brennan, the mother of his first child). In that respect he was an exception that proves the rule. To the extent that power is the result of idol making and idol playing, it will almost always distort our deepest relationships. That distortion does not necessarily have to take the form of divorce; for every family visibly broken by a powerful member's incapacity to keep his promises, there is another where spouse and children know the equally cruel reality of unavailability and unreliability. As the funny but also sadly cynical T-shirt puts it, "Behind every great man is a woman rolling her eyes."

Like all cynicism, that T-shirt expresses something all too true, but also not true at all. True greatness and true power is faithful all the way down, including humbly quick to admit limitedness, sin and brokenness, and to ask for forgiveness. Behind all of the greatest, and some of the most powerful, people I have personally had the good fortune to know are spouses, children and friends who have been deeply known and loved. One friend, a prominent pastor, has guarded a decades-long marriage to a wife with a difficult chronic disease. Another friend, leader of a major institution, patiently cares for a daughter with profound cognitive deficits. A CEO has lived gracefully and humbly with several disabilities, including a degenerative nerve disease, while also saving and creating thousands of jobs by leading successful turnarounds of several public companies. They are only the most dramatic examples of people with great power who do not use their power to grasp at opportunities to demonstrate their godlike freedom from constraint, or to discard obligations that threaten to expose their creatureliness and limits. Instead they have become more like the true God the more they embrace everything that has been given them, including their own and others' limits and pain.

All these friends bear eloquent witness that wielding significant power does not require the kind of narcissistic infidelity that Jobs indulged that evening. Infidelity is not just a matter of breaking marriage vows or unspoken romantic commitments. Infidelity is the name for what happens any time we renegotiate our promises unilaterally, for our own interests, when they turn out to constrain our dreams of what our life should be. Infidelity is rooted in an implicit belief that if we honor the promises we have made, we will miss out on what we are really made for. Once again we see the power of zero-sum thinking—the calculation in even such a fertile and creative mind as Jobs's that one has to choose between the dull but real duties of leadership (dinner with the sales team) and the true joys of life (the "something special" Tevanian referred to).

Of course, the opposite is closer to the truth. It is not those who keep their promises who end up bereft, but those who have been seduced into god playing. One goal of discipleship is to shape our lives so closely after Jesus that we understand, with Paul, that "all things are yours," whether "the world or life or death or the present or the future—all belong to you, and you belong to Christ, and Christ belongs to God" (1 Corinthians 3:21-23). There is nothing good that we have to grasp and wrest out of the hostile world's clenched fist. Everything good has been and will be given to us.

Lurking behind every page of Isaacson's biography, and many of the worshipful responses to Jobs's life, is an assumption that is sometimes stated outright: that Jobs's eating disorder, fits of rage and unreliability were all the inescapable corollaries of his creative genius—that to take away his hypercontrolling personality would also have been to rob him of the very qualities that made him such a brilliant designer and leader. Not for the first time has our culture concluded that greatness excuses, or indeed requires, this kind of soul sickness. Ernest Hemingway's alcoholism and despair, which eventually led to his suicide, were long seen not only as not detrimental to his writing but essential to it.

This assumption is a lie, an especially cruel lie if it is allowed to minimize the human cost of Jobs's god playing to the persons who were most dependent on him for love and support, not least his first child, with whom he had such a strained relationship. Nothing is gained and much is lost when a life spirals into idolatry—no matter how much creative image bearing may also be preserved by the mysterious workings of common grace. Had Jobs been able to turn from his more extreme forms of god playing, his life might have yielded much more, not less, lasting cultural fruit.

## TAMING POWER

What wretched creatures we are, even and especially with all of our power and privilege! What can deliver us from our entanglement with sin and death, even and especially at the height of our powers? The Christian tradition has a simple and sobering answer. We will need the spiritual disciplines.

The spiritual disciplines are not like the kinds of discipline that most of us have mastered to some extent. No one acquires substantial creative power, after all, without certain kinds of discipline. The ability to concentrate and work hard, the commitment to practice an instrument or craft or sport over and over, the willingness to defer gratification in hopes of a larger future reward—all of these, especially if learned and practiced from an early age, give us options and opportunities that less-disciplined people may well miss.

For this reason one rarely encounters people with substantial creative power who are truly undisciplined. Steve Jobs may have been unwilling to tame his temper or show up to dinner engagements, but he was ferociously disciplined in other aspects of his work life and, indeed, in his approach to food. And while any discipline can become an idol, many of these disciplines are genuinely good pathways to image bearing. When I discipline myself to sit and write, pushing aside the distractions that arise from the world outside and from my own heart with its fantasies and fears, I become more like the person I know I can be at my best: calm, hopeful, careful, clear.

And yet the disciplines that lead to power are not enough to prevent the worst forms of god playing—in fact, they can reinforce it. Practicing an instrument day after day can be a humbling, grounding experience of gratitude and human flourishing, but for some professional musicians it also becomes a furious pursuit of ambition, competition and even addiction. A capacity for intense, focused work can be the sign of mature commitment to excellence, but it can also become a barrier to true dependence on and intimacy with God and other people. And, of course, in the realm of faith itself the disciplines of personal prayer and spirituality can either lead to genuine faithfulness or become the sources of idolatrous and unjust pride. Jesus tells the story of a meticulously disciplined Pharisee who prays in the temple steps away from a wretched tax collector—telling us that the repentant tax collector went home justified while the self-congratulating Pharisee did not. The more successful we are at the disciplines that lead to power, the more at risk we are from their shadow side, and the more we become exposed to the perilous freedom granted to those who have accomplished something in the world. It is then, if it is not too late, that we need to embrace the disciplines that tame power: the disciplines that make us more deeply and truly image bearers of the true God.

So anyone who desires to use their power for image bearing rather than god playing needs to embrace not just the disciplines that lead to success but the disciplines that lead away from it. The classical Christian tradition has emphasized three practices that radically interrupt lives of power and privilege: solitude, silence and fasting. Each of these practices involves the intentional pursuit of secret defeat, the perfect antidote to a life of sociable success. And each of these contributes to shaping us into image bearers who can use whatever power we are given humbly and wisely.

The spiritual disciplines, and all disciplines that tame power, are in some ways like the disciplines that lead to cultural power. They require patient, repeated choices, and only reward those who practice them over long spans of time. Yet in other ways they are quite different. On the one hand, they are so easy that any adult human being can do them. There are no particular skills required to be alone, to be silent or to abstain from food. Yet on the other hand, they are so difficult, and so perfectly calibrated to reveal the true condition of our hearts, that no one can "succeed" at them. Indeed, the secret of the classical spiritual disciplines, and all disciplines that tame power, is how reliably they lay waste to whatever sense we may have of ourselves as competent agents in the world.

Take fasting and food, where I can offer a personal testimony to the humbling effect of the disciplines. My annual fasts during the seasons of Advent and Lent are darkly comical reminders of how completely undisciplined I truly am in my relationship with food. No matter how minimal the fast I set out to practice—one Lent it simply was leaving milk out of my tea—I find that I am almost never able to keep it to the end. Among the most pitiful moments of my life was that day, about two weeks into Lent, when I desperately and furtively opened the refrigerator, fully aware that I was breaking the most minimal fast conceivable but feeling completely unable to go on without milk in my tea. It was the sweetest, and the bitterest, cup of tea I have ever had.

When we practice the spiritual disciplines, we discover how deep runs our commitment to our own autonomy and comfort, and how addicted we are to the approval of others, the sound of our own voice, and the satisfaction of our appetites. For those whose creative power has emerged from sociability and success, sufficient amounts of solitude and silence will ruthlessly unmask how dependent we are on others' approval and affirmation. We discover how much we rely on them to shield us from our own failings, regrets and fears. Indeed, we have used our power and privilege to shield us from deeper, darker forces that the desert saints knew as demons, which have always been present to us but do not make themselves known until we begin the pursuit of the disciplines.

It is by no means necessary to take a weeks-long vision quest into the wilderness. For anyone who has succeeded in our always-on, noise-filled culture, an hour alone in a quiet room without the Internet, without recorded music, and without a reassuring to-do list to accomplish is more than enough to reveal the true state of our hearts. I dare say that most readers of this book will never have attempted even an hour of solitude and silence—and that many of us who try such a elementary discipline for the first time will find ourselves quite unable to "watch and pray one hour." So deeply are we invested in the reassuring trappings of our power and unaware of our real spiritual poverty.

There are other important disciplines that can or must be done in community: the practices of sabbath, confession, study, tithing and prayer. These disciplines, too, share the essential paradox of simplicity and difficulty. Yet all these sociable disciplines are subject to subtle or overt distortions from our pursuit of power and privilege (as when a pastor spends most of his study and prayer time preparing for the very public and powerful act of preaching). The solitary disciplines are fundamental precisely because they bring an end to our playing god: there is no audience, no one to play to except our severely merciful Creator, who graciously uses these disciplines to confront us with the depth of our idolatry and injustice.

Yet strangely enough, as we practice the beautiful defeat of both the sociable and solitary disciplines, we find ourselves living more and more lightly in the face of power and privilege—our own and others'. If we want to be the kind of people who can take up power, and lay it down, the disciplines are the only adequate preparation.

## THE DISCIPLINE OF DISHES

While any serious Christian life is built around the classical spiritual disciplines, there are important disciplines that are far less dramatic than solitude, silence and fasting. Some of the best disciplines for taming power are very small.

One of the dull but real duties in my life is doing the dishes that accumulate with astonishing speed in our family kitchen. Yet for many years my work has taken me away from home several times a month, and the hours preceding a trip are often consumed with last-minute preparations for the meetings or speaking engagements that will greet me when I arrive. The last thing on my mind, I have found, is the mundane maintenance of our family life that will have to continue while I am away.

But while I am off being treated with absurd courtesy and being showered with the accoutrements of power—the wireless microphones that amplify my voice, the gracious introductions that amplify my accomplishments, the always polite and frequently enthusiastic applause, the meals out with old and new friends—there will still be dishes accumulating in the kitchen. In the last minutes before leaving for the airport, those dishes seem like the least important thing I could possibly attend to, which is exactly why one of my personal disciplines is, whenever possible, to do them all before I leave. Many times I've torn myself away from revising a talk, tweaking a set of presentation slides, or rehearsing a piece of music in order to plunge my hands into hot, soapy water and deal with the dishes from last night's (or, to be honest, last week's) dinner.

Doing the dishes serves an immediate, practical purpose. But I have come to see that it serves an even more important role in shaping my relationship to my own power. Dirty dishes remind me of my own creatureliness, my implication in and membership in the world's glorious mess. Even the most delicious feast comes with responsibilities to patiently restore the world. The dirty dishes remind me, too, that I am embedded in relationship with other glorious and messy human beings. I don't just wash my own dishes, cleaning up after myself in a neat tit-for-tat, but my family's and our guests'. As I lavish soap over the leavings of their nurture and refreshment, I am prompted to see how physical our love and friendship are—not just warm feelings but the tangible sharing of the very goodness of the world, always accompanied by our need for grace for all that we leave behind.

Most of all, doing the dishes on deadline (more than once, while the taxi waits outside our house) challenges and undermines my zero-sum calculus of opportunity. I wash plenty of dishes when I am not going anywhere, but it is the pre-travel dishwashing that is the real test of my oddly powerful life. It is only in those precious moments before I leave that it becomes clearest that serving my family feels, and is meant to feel, *costly*—that it limits, and is meant to limit, my own exercise of godlike freedom and significance within the bounds of a more deeply Christlike, image-bearing set of commitments and smallness.

As I spend valuable time with my hands in the sink, I am challenged to trust that "all things are mine"—that the God who has called me to speak to a thousand people has also called me to clean this pan, and vice versa, and I have been given all the time I need, and more, both to serve my family's mundane needs and also to use my gifts in public. I can plunge my anxieties about being sufficiently prepared and getting to the airport on time into the hot water, turning my dishwashing into a prayer for those I will greet at the other end of my travels and a prayer for those I am leaving behind. The honest truth is that not once have I ever felt any reason to regret my time spent serving my family this way, whereas more than once, having left a sink full of dishes behind in self-imposed hurry, I've been haunted by regret and the painful awareness of how little I trust God and how thin my love for my family is.

My predeparture dishwashing is a discipline—a practice deliberately chosen to chasten and form my false god playing into something more like true image bearing. For a person with a public religious life, it answers the essential quality of spiritual practices articulated by Jesus in the Sermon on the Mount: it is done "in secret," out of public view and of little conceivable interest to anyone else.

Or at least it was, until I engaged in this little act of authorial alchemy, turning a mundane, unremarkable activity into an object lesson in spiritual disciplines—meaning that it has become, or could become, merely one more contribution to burnishing my public image. Now it will have to be supplemented by yet more commitments to small, unremarkable things that are truly kept secret, never used in any book or lecture, known only to those who know me best or not even to them, not even known by the hand not involved in them. The pursuit of a mature life, a life that can bear the weight of image bearing, is in many ways the continual accumulating of more and more secret disciplines, until we are fully formed in the image of the one who confronted every temptation, every opportunity for the misuse of power, and always and only bore the true image in the midst of it all.

## THE INTERRUPTIBLE GOD

One of the many remarkable things about Jesus of Nazareth is the abundant evidence that his life was shaped by spiritual disciplines. From childhood on, Jesus' life was built around weekly observance of the sabbath and annual pilgrimages to the temple. The Gospels report that he would regularly rise before dawn to pray. Before his public ministry began he spent forty days in none other than solitude, silence and fasting.

Yet the same Gospels that report Jesus' rhythm of spiritual disciplines also reveal a remarkable ability to improvise and change plans on the spur of the moment. Jesus would spot a tax collector in a tree and invite himself over to dinner, stop to listen to a blind beggar calling from the side of the road, and allow a perfume- and tears-laced interruption by a woman of ill repute during a formal dinner at the home of a Pharisee.

We might think that Jesus' openness to interruptions and changes of plans was much like the impulsiveness of powerful people like Steve Jobs. And in one sense, it was—Jesus was never bound by the narrow expectations of others. But when we examine Jesus' changes of plans more closely, we discover an unmistakable pattern: Jesus' changes of plans almost always took him in the opposite direction of his own privilege. The purpose of every one of Jesus' improvisations was the restoration of image bearing in places where it had been lost. He exercised his power to interrupt in others' interests, never his own.

Perhaps the most remarkable story of Jesus' interruptibility is narrated in the fifth chapter of the Gospel according to Mark, as Jesus is on the way to the house of Jairus, a synagogue ruler whose twelve-year-old daughter is dying. Jairus has all the markers of power in his society—his gender, his position, a house full of servants—but has been brought low and powerless by the illness of his daughter and has come humbly to Jesus. A miracle in Jairus's house would surely be an asset to Jesus' Galilean ministry, and as they make their way there Jesus and Jairus are surrounded by the large crowd that could be expected to gather when a charismatic visitor and a local leader were in the same place, brought together by a crisis.

Yet the story is decisively, and from Jairus's point of view it seems fatally, interrupted by another person whose description compresses nearly every marker of disempowerment: "A woman was there who had been subject to bleeding for twelve years. She had suffered a great deal under the care of many doctors and had spent all she had, yet instead of getting better she grew worse" (Mark 5:25-26 NIV). She is a woman; she is chronically ill with an illness that would leave her perpetually "unclean" and cut off from the community, while also preventing her from childbearing; she has suffered and lost everything. Jairus had approached Jesus and boldly (though humbly) fallen at his feet; she sneaks up from the back, not daring even to call his name. And while we know Jairus's name, her name we do not know. All we know is that her faith draws "power" from Jesus, causing him to stop, search and listen to "the whole truth," and at last send her off with the tender words, "Daughter, your faith has healed you. Go in peace and be freed from your suffering" (v. 34).

This daughter's healing comes at a great cost for Jairus's daughter. During what can only have been a long and patient conversation, "those from Jairus's household" arrive to tell Jairus that the child has died. The interruption has saved one anonymous daughter, but seemingly has doomed another prominent one. But Jesus now presses on, ignoring the resigned fatalism of Jairus's servants, and arrives at the house of the powerful man—only to close the doors so that no one but the parents and three disciples will see the ensuing miracle. The resurrection of Jairus's daughter takes place out of sight, and the parents are enjoined to say nothing about it, so that the crowd outside might well suppose that she had merely recovered rather than been resurrected. The anonymous daughter is healed publicly; the prominent daughter is healed secretly.

No story shows more clearly Jesus' utter disregard of human privilege— disregard, not antipathy or distaste. He is swayed neither by Jairus's prominence nor by the woman's poverty, but by the faith and desperate need of each one. Jesus is not a strategic political calculator, currying favor with the local leaders; nor is he a revolutionary, ostentatiously undercutting the powerful. He is a restorer of daughters, known and unknown, socially central and socially marginal. And while he is indifferent to human power, he is so exquisitely aware of his own power to restore health (which is simply another way to say flourishing image bearing) that the slightest faithful brush with his cloak brings him to a halt, not content to have power flow anonymously and disconnectedly, searching out relationship with the ones who seek him.

Over and over in the Gospels, Jesus interrupts his agenda for those who have nothing to offer him but need everything from him. And over and over, as behind the closed doors in Jairus's house, he ensures that when his agenda is interrupted by someone who could benefit his cause, any potential accumulation of privilege is averted. When crowds gather in Peter's hometown after the healing of Peter's mother-in-law, Jesus and the disciples sneak off before dawn; when the throngs who were miraculously fed seek to make him king by acclamation, he gets in a boat and crosses to the less receptive side of the lake. When the woman enters Simon's house to break a jar of pure nard over his head, he interprets her lavish offering: "She poured perfume on my body beforehand to prepare for my burial" (Mark 14:8 NIV). Jesus has no need to stockpile power or impulsively grasp at what he wants or needs; he knows as deeply as a human being can know that "the Father had given all things into his hands" (John 13:3). Living in the reality of infinite abundance, he can steer his course ever more directly toward the abyss of powerlessness from which no one has ever returned, stopping only to restore the true image in anyone who asks.

This improvisational, interruptible life that was Jesus' can be ours as well; it is, in fact, the surprising result of the spiritual disciplines. By gradually confronting and weaning us from our god playing and its associated undercurrent of scarcity—by making us into the kind of spiritually poor people who fall down at Jesus' feet and reach for his cloak—the disciplines form us into the kind of people who interrupt our agenda for others rather than interrupting others for our agenda. They make us people who have a holy indifference to worldly power and a passionate commitment to using the power we have been given, which is everything we need and more, to restore the image of God in the world. So ultimately, the spiritual disciplines—the disciplines that lead us away from power into deserts both literal and spiritual, that are

designed to tame whatever other kind of power we have acquired—
actually have a great deal in common with the disciplines that lead to
power. They are the path to flourishing, not just for us, not just for the
"something special" that each of us secretly hopes for, but for a world
groaning to be made new.

# THE SABBATH LADDER

*G*leaning is one of those biblical words, and ideas, all but lost to those of us who live in postindustrial societies. It is the subject of one of the more remarkable commands in the book of Leviticus, placed right in the midst of commandments of the gravest importance about idolatry and injustice, and it culminates with the solemn name of the Lord who gives it:

> When you reap the harvest of your land, you shall not reap to the very edges of your field, or gather the gleanings of your harvest. You shall not strip your vineyard bare, or gather the fallen grapes of your vineyard; you shall leave them for the poor and the alien: I am the LORD your God. (Leviticus 19:9-10)

We see the practice of gleaning at work most vividly in the book of Ruth, where widows and foreigners like Naomi and Ruth are able to follow the harvesters, gathering enough grain from the corners of the fields that they can support themselves. Gleaning is not charity, in the sense of passively received handouts that take the place of work; rather, leaving the edges of the field unharvested and the grapes between the vines ungathered makes it possible for "the poor and the alien" to participate in the dignified productivity of harvest. Faithful agriculture will, like the fields of the prodigal son's father, produce "bread enough and to spare," so that every member of the community has the opportunity to experience the abundance of good work.

But gleaning requires discipline on the part of the landowner and the harvesters. Gleaning is a discipline that tames power, placing limits on the temptation to idolatry and injustice. You might think a diligent harvester's job would be to extract the maximum amount of grain from the field and the greatest tonnage of grapes from the vines. Instead, the discipline the Lord required of Israel was *not* to do everything within their power, *not* to push their own productivity to the limit—to intentionally leave margins that made room for others to participate in the economy of the community (and perhaps, as in the book of Ruth, to get to know a distant relative a bit better).

The practice of gleaning raises suggestive questions about our own economy. What kind of margins should be left at the edges of modern economic sectors so that the unemployed can still do meaningful work, and the poor have opportunities to provide for their own families rather than standing in line waiting for others' generosity? In the restaurant and grocery sector, with their close links to agriculture, for-profit companies and not-for-profit organizations have partnered to ensure that the abundant leftovers of modern food service become available for the clients of food banks—though these efforts could be much improved by creating opportunities for the dignity of harvest rather than the passivity of handouts.

But the practice of margins and gleaning has more than just an economic application. It applies wherever there are dramatic disparities in power. Precisely because our power is the result of genuine image bearing, a genuine human calling to have dominion over the world in God's name, the human hunger for power is insatiable. We seek greater opportunities to use our gifts for a good reason: we are meant for far more. It is not wrong to want to "expand our territory" (in the words of the Old Testament figure named Jabez). But the more our territory expands, the more we must embrace the disciplines that make room on the margins for others to also exercise their calling to image bearing.

Indeed, in the wider context of Leviticus, leaving margins along the fields for gleaning is just the first step on a ladder of disciplines. Each one is meant to *limit* Israel's agricultural productivity in the name of preserving the possibility of true image bearing, not just for Israel but for any human being who sojourns among them as stranger or slave. Every day when the workers harvest, they will leave margins; every week, they will observe a day of sabbath, leaving the crops to grow on their own; every seven years they are enjoined to leave the field alone entirely and live simply on whatever may come up without active cultivation; and every fiftieth year (that is, after seven sevens) they are to celebrate the extraordinary festival of Jubilee, where debts are forgiven, land that has been pledged as security for debts is returned to its original family, and slaves are freed. At each stage of this escalating "sabbath ladder" the powerful are asked to relinquish more of their power and, especially, their privilege—the accumulated fruits of their successful exercise of power. On a daily basis they are to hold back from wringing the last possible ounce of produce from the land, but at intervals of weeks and years and most of all once a lifetime, they are to prodigally withhold the rightful exercise of their power. *Not* because God does not intend wealth to be invested productively and yield an abundant harvest, but because both the wealthy and the poor are image bearers, and only by climbing the sabbath ladder will the powerful be assured that they are making room for others to glean, to rest and to feast.

What does the discipline of margins for gleaning look like for those of us who do not own fields or vineyards? In essence, it seems to ask that in every area that we are especially competent, we must ensure that our productive work does not crowd out other image bearers. Part of our responsibility with our own power, oddly enough, is not to use it as much as we can.

In the fall of 2011 I had the opportunity to exercise a certain amount of power by writing an essay for the *Wall Street Journal* after the death of Steve Jobs. Though the circumstances that gave rise to the piece were tragic, the opportunity to offer a Christian reflection on the meaning of Jobs's life seemed like an image-bearing moment. There was also, inevitably, the heady experience of realizing that two pages of a national newspaper had been devoted to my words and that my careful work had opened up relationships with editors I had not previously known—the kind of "break" every writer hopes for.

A few weeks later, in fact, the editors reached out to me again, asking if I was interested in writing a similar essay on the football player Tim Tebow. Now, to tell the truth, I am pitifully uninformed about football, but no cultural commentator could miss the significance of this openly Christian quarterback during his first season in the NFL, along with his efforts to use his power—his fame and football prowess—to point to something greater than the game itself.

In a given year, hardly anyone has two shots at the coveted two-page cover story in the *Journal's* weekend Review section. Every worldly calculation would have said that I should say yes to the invitation and get to work, patching up my football knowledge with some quick visits to Wikipedia and maybe even ESPN.com. Never mind that to do so would have taken me to the absolute edges of the field I know how to cover as a journalist, that I would have been reduced to picking up the grapes dropped by other better-informed writers, and that the invitation came in the midst of an already packed week. I am fairly sure that had this same sequence of events happened when I was thirty years old, I would have said yes in an instant and gotten feverishly to work.

But instead, I chose to leave this particular field unharvested—at least by me. As it happened, just a few weeks earlier my friend Patton Dodd, an experienced, insightful journalist who also happened to be (as I could tell by his Facebook posts) a devoted Denver Broncos fan, had told me about a writing project he was completing, an ebook on Tim Tebow and his Christian faith. I wrote the *Journal* editor, declining the assignment but suggesting they take a look at Patton's ebook and giving them his cell phone number. That weekend, Patton's article was on the front page of the *Wall Street Journal* Review, followed over the next few weeks by Patton's appearing on most of the major sports radio and TV networks for interviews about his timely and controversial subject.

I would have to be more of a saint than I am not to have tracked the success of Patton's article with keen attention. But I would be less of a saint than I am becoming if I didn't cheer as my friend got the opportunity to reap a much richer harvest than I could ever have managed. The truth is that while I suppose I could have written a competent article about Tim Tebow, Patton was the right one for the job. And far beyond any effect my not writing, and Patton's writing, may have had on his career and mine, I am sure beyond any doubt that there was a greater abundance of grace and truth in the major media in the weeks following his article than there would have been if I had attempted to reap that harvest by myself.

Making room for gleaning does not just ensure that others can eke out a dignified living even in straitened circumstances; by preserving the conditions for fruitful image bearing for every person in our circle of influence, it also makes room for abundance and flourishing far beyond the mere provision of basic needs. The book of Ruth, indeed, is one of the many reminders sown throughout the Bible that our small disciplines make room for extraordinary infusions of God's grace into history. Boaz and his workers were simply obeying the Levitical law to make room for the poor, widow and alien, and if all that resulted was the provision of food and dignity to a few Moabite image bearers, that would have been enough. But in the providence of God, a gleaner named Ruth was able to meet a kinsman-redeemer who could not only rescue her and her mother-in-law from exile, but become with her the ancestor of the kinsman-redeemer of the whole human race. In the very margins of the field where Boaz left room for gleaning, God was planting the seeds for the ultimate abundance of history.

Indeed, from a cosmic perspective it is not just human beings who make room for gleaning. The Creator of the universe spoke uncountable galaxies into being, and at the fringes of the vast cosmos created by his Word and sustained by the Spirit, he placed us. Compared to the power and creativity that brought the universe into existence we are infinitesimal and poor. Modern science is showing us in detail how utterly dependent we are on things far beyond our control, from the fine tuning of the cosmological constants to the fusion furnace of our own nearby—but not too nearby!—star to the millennia's worth of creatures whose death and decay gives life in the few inches of soil in which everything grows. Perhaps even more amazingly, the bewildering field of quantum mechanics suggests that at the very core of the universe is uncertainty and, therefore, freedom. For all our utter dependence on the creative power of God, he has carved out for us a habitable environment of dignity, freedom and possibility (as well as the risk of falling and failing). At the edges of the vast fields of stars we do our little work, sowing what we could never have provided for ourselves and harvesting what we have not sown. We are all gleaners. When we ensure that our use of power does not extend to its absolute limits but freely limit our power so that others can themselves harvest, we are doing exactly what the Creator God himself has done. To make room for gleaning is to play the true God.

## SABBATH

Making room for gleaning limits and disciplines our daily exercise of power. Any of us who possesses any significant power should ask each day what we might leave *un*done that day for the sake of others' creativity. But on a weekly basis we are commanded not just to leave margins around our exercise of power but to withdraw from it altogether. In the practice of sabbath, as of making room for gleaning, we once again play in the footsteps of the Creator God, whose work was not without rest and within whose sabbath all the rest of the story has unfolded.

The sabbath is more familiar to us than gleaning, and in recent years not just Christians but our society as a whole have been embracing—well, at least gingerly sidling up to—the possibility that restless, work-filled lives are not as good as lives with regular rhythms of ceasing and feasting. Yet it is extraordinary how few Christians make any concerted effort to keep the commandment of sabbath rest. We have somehow twisted Jesus' pithy rebuke of the Pharisees, "The sabbath was made for humankind, and not humankind for the sabbath" (Mark 2:27) from a warning against legalism into a license for neglect. We seem to forget that in the very next breath Jesus asserts, "so the Son of Man is lord even of the sabbath" (v. 28), thus asserting his lordship over—not exemption from or indifference to—this very good gift from God to his image bearers.

There is perhaps no single thing that could better help us recover Jesus' lordship in our frantic, power-hungry world than to allow him to be Lord of our rest as well as our work. The challenge is disarmingly simple: one day a week, not to do anything that we know to be work.

But as soon as this simple definition is laid out, the objections begin. Someone has to cook and do the dishes, right? Well, no—for one thing, as Jewish families know well, the cooking can be done the day before and the dishes will wait for the next. And for those of us not bound by the details of the Jewish halakha, in most households there is someone for whom doing dishes is *not* work, not part of our daily calling but a diversion from it. In our own household, where doing the dishes is part of my daily maintenance of our shared life, I will often get up from my Sunday afternoon nap to find that my wife has done the dishes for me. Conversely, Catherine somehow manages to fit cooking in to the family routine along with her demanding research and teaching; so on Sundays, more often than not, I do the cooking instead. We are not legalistic, though, about either dishes or cooking; we save that for our computers, which are firmly shut Saturday night and not reawakened for twenty-four hours.

There is so much more to sabbath than what we stop doing, but for the purposes of disciplining power, simply stopping matters a great deal. The God whom we are meant to play is a God who stops. Indeed, in Genesis 1's creation account God stops every day, as the day comes to an end, in order to celebrate what he has done with the benediction of goodness. (While surely it is true that the Maker of the world neither slumbers nor sleeps, the Creator of Genesis 1 does not pull all-nighters.) Likewise, in the Garden of Eden we find God walking (not working) in the cool of the day. But on the seventh day God stops not only to bless but to "hallow" or set apart the sabbath. The holiness of God is revealed not just in what he does but how he rests.

There is no quicker way to discern our god playing or image bearing than to take the measure of our sabbath observance. The point is neither to outdo one another in extreme acts of sabbatarian asceticism nor to find the finest possible line between work and rest—it is simply to ask ourselves and be asked by our friends, Is there a day a week when we can honestly say that we do not work? In particular, as our power has increased, what has happened to our sabbath observance? Has it become deeper, faithful and more joyful, or has the idol of false god playing driven us ever more toward busyness and 24/7 control? One reliable sign that you are worshiping, and playing, a false god is when your power has increased but you find yourself on an ever-steeper treadmill, less and less able to rest.

As with all the best spiritual disciplines, sabbath observance serves perfectly as both diagnosis and prescription. Our ability to disengage from the activities that give us identity, meaning and agency in our public worlds will tell us volumes about whether our activity is fruitful image bearing or increasingly desperate god playing. And if we do keep the laptop closed, let text messages go unanswered and billable hours uncollected, we will learn a great deal about our own spiritual condition. In the resulting quiet, the worship shared with others, and hours of unstructured time, do we find ourselves anxious or content, fearful or confident, peaceful or restless, depressed or joyful?

In recent years sabbath has told me (and my family) more than I really wanted to know about the extent to which I was failing to leave margins for gleaning in my daily work. Too often I have retired, exhausted, for a long nap after church (and on too many weeks I have been too tired to take much joy in going to church at all). As the end of the day approaches, low-grade irritability and depression at the demands of the coming week have been evidence that my life, for all its appearance of satisfying work and gratifying influence, is infected with idolatry and is probably therefore perpetuating injustice, distorting the way I treat other image bearers. I rarely feel such clear signs of fatigue and anxiety on days that are filled with travel, meetings and assignments—only when I stop to rest. Without sabbath, I would be dangerously ignorant of the true condition of my soul.

But sabbath is prescription as well as diagnosis, the path toward a cure for our god playing. Properly observed, sabbath is a weekly practice of the generosity and goodness of God. Without our having to work one bit, we find we are sustained and even lavishly provided for; we taste and see that the Lord is good. Indeed, in the marvelous economy of God, it has been the experience of countless disciples that the more faithful and trusting our weekly rest, the more real fruit we have to celebrate from our weekly work. What idol ever granted its worshipers this kind of rest? Just as the cessation of work is an incentive to make the work on our other days more focused and faithful, the promise of sabbath's weekly festivity—not some distant holiday or vacation, but every seventh day!—reorients us toward the truth about God and God's very good world.

## THE UNTHINKABLE SABBATH

It is surpassingly ironic that the most powerful people in the world often are the ones who believe most firmly that sabbath is unrealistic. The ones you might think would have the right to doubt whether weekly rest is advisable would be those who live, like most of the Bible's original readers, within the horizons of subsistence agriculture and its terribly thin margins for error. Yet as our technological capacity has expanded and our economy has generated undreamed-of wealth and opportunity for billions of people, many Americans seem to have become more convinced that a day of rest is unthinkable, even unpatriotic.

The unthinkable sabbath is closely related to the demands of advanced capitalism for a distinctly ungleaning-friendly level of productivity from capital assets. Factories operate three shifts, seven days a week, because that is the way to extract the maximum productivity from machinery. Costly buildings on costly land can return more in retail sales to their owners if they are open on Sundays. If you have promised your investors that you will squeeze every possible penny of productivity from the assets purchased with their dollars (that is, if you have been seduced into a contract or economic system that makes no provision for gleaning), a true sabbath starts to seem like an impossible indulgence. And to be sure— unlike agricultural land, animals and people—well-maintained machines can in fact operate round the clock and round the week. Even the most diehard sabbatarians rely on this unique feature of industrial technology if they do not switch off the electricity and other utilities altogether on Saturday night. Certain features of this very good world do not, in fact, have to be switched off to be kept good. (Some sources of electricity, in fact, such as hydroelectric and nuclear power, cannot be prudently disconnected on a weekly basis; they produce a steady output day after day.)

But what is thankfully true and good for these features of the physical world is not true and not good for creatures. Sabbath was made for humankind, and for the creatures with whom we share the world. And for people, animals and land (which is not an inert substance but a wondrously complex living system of fellow creatures), sabbath is not just realistic but so absolutely necessary that to ignore it is itself unrealistic. Faithful observance of the sabbath may or may not require that we idle a factory or a store one day a week, but it unreservedly requires that image bearers, and every creature that can only flourish when image bearers are properly exercising their dominion, be allowed to rest. Not to do so is idolatry—and idolatry, no matter how promising it seems at the beginning, is the ultimate and greatest unrealism.

So those who are stewards of capital goods like factories and stores must, if they are to be lastingly fruitful, provide a way for everyone affected by their power to truly rest one day a week. Even in our hypercompetitive, gleaningless economy it is possible to observe an organization-wide sabbath. Many Christians are familiar with the privately held restaurant chain Chick-fil-A, which is closed every Sunday in consistently profitable defiance of retail wisdom, but the successful electronics retailer B&H, owned by Orthodox Jews, not only closes its massive (and endlessly tempting) Ninth Avenue store in Manhattan every Saturday in order to keep the sabbath, but turns away orders on its website for those twenty-four hours as well. If these businesses, operating in two of the most competitive segments of retail, can succeed, there is no reason that many more enterprises cannot follow suit.

In an individualistic society, sabbath can easily seem like a private question of personal piety. But few other disciplines reveal so directly that both idolatry and injustice are necessary categories for the stewardship of power. Personal sabbath observance is all well and good, but as Isaiah cried out six centuries before Christ, sabbath raises the even more pressing questions of how we are treating those over whom we have power:

> Look, you serve your own interest on your fast day,
>     and oppress all your workers. . . .
> If you refrain from trampling the sabbath,
>     from pursuing your own interests on my holy day;
> if you call the sabbath a delight
>     and the holy day of the LORD honorable;
> if you honor it, not going your own ways,
>     serving your own interests, or pursuing your own affairs;
> then you shall take delight in the LORD,
>     and I will make you ride upon the heights of the earth;
> I will feed you with the heritage of your ancestor Jacob,
>     for the mouth of the LORD has spoken. (Isaiah 58:3, 13-14)

Who depends on us for the exercise of their own image bearing? We are responsible not just for ensuring that we can rest one day out of seven but that they can too. In a consumer economy this includes not just the "workers" whom we may directly employ or supervise, but the people who serve us at gas stations, restaurants and retail establishments, and those who work behind the scenes to make our lives go smoothly, from the custodial staff at our church to the employees of the local utilities. The point is not so much to avoid all commercial entanglements of any sort on the sabbath; that is not really possible in a complex economy. And in a religiously pluralistic society there may well be three different days of rest represented among the religions of those who serve us (Friday for Muslims, Saturday for Jews, and Sunday for Christians and *New York Times* readers). Rather we need to ask whether those who are directly or indirectly employed by us are free to honor the sabbath pattern of rest and work. If the answer is no, what might we do, whether through changing our patterns of consumption or advocating for different labor laws and practices, to include them in the circle of those who are able to play the true, sabbath-making and sabbath-taking Creator God?

If we do not ask these difficult questions and simply settle for piously observing our own private sabbaths, we run the risk of playing a false god—a god whose leisure is purchased at the price of others' labor and whose abundance comes at the expense of others' deprivation. True sabbath practice expands in ever increasing circles until every creature experiences the blessings of both meaningful work and abundant rest. If we are not helping to create and sustain systems that allow for sabbath, our own rest will be nothing more than an expression of privilege and power, and it will be, or should be, troubled by the prophets' denunciations.

## FROM SABBATH DAY TO SABBATH YEAR

From the barely imaginable practice of sabbath we turn to the truly inconceivable practices beyond it. In the book of Leviticus a weekly sabbath is just the bottom rung on a ladder of sabbath practices that extend over years and generations—for every seventh year, Israel was commanded to forgo active agriculture altogether:

> Six years you shall sow your field, and six years you shall prune your vineyard, and gather in their yield; but in the seventh year there shall be a sabbath of complete rest for the land, a sabbath for the LORD: you shall not sow your field or prune your vineyard. You shall not reap the aftergrowth of your harvest or gather the grapes of your unpruned vine: it shall be a year of complete rest for the land. (Leviticus 25:3-5)

For an entire year the people of Israel would let the land lie fallow. Just as they bore the image of God by working the land, sowing in it and reaping from it, they would also bear the image of God by resting and letting the land rest.

Today, of course, we know that there are good agricultural reasons for letting fields "rest," and even in biblical times there must have been some inkling that a fallow year would allow nutrients to be replenished and ecological diversity to be maintained. But if a weekly sabbath demanded a certain amount of faith and trust, a "sabbatical year" must have required tremendous discipline from people whose entire sustenance came from the land. It would require advance planning, storing up sufficient grain in the years preceding the sabbath year. It was a kind of gleaning to the seventh power, since during the sabbatical year the poor, who had no land of their own to harvest, were free to harvest anything that came up (Exodus 23:11).

But the sabbatical year's implications were not just agricultural—they were cultural. People who did the demanding work of agriculture six years in a row would find themselves with very little to do for an entire year. What would replace the labor of agriculture if not all sorts of other kinds of culture? The seventh year would become an ideal time for pilgrimage, for worship and study, for sport and song. The seventh year ensured that even people whose existence was largely defined by subsistence would explore the broader and deeper implications of image bearing.

Most Westerners do not work directly with or on the land, but to have a healthy relationship to our own power we would be well advised to ask what a sabbatical year might mean for us. In our culture *sabbatical* is a term reserved almost exclusively for teachers and scholars (and the occasional fortunate pastor) who are granted a year off to allow their teaching to lie fallow and to pursue other callings. The sabbatical year in academia is not a vacation—"time off" without goals or accountability. Rather, it is an opportunity to expand and redirect one's vocation, to explore what we may be called to next.

If weekly sabbaths seem out of reach for many of us, a sabbatical year must sound like fantasy. Assuming we do not work in an institutional setting like a university or church that will pay for our time, how could we ever afford to withdraw from our day-to-day productive activities for an entire year?

This question was exactly what the Israelites asked about their own sabbatical year, and God had a very specific response recorded alongside the Levitical law: "Should you ask, 'What shall we eat in the seventh year, if we may not sow or gather in our crop?' I will order my blessing for you in the sixth year, so that it will yield a crop for three years" (Leviticus 25:20-21). The commandment came with the provision to keep it; all Israel had to do was be prepared to harvest the abundance in advance and steward it over the following years of rest and return to ordinary work.

And in fact, in Western societies we are familiar with the idea of laboring while planning and saving up for a future when our activity will not be economically productive. We call it "retirement": many years of leisure after decades of hard work, ideally filled with enjoyable travel and time with extended family and friends. Many Americans have no trouble, at least in principle, with the idea of people saving up for their retirement years (though having the means and the will to save *enough* is a different matter).

As it turns out, retirement and sabbatical require similar amounts of time. If one were to start full-time work at twenty-one and retire at the age of sixty-nine, then hoped to enjoy an "active retirement" until, say, seventy-seven before being more constrained by the limitations of old age, the forty-eight years of work would be matched by eight years of retirement—exactly the 1-for-6 ratio of the sabbatical year.

Yet modern "retirement" is far less healthy than the 1-for-6 pattern of Leviticus because all the years of leisure are piled up at the end of one's life. Two years of rest are not twice as satisfying as one, and ten years are assuredly not ten times as satisfying. Leisure has sharply diminishing returns, especially when there is no meaningful work ahead of us to which we might apply the insights and energy gained during our year of rest. Image bearers are not meant to take a permanent vacation from responsibility and creativity. The retirement model not only asks us to soldier through an entire working life without ever benefiting from the rest and refreshment of a sabbatical year, it gives us no wider cultural purpose for our retirement years than our own leisure and pleasure.

As more and more people who have the luxury of retiring are finding out, endless unproductive leisure is something to be avoided, not sought. A cruise may feel like heaven for two weeks, but it would feel like hell after two years. And at the same time, the gifts of modern medical care and the shift to less physically demanding work mean that there is no good reason for many people to cease working at sixty-five or sixty-nine. So why is there a vast industry designed to channel our planning and saving toward the dubious reward of retirement, and none designed to help us plan and save for periodic sabbaticals?

I recognize that there are vast complexities in implementing a sabbatical vision for any one individual, let alone a whole society. All I am really trying to do is to awaken us to our odd situation. Working without extended periods of rest, we dream, plan, save and strive for a vision of the good life that will come in our later years. But in practice that dream may turn out to be just a disappointing, diminishing form of idolatry. And should we discover at that point that retirement is not as satisfying as we had hoped, it will be difficult if not impossible to change course and make different choices. Meanwhile, we think Scripture's much more realistic, beneficial and achievable vision inconceivable.

The sabbatical year is both a discipline toward power and a discipline that tames power. Sabbaticals force us to relinquish our sense of indispensability. So they subvert the god playing that can afflict custodians and CEOs alike. The truth is that others are fully able to fill the roles we set aside. This humbling reality can help us return to work with a more sober sense of our own importance and abilities, as well as providing organizations with a deep "bench" of people who have grown in their capacities during one another's absence.

The benefits of sabbatical could apply to families as well as firms. After a stay-at-home mother has been parenting full time for the better part of a decade, couldn't the older children and the father grant her a sabbatical leave from many of her household responsibilities? They could learn to cook and clean in her place while she takes on a temporary assignment outside the home or pursues a formal or informal course of study.

At the same time as a practice of sabbatical years would tame our power, it would lead us toward true creative power. I have had two sabbaticals in my life, year-long interruptions in my life's routine: first a year off between my sophomore and junior years of college, and then a year with no formal employment at age thirty-five after the magazine I had edited failed and our family moved to a new city. The first was a much overdue sabbath after fifteen years in school, all the more crucial for my spiritual health and vocational development given how much success and satisfaction I enjoyed in academic environments. Instead of spending more time in classrooms, I temped for a mid-level executive at a corporation in Boston, apprenticed at a retreat center in Georgia, and traveled around the eastern United States performing as a singer-songwriter to groups of three to thirty-three people in tiny halls and churches. Each of these was a profoundly humbling experience, but each was also an opportunity to meet people from a far wider range of regions, backgrounds and economic circumstances than I ever would have on my educational track.

I wouldn't have sought the second sabbatical, which came on the heels of failure. But that year allowed me to focus on settling our family into a new home, schools and community just as my wife was embarking on a challenging new work assignment. And in the quiet time in between I mulled over and eventually wrote the proposal for the book that became *Culture Making.*

These fallow years, which were not at all like vacations and were by no means easy, were profoundly formative for the person I have become. Whatever creative contributions I have managed to make to the world emerged largely from the crucible of these two years. My wife Catherine, meanwhile, has the great fortune to work for a college that makes sabbaticals possible for its faculty, and she too has benefited, along with our family, from these opportunities to stop, explore, reflect and seek a vision for the next phase of her calling.

Sabbaticals are a tremendous privilege in the most precise sense of the word: the accumulated benefits of past exercises of power. I realize that even raising the idea of a sabbatical year, in our unjust (that is, idolatrous) society, will provoke envy and discontent for many readers who feel they have no such option. But it is crucial that we recognize that the sabbatical year was a privilege *commanded by God* for the people of Israel. The Creator God is not an idol who extracts endless work while dangling the promise of eventual leisure—he is an abundant God fully capable of providing everything we need to be faithful to his cosmic pattern of work and rest.

Why can't we imagine a sabbatical year being possible for every image bearer—for students in the midst of their years of schooling (the AmeriCorps national service program in the United States is an example), laborers after six years of hard work, fast-food workers who live from paycheck to paycheck, or CEOs who require "key man" insurance that implies their utter indispensability? The fault is not in the realism of the biblical pattern for life but our shared lack of faith and imagination, and our reluctance to work and save diligently in the six years in order to provide a way for our work to lie fallow in the seventh.

The point is not to erect another legalistic hurdle that neither we nor our children will be able to bear, but to hold out hope for a sabbath-shaped life that would both tame our power and greed and would release untold human capacity in the midst of, rather than at the end of, the years we are given on this earth. God intends this kind of abundance for all of his image bearers. Doing the hard and careful work to make sabbatical years possible for ourselves and our neighbors is one of the best contributions we could make to the flourishing of the world.

## JUBILEE

There is one more step on the biblical "sabbath ladder." Beyond gleaning, sabbath days and sabbath years lies the "sabbath of sabbaths," the seventh year of the seventh cycle of sabbatical years. This year, unlike the sabbath years, was not just a year of rest, letting crops and workers lie fallow. The Jubilee year was to be a time of dramatic activity, beginning with a trumpet blast and continuing with a mass migration that would make Thanksgiving in America or the New Year in China look tame.

For in the Jubilee year the people of Israel were to reset their status, privilege and power by returning land to its original owners and canceling the debts accumulated in times of personal or national crisis. Every forty-nine years the lucky and the hard-working would give up their excess gains, and the less fortunate and less diligent would get another chance to work the land that had belonged to their parents. A multigenerational system of indentured servitude and caste, like the one that had existed in

Gudiyatham before World Vision's intervention, would never emerge among a people who practiced Jubilee, because every generation would remember and anticipate the time when debts would be forgiven and privilege would be released. Jubilee would guard the image-bearing dignity of every member of Israel, undermining patterns of accumulated wealth that might eventually lead some to play god and others to shrink into the broken images of persistent poverty.

The premise of Jubilee was the goodness of God, the true God who had chosen a people from among the peoples, given them an abundant land, and called them to bear witness in the midst of the nations to his goodness. Through Jubilee, as through every other step on the sabbath ladder, Israel would be reminded, and would remind the world, that power was not an achievement but a gift, that prosperity comes not from idolatry or injustice but from gratitude and generosity, that wealth does not have to be hoarded and debts are meant to be forgiven.

Jubilee would be a way of playing the true God at the most visceral level of land, wealth and work—playing the God who cancels debts and gives the homeless a home. Imagine the joy of grandchildren moving back to land their grandparents had been forced to mortgage in time of famine or disease, the astonished gratitude of slaves seeing their documents of indenture ripped into pieces, the stunned delight of people who had been dutifully paying off debts realizing that next month they owed nothing. And imagine the relief and hope that might well up in the powerful who extended that kind of mercy and opportunity, the freedom from the subtle chains of privilege and the release from the slowly growing resentment of those less fortunate. You can understand why the result might be a full year of celebration and worship.

All this might have been true, but we have scant evidence that Israel ever actually obeyed the Jubilee instructions. Certainly there is no record in Scripture itself of a Jubilee year being carried out. We hear about it in the pages of Deuteronomy, as Israel prepares to enter the land; we hear about it again in the clarion call of Isaiah and the prophets to worship and justice; but in the historical books, not a word.

This is not so surprising. For the histories make it clear that Israel was constantly tempted by idolatry. Once in the land, surrounded by seemingly powerful alternative gods and conformed to the prevailing social and economic systems those gods legitimated, God's chosen people faltered early and often, individually and systemically, in their worship and in their obedience. In the failure of Israel ever to implement the Jubilee year, we see the economic and cultural counterpart to the failure of Israel ever to fully cleanse their hearts of the temptation to run after other gods.

The Jubilee year, if practiced, would have led to a kind of flourishing that no human society has seen. But just as idolatry and injustice are linked, so are justice and worship. An Israel that never managed to worship the true God with a pure heart also never managed to play that true God to the depth of generosity that the Jubilee year would have required.

And so the Jubilee stood for Israel, as it does for us, on a distant horizon: the picture of what would happen if people so trusted their Maker and Redeemer that they did not need to cling to privilege and status; the promise to the downtrodden that one day they too would be flourishing image bearers with authority over part of God's good world; the warning that everything we cling to apart from God will one day be torn from us, that the only lasting good is the one that is given us as a gift. That Jubilee was never fully enacted is the same as saying that the true God was never fully worshiped and obeyed.

But Jubilee was never forgotten. The true God never gave up on his people and the flourishing that his image bearers were meant to bring. When Jesus began his ministry, he found the place in the scroll where Isaiah revived the hope of the Jubilee year and read it aloud (Luke 4). Wherever Jesus went, there were foretastes of Jubilee.

## LIBERTY THROUGHOUT THE LAND

Is Jubilee possible in our own time? We live in a vastly different economic and cultural world than the land-based economy of ancient Israel, and the nations of the earth are not subject to the same law that was given to God's chosen nation. But we will find echoes of Jubilee whenever individuals, families, communities and nations embrace the twin ideas of the cancellation of debts and the surrender of privilege.

Among the great innovations of Anglo-American law is the invention of bankruptcy. Before the invention of bankruptcy, those who ran up excessive debts were subject to debtor's prison—a one-way ticket to despair that, obviously, made it almost impossible to repay even a fraction of one's debts. The dependents of debtors were often left without any support and cut off from the prisoner. Bankruptcy replaced this dead-end system by providing a legal means for discharging obligations that cannot be repaid.

We don't normally think of bankruptcy as a good thing, and going bankrupt is no fun, by design. But the institution of bankruptcy is actually a little piece of Jubilee in an economic system. Bankruptcy ensures that debts do not ensnare generation after generation. It extends mercy and a measure of dignity even to debtors—in ordinary bankruptcies, for example, one cannot be forced to give up one's home no matter how great one's debts. In the United States, in an unmistakable echo of the biblical pattern, the cancelled debts of bankruptcy cease to appear on a credit report after seven years.

Oddly enough, the possibility of bankruptcy contributes to flourishing. Not long ago I had dinner with an attorney who represents creditors in bankruptcy cases. Every day he tries to collect money from debtors through the legal system. He has seen every possible abuse of the bankruptcy system, and no doubt the debtors on the other side sometimes resent his efforts on behalf of his clients. But he told me, "As a Christian, I am glad bankruptcy exists. We are so much better off as a society with it than without it." He laughed. "Sometimes my clients don't like to hear that. But it's true."

Bankruptcy provides even failed entrepreneurs a second, or even third or fourth, chance at creating wealth. It puts a limit on the damage that can be done to image bearing by even the most foolish financial choices. Of course bankruptcy comes with all the same moral hazards that the Jubilee year would have posed: why avoid debt if you know you'll never have to pay it back? And yet creditors find a way manage that risk. In the end, economic systems that provide for bankruptcy are more robust than those that do not, and nations with strong bankruptcy protections have more new businesses and economic vitality than those that do not. Like Jubilee itself, bankruptcy sounds like it could never work, but this impractical system actually makes room for a kind of flourishing that a merely practical system would not allow. It is a system for creatures, not would-be gods.

Another remarkable example of Jubilee-like patterns arose among a few extremely wealthy individuals at the turn of the twenty-first century. Led by American investor Warren Buffett and Microsoft founder Bill Gates, over eighty billionaires from around the world have signed a "Giving Pledge" to give at least half their assets to charity. For those of us without billions in assets, it is easy to be cynical about such a pledge: we'd be happy, we think, to keep half of a billion dollars for ourselves and give the rest away.

Of course the Giving Pledge is no vow of poverty, but neither was Jubilee. And to laugh off the public generosity of billionaires is to greatly underestimate the power of the false god of money. No one makes a billion dollars by accident. They make it by founding and tending enterprises that create wealth. And those enterprises and the wealth they create quickly become, for many who pursue them, false gods who ensure that their worshipers never, ever have enough. To give away money, in any substantial fraction of one's assets, is to topple that false god. (If you doubt this is true, you can simply contemplate giving away half of your own assets. But I'm no billionaire! you may protest. True, but even with half your current assets you would probably seem as wealthy to the bottom billion of the world's population as billionaires seem to you. Why would it be so hard to give away 50 percent?) The Giving Pledge is a sign of Jubilee—the privileged relinquishing their accumulated benefits, releasing them to the control of others so that others can tend and contribute to the world.

Money is just the most countable, fungible form of power. But even in a money-based economy, land, the focus of the biblical Jubilee, can still be significant. In many countries, especially the United States, the place where you live determines your access to perhaps the most important form of nonfinancial power in the world: primary and secondary education. School districts in the United States and many other countries vary drastically from one jurisdiction to another. Land in "good" school districts can command much higher prices than in "poor" school districts. Some children, through privilege, attend schools that are the envy of the world; others attend schools that teach little and only reinforce disappointment, chaos and failure.

What would Jubilee look like in a broken, geographically based educational system? I know more than one group of prestigious university graduates who have moved into urban neighborhoods with "poor" schools and are raising their children there. They could easily live in more affluent locations, but they choose to relinquish that option in order to make new friends, love new neighbors and contribute to the rebuilding of broken institutions. Similarly, I am told by reliable sources that a strikingly disproportionate number of successful candidates for Teach for America are motivated by their faith. They are investing their privilege—their elite educations and all the experiences and resources that equipped them to acquire them—in places where power seems distant and the world seems cruel. And every urban school has more than a few teachers and administrators who could easily find jobs elsewhere, but stay in difficult situations from a deep sense of calling.

These individual and communal decisions are remarkable. But if we are serious about Jubilee, we must ask what institutions and structures could be created or cultivated in our society to make it possible not just for powerful people to opt in to troubled places but for the less powerful to opt out. One of the most remarkable reforms in this area has been the ending of mass public housing in many American cities, replaced by "Section 8" vouchers that allow poor families to live in urban or suburban neighborhoods of their choosing. The demolition of huge apartment blocks of public housing has not been a simple matter, but it has had at least one beneficial effect: parents who once were limited to a single school district now have more choices about where their children grow up and go to school.

Such policies are never perfect, and the best policies are a poor substitute for transformed people who invest sacrificially in restoring the image in places where it has been lost. If ancient Israel was never able to obey the Jubilee laws, any more than it was able to worship and serve only the true Creator God, we will probably never see a full institutional expression of Jubilee in our own societies. But we can use our power, and surrender our privilege, in ways that anticipate the "acceptable year of the Lord."

# THE END OF POWER

In the end, we have very little power. We began our lives utterly powerless; we will end them the same way. Our first breath was a cry, and so will be our last. In between we will forever lack the power we most would long for: the power to raise the dead. As far as physics can tell, our activity in the world is neither positive-sum nor zero-sum, but negative-sum—every increase of order and fruitfulness comes at the cost of greater disorder and decay somewhere else. No one has the power to turn back the remorseless one-way arrow of time. "Again I saw that under the sun the race is not to the swift, nor the battle to the strong, nor bread to the wise, nor riches to the intelligent, nor favor to the skillful; but time and chance happen to them all" (Ecclesiastes 9:11).

There is nothing more sure than this: all power will come to an end. To deny this—and every human being and every human institution devotes substantial energy to denying it—is to capitulate to the serpent's temptation: "You shall not surely die." "You will be like God." No. The serpent's promise is false. To chase after it leads us headlong into idolatry and injustice: idolatry, the worship of gods that will never deliver the power we seek, and injustice, the increasingly frustrated and violent attempt to coerce from the world and our fellow creatures the godlike immortality that will always remain out of our grasp.

But there is an end beyond the end. At the beginning of this book, we looked at the improbably good news of the opening chapters of Genesis, the chapters that anchor the rest of the salvation story in the claim that against all evidence, the world's story began good and very good. So at the end of this book we should remind ourselves of the chapters at the end of the Bible, just as hard to believe in their own way as the chapters at the beginning. For after the fruits of idolatry and injustice have been exposed for what they are and received the full measure of judgment, the final tableaux of Revelation bring impossibly good news.

The remade world is a city—the human institution with the greatest capacity for teeming diversity and durability over time. A city—that central biblical symbol of human power at its most concentrated, noble and corrupt. A city—that human creation so closely tied up with the principalities and powers that the apocalyptic visions speak of heavenly enemies and earthly cities in one breath: "Fallen, fallen is Babylon the great!" A city—not a generic city but a specific city, Jerusalem, "coming down out of heaven from God."

The inhabitants of that city are not a new and improved race of beings who would be suitable to the glorious new world. Instead they are specific, recognizable, redeemed people, beginning with those twelve brothers whose names are inscribed on the gates—Judah, Manasseh, Benjamin and the rest—and those twelve Galileans whose names are inscribed on the foundations—Simon called Peter, James, John and the other bumbling fishermen and zealots who all became witnesses and martyrs. Thronging the city are the "kings of the earth," the embodiments of national power bringing in the glory and honor of their nations, the specific achievements of human power working in the very good world.

Planted by the river that runs through the city is a tree, a specific tree: the Tree of Life "with its twelve kinds of fruit, producing its fruit each month; and the leaves of the tree are for the healing of the nations" (Revelation 22:2). A tree with twelve kinds of fruit, an entirely new kind of fruit every month, is a glorious tree, a fantastically flourishing tree, like no tree we have ever seen and yet very much like the trees we have seen. Its leaves carry not modest medicinal properties for one ailment or another, but for the deepest wounds of the human story, the miserable history of nation against nation, the wars that have been the most ferocious embodiment of idolatry and injustice. No less than these deepest wounds are named, known and healed in that city where tears are not forbidden but instead are wiped away.

And the lamp of the city is the Lamb. Not just any lamb, but *the* Lamb, marked forever with the signs of slaughter one wretched day on a wretched hill outside the gates, who now says to the stunned seer, "Behold, I make all things new" (Revelation 21:5 KJV).

Nothing in this city is new. As some friends of mine like to quip, Jesus says, "Behold, I make all things new," not, "Behold, I make all new things."

Nothing is new. But everything is made new.

Nothing and no one in this city has arrived by their own effort, their own expenditure of power, their own ascent into control or godlikeness. Everything and everyone in this city is there as a gift.

Nothing and no one in this city—as John makes fiercely clear—is numbered with "the dogs and sorcerers and fornicators and murderers and idolaters, and everyone who loves and practices falsehood" (Revelation 22:15), that typically biblical mashup of the practitioners of idolatry and injustice, indistinguishable from one another in the end because they all degrade and deny the true image. All that crazed quest for godlikeness has been put aside.

Yet the quest is put aside at the very moment, strangely enough, that it is achieved. When John, overawed by his angelic tour guide, falls down to worship him, the angel stops him without a moment's hesitation: "You must not do that! I am a fellow servant with you and your comrades who hold the testimony of Jesus. Worship God!" (Revelation 19:10). The city is full of the redeemed in glorious robes, any one of whom (as C. S. Lewis famously said of our fellow human beings in glory) we would be strongly tempted to worship. But they are all fellow servants, prophets and comrades serving the Lamb.

## THE COMMUNITY WHERE POWER FINDS ITS END

That beautiful city seems a long way off at this moment in history—at every moment in history. But there is a place where the ways of that city are meant to be practiced in advance and anticipation: the church. Indeed, the whole reason for John's Revelation is to encourage the churches strewn around the rim of the Mediterranean to lift up their eyes from the imperial power of Rome and every earthly Babylon. John is commissioned to bring these churches a vision of ultimate reality, in all its glory and justice, so that they can live faithfully, candles set in lampstands in a dimly lit world.

The church is—or should be and can be—the place where all our power is put in the perspective of God's great story of creation, redemption and new creation. Like Israel before it, the church does something that no other human community can do: bear witness, by name, to the true Creator, Redeemer and Sustainer of the world, and proclaim and live his ways in the midst of a world that insists on its own way.

This is the reason it is so foolish and short-sighted to say, "We don't have power in our church." The church, as a human community, pulses with the inescapable power that comes with image bearing. The church, as a fellowship of sinners, includes and at its worst enables every possible species of god playing. But as a community called into being by the Holy Spirit, the church most importantly is caught up in the resurrection power that will ultimately bring the world to judgment and renewal. Far from being aloof or detached from power, the church is all about power—the end of power, meaning the purpose of power, the taming of power, and the unleashing of power for true flourishing.

*The church proclaims the true story of power.* By telling the whole story from Genesis to Revelation, with its astonishing bookends of good, very good and glorious news, the church recognizes and affirms our human ambitions and aspirations, placing them in the context where they truly make sense and can find their rightful place. By telling the full truth about idolatry and injustice, not least by recalling the stories of how our own heroes fell into compromise and foolishness, the church makes clear just how damaging our pride is to ourselves, our neighbors and the whole groaning creation. And by recounting over and over the immense cost of redemption, the church leads us to abashed and grateful humility before the one who gave up everything for us.

*The church reminds us of the end of power in death.* Around churches of an earlier era were cemeteries, where the faithful of past generations slept, awaiting the resurrection. Most readers of this book are more likely to attend a church surrounded by parking lots than a cemetery. But even without that visible reminder, any church worth the name must learn to bury its members. One unhappy side effect of American Christianity's accommodation to youth culture has been the formation of congregations that have no significant intergenerational membership, no elders who are facing frailty and death, no one to say goodbye to and commend to the perpetual light of Christ. Such churches may be full of youthful vitality, but learning to proclaim the resurrection life in the face of grief and loss is essential to spiritual maturity and true spiritual power.

But it is not just through funerals that our worshiping communities remind us that all power comes to an end. Whenever we share the eucharistic meal we "proclaim the Lord's death until he comes again." Whenever we baptize new believers, immersing them in water, we bury them by baptism into death, uniting them with a death like Christ's (Romans 6:4-5). Indeed, initiation into both biblical worshiping communities— Israel and the church—began with a disabling act (at least, in Israel's case, for men): circumcision and baptism. Only after we have been laid low are we able to rise. The sacraments of the church are rehearsals of the end of power, putting our own power to death in baptism and then approaching with trembling awe the memorial of the moment when God's own Son gave up his power.

*The church celebrates a greater power in worship.* Even as we put our own power to death, we find ourselves caught up in something greater than any human being or human institution could conjure up by our own efforts. Whether in the dancing of the church in Africa, the soaring interior spaces of Europe's cathedrals, the bottomless depth of Russian chants, or even the decibel levels of a stadium full of passionate college students singing their hearts out to God along with the wail of guitars and the thudding of drums, no human experience compares to the worship of the people of God made alive by the power of the Spirit and the hope of resurrection. Of course, all these experiences can be replicated in part by skilled performers in perfectly secular settings, and even there, image bearing can happen along with moments of astonishing transcendence. But only in worship is there the context and the pretext for the joyful self-forgetfulness that unleashes the glorious presence of the Holy One, the one who fully dwells where there are no competitors for his glory.

The church exists to help us put to death our unholy addiction to playing god, to die to our selves and rise to the exercise of true selfhood, "having nothing, and yet possessing everything" (2 Corinthians 6:10). It exists to make possible for our stewardship of power the blessing Galadriel offers to Gimli in *The Fellowship of the Ring*, even as it echoes her stark refusal to make any absolute promise: "I do not foretell, for all foretelling is now vain: on the one hand lies darkness, and on the other only hope. But if hope should not fail, then I say to you, Gimli son of Glóin, that your hands shall flow with gold, and yet over you gold shall have no dominion."

We need worship. Only in the context of true worship can we hope for power to flow through us without having dominion over us. Christian worship gives us the words, the songs and the actions that train us to play the God we were meant to play. In worship we loosen our grip on power, and power loses its grip on us. Through confession, fasting, celebration and feasting we become spoiled for anything less than the true power that, unlike any human power, can raise the dead, can heal the nations, can hold everything forgotten in memory—the power that will ultimately build a city where the redeemed will sing to the Lamb.

## YOU SHALL NOT SURELY DIE

There is an old and valuable Christian tradition that sees the cross as a holy trick played on the devil. In this tradition the devil is simply not able to imagine that the Son of God can go down to death and return from the grave. To the devil, death is death—powerlessness is powerlessness. Thus he lies to the original image bearers in the garden, "You shall not surely die," believing just the opposite, that once they have tasted the fruit they will belong forever more to his dominion of death. Thus he tempts Jesus in the desert, inviting him to throw himself from the pinnacle of the temple and be rescued by the angels—betraying the devil's conviction that a truly powerful God would never allow his own Son to die. The imaginative minds who sustained this tradition pass on the stories of Satan watching in joyful disbelief as God, to all appearances, gives up on Jesus—of the raucous party in the depths of hell on Holy Saturday, as all the enemies of God mock and rejoice—and then the horrifying sound of the tomb opening up above them Sunday morning, the stone rolling away, the voice that commanded creation now commanding the Son to come forth. Satan is cheated, foiled by his own certainty that death, his special domain, is the ultimate power. He does not know, until it is too late, that death can be defeated.

The last enemy to be defeated is death. Death puts an end to all power, and the death of the cosmos is as sure as the death of every person. But the Christian testimony is that death has been defeated by death itself. Rather than counting equality with God something to be grasped—rather than gripping and being gripped by the power the world knows and understands—the one who was the very image of God empties himself, takes on the form of a servant, and goes to death, even death on a cross. God's power never was as small and constrained as the devil thought. God has nothing to fear even from death, the end of power.

And neither do we. That is why we can be so reckless with our privilege, so unconcerned with status—because we are grasped by the life-giving power of God. That is why we can face even our own death, and the death of those we love, with hope—because the creative power of God raised Jesus from the grave. The resurrection is the beginning and end of all power worthy of the name, which is why all other powers, according to the great hymn of Philippians 2, will eventually bow before the name of the one who did not grasp power.

Our power will come to its end, one way or another, in protest or praise of the only true power that created, redeemed and sustained the world. It is faith, hope and love that abide, not sex, money and power—all three of these fleeting gifts only exist to draw us toward those lasting realities. All the disciplines that guide and guard our use of power, all our practices of worship, are ways of dying to ourselves and letting Another live in us so that the power at work in us is the power of creation and new creation, not the devil's petty powers of coercion and death.

What we do with our power is ultimately a sure guide to what we will do with the God who claims the power to raise the dead. Either we will grip ever more tightly to our own power in fear of its disappearance, or we will become bolder and bolder in our use of our power to prepare for its ultimate end: the restoration of the world's shalom by the world's power-yielding, powerful Creator.

## ABRAHAM'S FEAST

In the Tretyakov Gallery in Moscow hangs an icon by the fifteenth-century iconographer Andrei Rublev commonly known as *Rublev's Trinity*. Rather than attempting to portray the three persons of the Trinity in the abstract, Rublev paints a specific biblical scene: the three angels who visit Abraham and Sarah in Genesis 18 to promise that Sarah will bear a son, and who seem even at this early point in the biblical revelation to be more than mere messengers, a kind of early intimation that God is most fully known through three persons in loving union.

Centered in the background of the icon is a tree that figures oddly prominently in the Genesis story. Abraham invites his guests to sit under this tree, suggesting they have "a little bread" to eat, but then rushes off to prepare an absurdly lavish feast of cakes and curd and freshly roasted veal. When he ultimately returns to serve the feast, after what must have been quite a long delay, he stands under the tree while his guests eat. Rublev shows us the three visitors under that tree, seated at a low table on which a small piece of bread has been placed, waiting for Abraham to finish preparing the larger feast in the house in the background.

Each of the figures wears a different colored robe, but there is a clear family resemblance among them. They are slender and fine of features, with long braided hair, neither firmly masculine (like the Christ of the Orthodox Pantocrator icon) nor distinctly feminine (like the Madonna holding her child). Each is gazing at the others, each one's head bowed in another's direction. Their expressions are kind, affectionate and above all patient. These angels of God are content to wait while Abraham prepares the meal. They have come to set in motion the chain of events that will save the nations—the birth of Isaac, the preservation and flourishing of Abraham's descendants, the arrival of the Anointed One, the breaking open of the gospel into every nation—but for the moment they sit, contemplate and wait. There is no hurry, and yet there is no delay.

The world is already torn, and these same messengers will go on to pronounce God's judgment on cities that practice idolatry and injustice. A few lines of the story from now, Abraham will be bargaining with the Lord, pleading for the salvation of the cities down the road if just fifty, then forty-five, then all the way down to ten, righteous people can be found. At no point in this negotiation, even as Abraham trips over his apologies for daring to bargain with God, does the Lord show the slightest impatience. Abraham is an image bearer, interceding on behalf of the broken idolatrous world with the world's Creator. Abraham cannot know that there is not even one righteous to be found in the cities of man. Abraham cannot know that his pleas will only be answered when one of his own descendants becomes the true image bearer. He certainly cannot know that his pleas will ultimately be answered by the self-giving of the very Lord he pleads to for mercy—that one of his guests will offer himself as the single righteous person for whose sake, and by whose sacrifice, the world will be spared.

All this is in the future at the moment Rublev captures. For now, Abraham prepares his own absurdly abundant feast—and here too, just off stage, he is an image bearer, reflecting his own Maker's teeming generosity, making the good world very good with his creative care. To me Abraham's feast is a kind of parable of both our work and our worship. God has arrived in our story, bearing news of a future better than we ever could have imagined. The barrenness of our lives is not the last word. Instead there will be descendants like stars in the sky. So while God waits patiently over our little offering of bread, we practice the abundance of good, creative work and lavish, open-hearted worship, making something that might be worth offering to the King of kings.

Bustling about in the house, preparing the best feast he can offer, Abraham is a comically unwitting participant in a grand drama he cannot even begin to imagine, a story held in the loving nods of each member of the three to one another, their faces both serious and glad, as if they are saying to one another, "It is good." "You are my beloved Son, with whom I am well pleased." "It is finished." "Behold, I make all things new."

The three sit under the tree, which curves and bends like a live oak. It is luxurious with leaves.

# EXPLORATION

## LUKE 15—PRODIGAL POWER

Jesus' best-known parable is, among many other things, a story of power at its best and worst. "There was a man who had two sons" (Luke 15:11-32). This is a family with wealth, property and prospects—all put in jeopardy by the younger son's demand for unaccountable autonomy from his father. The common wealth which has been held in trust is to be divided and, soon enough, squandered. The father could rely on the coercive power available to him in a traditional society and squelch the son's rude request with a word. But he submits to this scandalous breach of relationship and abandons the principles of sound financial management, apparently without complaint. The way he gives in to his son's rebellion is one of the great and fearful mysteries of this story, and it speaks volumes about a power that ultimately depends not on compulsion but on love.

The younger son's god playing is decisive and, at first, effective. In a matter of a few hours he shakes off the dusty dreariness of small-town life and his entanglement with his father and brother (the brother, to be fair, may have been rather hard to get along with). He is able quite literally to cash in his privilege in the form of travel, entertainment and leisure. His brother (or his brother's imagination) contributes the possibly fabricated detail that he wastes his inheritance on harlots, but the details of how the money is spent are not important. The real problem is that his use of his privilege is all-consuming and fruitless. The wealth that had apparently been so productively employed in his father's farm, producing abundance year after year, turns inert and fails all too quickly in the far country when it is severed from partnership, community and discipline. Unfortunately we can be fairly sure that the younger son is not the only one harmed by his misuse of his wealth. Gresham's Law, "Bad money drives out good," applies to the misspending of any resource. Think of the impact on the economy of the far country, and the choices of its citizens, when this free-spending young man arrives. Everyone around him will be sorely tempted to follow him into the ditch of idolatry and injustice, as they chase the profits to be made from his pleasures, in spite of their diminishing returns.

It may just be that Jesus intends to jog our memory of another famous younger son, also a bearer of great privilege, who found himself in a far country, cut off from his father and brothers—Joseph son of Jacob. Joseph, too, had been dangerously reliant on his father's favor and just as estranged from his elder brothers as the son of Jesus' parable.

But Joseph's journey to the far country of Egypt is the very opposite of the unfortunate prodigal's. Rather than starting with everything and ending up with less than nothing, at the mercy of the same famine that was ravaging his new foreign neighbors, Joseph started his journey to the far country with only the bare remnants of his faith and identity. Yet he ended up as a steward of power and privilege, overseeing a time of unprecedented prosperity not just for himself but a whole nation. And when famine struck his adopted land, his prayerful and prudent stewardship of power and wealth had warded off the worst effects of famine for himself, Pharaoh's people, and ultimately even the brothers that had cast him off.

Joseph was a model of image bearing, of power used well—though only after his prideful dreams were chastened twice over, first by being trafficked into slavery by his brothers, and then when he was falsely imprisoned on the word of Potiphar's wife. Thus chastened, Joseph became trustworthy in the use of power, and his use of his power resulted in lasting abundance.

## ENOUGH AND TO SPARE

The younger son of Jesus' parable, caught up in the false promises of god playing, brings no such blessing to his own far country when famine arrives. It is only at the end of his resources, when he has been reduced to the shameful level of feeding pigs, that he "comes to himself." He realizes that rather than being a stingy god player who produces diminishing returns, his father is a steward of power whose stewardship produces abundant returns. The many servants in the household have "bread enough and to spare," suggesting that in this highly unusual household even the servants are entrusted with abundance that they can then use in turn to be generous and fruitful.

Yet in this dawning awareness the son still greatly underestimates the lavishness of his father. The son makes a plan: he will return to his father just like Joseph's brothers, face down, asking for forgiveness and pleading to be treated as slaves. But this father is a steward of abundance not just in his economic dealings but also in his response to sin, failure and injustice. The son's well-rehearsed plan to accept a diminished status in his father's house, subject to the coercive power and distance between a master and slave, is smothered by his father's exuberant greeting. And here is where the parallels with the story of Joseph are especially hard to miss. For what is the very first thing the father shouts for as he embraces and kisses his son? "Quickly, bring out a robe—the best one—and put it on him." Once upon a time another doting father had fashioned a splendid robe for his favored younger son, only to see the robe torn and covered in blood, and the son seemingly dead and gone. But this father brings out the best robe for the very son who had brought him dishonor and shame, who had taken the inheritance and left his father for dead.

The parable, of course, has an uncomfortable sequel that reminds us that idolatry and injustice can take subtle forms. In the father's house—or at least in the fields outside—the older brother has labored thanklessly for "all these years . . . working like a slave for you, and I have never disobeyed your command." This brother has never perceived the abundance at the heart of his father's creative power; instead his only model of power is command and coercion. It seems surpassingly unlikely that a householder whose servants have "bread enough and to spare" would actually begrudge his own son a young goat for a party. Much more likely, trapped in his self-made prison of zero-sum power, the son has never asked.

If the younger son's essential failure is to seek to cash in on all his power and privilege in order to purchase a life of autonomous god playing, the elder son's failure is never to seek to turn his power and privilege into abundant celebration rather than grating effort. Like the dwarves in the stable in C. S. Lewis's *The Last Battle*, he is surrounded by countless resources but can only see dirt and straw—caught in a perpetual famine of his own resentment. He cannot see the true power that has always pulsed in the household of the father, waiting for both sons to come to themselves and come home, the power to transform shame into honor, wrath into compassion, the lost into the found, and death into life.

In his indispensable book *The Return of the Prodigal Son*, Henri Nouwen boldly invites us to imagine ourselves not just in the place of the younger son, and then the elder one, but also in the place of the father. Many of Jesus' parables are waiting for this kind of attention—his shepherds, widows and vineyard owners are not just clues to the true nature and identity of God, but to what we are meant to become by grace. But for us the path to becoming the shepherd requires first recognizing that we are the lost sheep; to become the searching widow, we must understand that we are the coin lost in the cranny; and to become the father requires first coming to terms with ourselves as his equally foolish, equally prodigal children. And that is, in a nutshell, what discipleship is about. In the crucible of discipleship we come to see just how distorted our vision for our own power has been and how small we have become, but we also discover just how lavish our Father's goodness is and how much glory is waiting for us, how much more we are meant to be.

The hard truth is that none of us—especially the most powerful—are safe with ourselves. To come to ourselves is to return from our far countries, whether they are over the horizon or just outside the house where the real, abundant feast can be found, and find ourselves clothed with the true Father's robe and ring. How can we become these kinds of image bearers? Only through the disciplines, community and worship that help us come to ourselves, arise in our right mind, and return from our prodigal power to the embrace of the only God worth playing.

At the nadir of the story of each son, each one is lost: all alone with his own mean fantasies and quickly diminishing idolatries. In stark contrast is the expectant, running, embracing, kissing, shouting father, who is also the one who leaves a party in progress in order to go out and plead for his son to come in. His power is embedded and expressed in the yearning for relationship, for the opportunity to foster abundance in the lives of his beloved sons.

This father, indeed, is what the various fathers of the biblical story— from Noah to Abraham, Isaac and Jacob, to David—never quite managed to be with their own families. He does what they rarely managed to do with their own power: use it for ever-increasing abundance and blessing. He is an icon of the true image. Indeed, in the holy hilarity of his greeting, the lavishness of his feast, and the eagerness of his pleading, we glimpse not just an image bearer but the very One "from whom every family in heaven and on earth takes its name" (Ephesians 3:15), whose image is meant to be refracted in his sons and daughters. Like him, we are meant to pour out our power fearlessly, spend our privilege recklessly, and leave our status in the dust of our headlong pursuit of love.

We are meant to do all this like him, because, far more than we ever dreamed or feared, we are made like him, and like him we will rise.

He is the God we are meant to play.

# ACKNOWLEDGMENTS

Thank you, first of all, to those who awakened me to the grip of power as I came of age, especially Bob, Mark, Mary and Christine.

Thank you to the countless hosts who have made space for my sometimes fumbling presentations on the topics of this book.

Thank you to Gary, Bethany and the other senior fellows of International Justice Mission's IJM Institute, and to the whole team at IJM who have been forerunners, partners and friends in the work of justice. Thank you to Lance and Debbie, Jonathan, Jeremy, Kent, and Jena, the staff and board of Equitas Group, for inviting me into your stewardship of power among the vulnerable.

Thank you to my neighbors Phillip, Dwight and Mark for repeatedly asking the question no author wants to be asked—"So, how's the book?"—and for your faithful prayers and bracing encouragement.

Thank you to Kathy and the team at Creative Trust for your wisdom and commitment.

Thank you to Andy, Jeff, Adrianna, Cindy and all the other remarkable people at InterVarsity Press for your patience and expertise. It is a privilege, in the very truest sense of the word, to work with you.

Thank you to Harold, Michael, Gabe, Greg, Katherine and Mark, among the many institutional leaders who have generously helped me to flourish. I thank my God every time I think of you.

Thank you to my thoughtful critics, who are not numerous enough. Each of you has been more helpful to me than a hundred friends.

A final thank you to Catherine, Timothy and Amy, my companions in life who know what a great fool I am. Thank you for sending me out so often, and welcoming me home.

# NOTES

In these notes I have tried to credit the principal influences on my thinking, while also pointing toward the source of direct quotations and particularly improbable statistics and assertions not documented in the text.

## Introduction

*p. 11*  Readers who want the real philosophical meat: In addition to the books mentioned, I discovered one published work that closely anticipates many of the themes of this book, especially in its critique of power as domination, Kyle A. Pasewark, *A Theology of Power: Being Beyond Domination* (Minneapolis: Fortress, 1993). Readers who turn to Pasewark will find many of the ideas I express stated with greater theological and philosophical precision, and with the kind of explicit dialogue with Foucault and his heirs that I decided to forgo in this book. James Davison Hunter briefly lays out the essential criteria for a theology of power, to which this book is one response, in chapter seven of essay two in *To Change the World: The Irony, Tragedy, and Possibility of Christianity in the Late Modern World* (New York: Oxford University Press, 2010), pp. 176-93. Another book, with a more limited scope, that makes related arguments in a readable and winsome way is Victor Lee Austin, *Up with Authority: Why We Need Authority to Flourish as Human Beings* (New York: Bloomsbury T & T Clark, 2010).

## Chapter 1: The Discovery of Power

*p. 19*  twenty-one million slaves: "21 Million People Are Now Victims of Forced Labour, ILO Says," International Labor Organization, June 1, 2012, www.ilo.org/global/about-the-ilo/newsroom/news/WCMS_181961/lang--en/index.htm. Advocacy organizations tend to use the higher number of twenty-seven million, based on the research of Free the Slaves' founder Kevin Bales. See Melissa Hogenboom, "A Tipping Point in the Fight Against Slavery?" *BBC News Magazine*, October 18, 2012, www.bbc.co.uk/news/magazine-19831913.

*p. 20*  Meeting with Jayakumar Christian: My visit and interview with Jayakumar Christian was described in "Powering Down," *Christianity Today* 51, no. 9 (September 2007), www.christianitytoday.com/ct/2007/september/14.38.html. Christian elaborates on his understanding of the role of "god complexes" in poverty in his book *God of the Empty-Handed: Poverty, Power and the Kingdom of God* (Federal Way, WA: World Vision International, 1999), which in turn is a major influence for Bryant Meyers's more readily available book *Walking with the Poor: Principles and Practices of Transformational Development*, rev. ed. (Maryknoll, NY: Orbis, 2011).

## Exploration: Genesis 1–2

*p. 31*    the only Christian doctrine empirically verifiable: Niebuhr gives as his source "The London Times Literary Supplement," and it may have been G. K. Chesterton who was writing, since this quote is also often attributed to him.

*p. 35*    the same kind of delighted dominion: For an especially important biblical theology of image bearing as "vice regency," see J. Richard Middleton, *The Liberating Image: The Imago Dei in Genesis 1* (Grand Rapids: Brazos, 2005).

## Chapter 2: Power Is a Gift

*p. 41*    money in a microeconomic system remains the same: What is true at the microeconomic level is not true at the macroeconomic level—healthy economies foster and reward productivity, and thus can actually create additional wealth, not just redistribute it.

*pp. 41-42*    Harvard Medical School faculty: "Case Studies," *The Economist*, May 6, 2010, www.economist.com/node/16067747.

*p. 44*    "absolute power corrupts absolutely": Lord Acton's first letter to Bishop Mandell Creighton, April 5, 1887, can be accessed in "Acton-Creighton Correspondence (1887)," *The Forum*, http://oll.libertyfund.org/index.php?option=com_content&task=view&id=1354&Itemid=262.

*p. 44*    induced abortions in 2003: "Facts on Induced Abortions Worldwide," www.guttmacher.org/pubs/fb_IAW.html.

*p. 46*    "My idea is that every specific body": Friedrich Nietzsche, *The Will to Power* § 636, trans. Walter Kaufmann and R. J. Hollingdale (New York: Vintage, 1968).

## Chapter 3: Idolatry

*p. 55*    creative power run amok: An important recent pastoral treatment of power and idolatry is Timothy Keller, *Counterfeit Gods: The Empty Promises of Money, Sex, and Power, and the Only Hope That Matters* (New York: Riverhead, 2011).

*p. 56*    idols demand everything and give nothing: I heard Jeffrey Satinover present these ideas at a lecture in the 1990s; they were further elaborated in his book *Feathers of the Skylark: Compulsion, Sin, and Our Need for a Messiah* (Grand Rapids: Hamewith, 1996).

*p. 56*    addiction as idolatry: An important theological treatment of addiction is Gerald G. May, *Addiction and Grace* (New York: Harper & Row, 1988).

*p. 63*    "To the horror of his friends and wife": Walter Isaacson, *Steve Jobs* (New York: Simon & Schuster, 2011), p. 453.

## Chapter 4: Injustice

*p. 76*  preservation of indigenous culture and language: Lamin Sanneh, *Translating the Message: The Missionary Impact on Culture*, 2nd ed. (Maryknoll, NY: Orbis, 2009).

*p. 77*  "life-changing" short-term trips: Robert Priest and Kurt Ver Beek, "Are Short-Term Missions Good Stewardship?" *Christianity Today*, July 5, 2005, www.christianitytoday.com/ct/2005/julyweb-only/22.0.html. Another resource for re-thinking the god playing that can lurk in our charitable efforts is the justly celebrated book by Steve Corbett and Brian Fikkert, *When Helping Hurts: How to Alleviate Poverty Without Hurting the Poor . . . and Yourself*, rev. ed. (Chicago: Moody Press, 2012).

## A Note: Evangelism and Social Action

*p. 79*  present-day suffering and "eternal suffering": John Piper, cited in "Cape Town 2010 Session Summary and Segment Synopsis," October 20, 2010, www.lausanne.org/docs/capetown2010/summaries/P120-Ephesians-3.pdf.

## Chapter 5: Icons

*p. 88*  An icon is a trustworthy image: An influential contemporary thinker who has elaborated on themes of the icon and the idol is Jean-Luc Marion, *God Without Being: Hors-Texte* (Chicago: University of Chicago Press, 1995). The themes of human beings as idols and icons are also explored in Scot McKnight, *Embracing Grace: A Gospel for All of Us* (Brewster, MA: Paraclete, 2005). Ben Witherington III uses the *imago Dei*, created, broken and restored, as the controlling metaphor for his two-volume work *The Indelible Image: The Theological and Ethical Thought World of the New Testament* (Downers Grove, IL: InterVarsity Press, 2009), and the "overture" to the first volume, "The Grand Story in Miniature," is a fine statement of the Wesleyan instincts that undergird my own statement of the theme in this chapter.

*pp. 91-92*  "Now this is his Word, our Lord Jesus Christ": Irenaeus, *Against Heresies* 4.20.4, Ante-Nicene Fathers, ed. Alexander Roberts and James Donaldson, vol. 1 (Grand Rapids: Eerdmans, 2001). Throughout this passage Irenaeus is using the inclusive Latin word *homo* that is translated here with the uninclusive-sounding "man"—he is referring to all human beings, not just males.

*p. 100*  one of the most famous folk parables: Hans Christian Andersen, "The Emperor's New Clothes," trans. Jean Hersholt, Hans Christian Andersen Center, www.andersen.sdu.dk/vaerk/hersholt/TheEmperorsNewClothes_e.html.

## Exploration: John 2

*p. 111*  "the third day" is a signpost: John also undoubtedly intends us to notice that this is the seventh day of his narrative—the completion of the first full week of his story of Jesus' ministry. The sign at Cana is the culmination and celebration of Jesus' first week of work just as the seventh day in Genesis was the culmination and celebration of the Father's creating work. I am grateful to an early reader of this section, whose name I have regrettably forgotten, for calling my attention to this.

## Chapter 7: Force, Coercion and Violence

*p. 133*      "All politics is a struggle for power": C. Wright Mills, *The Power Elite*, new ed. (New York: Oxford University Press, 2000), p. 171.

*pp. 133-134*  *Macht* and *Herrschaft*: Weber's definitions of *Macht* and *Herrschaft* are discussed in the fascinating, if not entirely current, entry by Leonard Krieger, "Authority," *Dictionary of the History of Ideas* (New York: Scribner's, 1968), 1:157.

*p. 136*      Surely *some* politics, perhaps *most* politics: Daniel Bell, "The Power Elite—Reconsidered," *American Journal of Sociology*, November 1958, pp. 238-50.

*p. 142*      Yoder placed under strict limits: Yoder's misconduct and subsequent discipline were covered in a series of articles in *The Elkhart* (IN) *Truth* in June-July 1992. See Ted Grimsrud, "John Howard Yoder's Sexual Misconduct (1992 Elkhart Truth articles)," *Peace Theology*, http://peacetheology.net/john-h-yoder/john-howard-yoder's-sexual-misconduct—part-five-2.

## Chapter 8: The Lure of Privilege

*p. 152*      David Beckham's contract: Kurt Badenhausen, "David Beckham Departs MLS After Earning $255 Million," *Forbes*, November 30, 2012, www.forbes.com/sites/kurt-badenhausen/2012/11/30/david-beckham-departs-mls-after-earning-255-million.

*p. 155*      At its worst, privilege is blindness: Amid the vast literature on race and privilege, one especially useful book from a Christian perspective for those from the dominant culture is Paula Harris and Doug Schaupp, *Being White: Finding Our Place in a Multiethnic World* (Downers Grove, IL: InterVarsity Press, 2004).

*p. 156*      Status is about your place in line: A helpful definition and discussion of status is found in James Davison Hunter, *To Change the World: The Irony, Tragedy, and Possibility of Christianity in the Late Modern World* (New York: Oxford University Press, 2010), pp. 257-58.

## Chapter 9: The Gift of Institutions

*p. 169*      institutions are essential for flourishing: The case for institutions has been made recently in stylish and readable form by Hugh Heclo, *On Thinking Institutionally* (New York: Oxford University Press, 2011). It may be a good candidate for the world's most boring book title (and, for that matter, cover), but in between the covers is a tremendously important and thoughtful rethinking of this topic. I am glad to declare how deeply in debt I am to Heclo and the several friends who alerted me to his book shortly after its publication.

*p. 171*      Institutions have four essential elements: While I have restated the ideas in my own words and may have not retained the nuances, I am grateful to D. Michael Lindsay, president of Gordon College, for some remedial tutoring in the elements of institutions as seen by the sociologists.

p. 184  "the one" and "the many" meet in "the three": This language is borrowed from Colin Gunton, *The One, the Three, and the Many: God, Creation, and the Culture of Modernity* (Cambridge: Cambridge University Press, 1993).

p. 188  the astonishing phenomenon of Japan's *hikikomori*: Maggie Jones, "Shutting Themselves In," *New York Times*, January 15, 2006, www.nytimes.com/2006/01/15/magazine/15japanese.html.

## Chapter 10: Principalities, Powers and Broken Institutions

p. 192  21 million adults attended a classical music performance: "'American Idol' Finale Audience Shrinks," *Wall Street Journal*, May 25, 2012, p. B6; Kevin Williams and David Keen, "2008 Survey of Public Participation in the Arts," National Endowment for the Arts, November 2009, p. 2, www.nea.gov/research/2008-sppa.pdf.

p. 203  Wright's useful modern metaphor: N. T. Wright, "On Earth as in Heaven," NTWrightpage.com, May 20, 2007, http://ntwrightpage.com/sermons/Earth_Heaven.htm.

p. 204  They are, in a word, institutional: Every account of the principalities and powers since is indebted to Walter Wink's life work, a series of books on "The Powers" that began with *Naming the Powers: The Language of Powers in the New Testament* (Minneapolis: Fortress, 1984).

p. 205  "The climax of Jesus's earthly ministry": Malcolm Muggeridge, *Confessions of a Twentieth Century Pilgrim*, quoted in Marva J. Dawn, *Powers, Weakness, and the Tabernacling of God* (Grand Rapids: Eerdmans, 2001), p. 72.

## Chapter 11: Becoming Trustees

p. 208  143 families had been enslaved: D. Madhavan, "522 Bonded Labourers Rescued Near Chennai," *Times of India*, April 29, 2011, http://articles.timesofindia.indiatimes.com/2011-04-29/chennai/29486830_1_revenue-officials-kiln-labourers.

p. 216  "I have almost reached the regrettable conclusion": Martin Luther King Jr., "Letter from Birmingham Jail," Martin Luther King Jr. Research and Education Institute, April 16, 1963, http://mlk-kpp01.stanford.edu/index.php/resources/article/annotated_letter_from_birmingham.

## Exploration: Philemon

p. 223  Paul's letter to Philemon is a power letter: While I dissent from its underlying cynicism, there are countless valuable insights in Norman R. Petersen, *Rediscovering Paul: Philemon and the Sociology of Paul's Narrative World* (Minneapolis: Fortress, 1985).

p. 225  "no man is the slave either of another man or of sin": Augustine, *City of God* 19.15, ed. and trans. R. W. Dyson (Cambridge: Cambridge University Press, 1998), p. 943.

p. 227  incarceration as "the new Jim Crow": The exact incarceration rate for the United States in 2009 was 756 per 100,000. See "World Prison Population List (8th edition)," King's College London, January 26, 2009, www.kcl.ac.uk/depsta/law/

news/news_details.php?id=203. The comparison of incarceration rates over time comes from the graph at "U.S. Incarceration Rates 1925 Onwards," *Wikipedia*, http://en.wikipedia.org/wiki/File:U.S._incarceration_rates_1925_onwards. png. A principal documenter of the racial dynamics of incarceration in the United States is Michelle Alexander, *The New Jim Crow: Mass Incarceration in the Age of Colorblindness*, rev. ed. (New York: New Press, 2012).

*p. 227*  Trisomy 21, better known as Down syndrome: In several different studies between 1995 and 2011, between 61 percent and 93 percent of parents who received a prenatal Down syndrome diagnosis terminated the pregnancy. See Amy Julia Becker, "Down Syndrome Prenatal Testing and Abortion—It's Complicated," *Patheos*, June 10, 2012, www.patheos.com/blogs/thinplaces/2012/06/down-syndrome-prenatal-testing-and-abortion-its-complicated.

## Chapter 12: Disciplined Power

*p. 234*  "How about Saturday?": Walter Isaacson, *Steve Jobs* (New York: Simon & Schuster, 2011), pp. 267-68.

*p. 239*  three practices that interrupt power and privilege: Among the many excellent resources for the classical spiritual disciplines, I am especially indebted to the work of Ruth Haley Barton, including *Invitation to Solitude and Silence: Experiencing God's Transforming Presence* (Downers Grove, IL: InterVarsity Press, 2004).

## Chapter 13: The Sabbath Ladder

*p. 252*  regular rhythms of ceasing and feasting: Judith Shulevitz started a remarkably broad, nonsectarian conversation about the value of sabbath. See her *The Sabbath World: Glimpses of a Different Order of Time* (New York: Random House, 2010). From a Christian perspective, Matthew Sleeth's *24/6* (Carol Stream, IL: Tyndale House, 2006) is winsome and compelling.

*p. 267*  teachers and administrators with a deep sense of calling: A recent Christian resource that gives many glimpses of educational Jubilee is Nicole Baker Fulgham's *Educating All God's Children: What Christians Can—and Should—Do to Improve Public Education for Low-Income Kids* (Grand Rapids: Baker, 2013).

## Chapter 14: The End of Power

*p. 273*  "I do not foretell": J. R. R. Tolkien, *The Fellowship of the Ring* (New York: Del Rey, 1992), p. 423. I was reminded of this passage by Timothy Keller.